EQUIVALENTS

DRIED BEANS

White, 1 pound : 2 cups, uncooked = 6 cups, cooked
Kidney, 1 pound : 2⅔ cups, uncooked = 6¼ cups, cooked
Lima, 1 pound : 3 cups, uncooked = 7 cups, cooked

PASTA AND CORN MEAL

Macaroni, 8 ounces : 2 cups, uncooked = 4 cups, cooked
Noodles, 8 ounces : 2½ cups, uncooked = 4 to 5 cups, cooked
Spaghetti, 8 ounces : 2½ cups, uncooked = 4 to 5 cups, cooked
Corn meal : 1 cup, uncooked = 4 cups, cooked

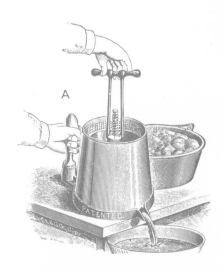

BREAD

1 pound dry bread crumbs = 3½ cups
1 pound bread, crumbled = 9 cups

EGGS

4 to 6 whole eggs, shelled = 1 cup
8 to 10 egg whites = 1 cup

SUGAR

1 pound brown = 2¼ cups, packed
1 pound granulated = 2¼ cups
1 pound confectioners' = 4 to 5 cups

FLOUR

1 pound white all-purpose = 4 cups, sifted
1 pound cake = 4½ cups, sifted
1 pound whole-wheat = 3½ cups

BUTTER

1 ounce = 2 tablespoons (butter the size of a walnut)
2 ounces = 4 tablespoons or ¼ cup (butter the size of an egg)
¼ pound = ½ cup (1 stick) or 8 tablespoons
½ pound = 1 cup (2 sticks)
1 pound = 2 cups

CHEESE

1 pound = 5 cups grated
1 pound = 2⅔ cups cubed

CHOCOLATE

1 ounce = 1 square (unsweetened)
6 ounces = 1 cup (1 package) semisweet chocolate pieces

NUTS

1 pound almonds, unshelled = 1½ cups nut meats
1 pound pecans, unshelled = 2¼ cups nut meats
1 pound walnuts, unshelled = 2 cups nut meats

SHELLFISH

1 pound cooked shrimp, crab,
or lobster meat = 2 cups

LONG GRAIN RICE

1 pound, uncooked : 2 cups, uncooked = 6 cups, cooked

The
AMERICAN HERITAGE
COOKBOOK

Students at a cooking school of the 1880's offer samples to their gentlemen friends.

The

AMERICAN HERITAGE
COOKBOOK

BY THE EDITORS OF AMERICAN HERITAGE, THE MAGAZINE OF HISTORY

RECIPES EDITOR

HELEN McCULLY

ASSOCIATE RECIPES EDITOR

ELEANOR NODERER

HISTORICAL FOODS CONSULTANT

HELEN DUPREY BULLOCK

AMERICAN HERITAGE PRESS

NEW YORK

THE KITCHEN COMPANION,

AND

HOUSE-KEEPER'S OWN BOOK,

CONTAINING ALL THE MODERN, AND MOST APPROVED METHODS IN

COOKERY, PASTRY, & CONFECTIONARY,

WITH AN EXCELLENT COLLECTION OF

VALUABLE RECIPES,

TO WHICH IS ADDED, THE

WHOLE ART OF CARVING, ILLUSTRATED.

Cover of The Kitchen Companion, *a cookbook published in Philadelphia in 1844*

TABLE OF CONTENTS

A WORD OF EXPLANATION

How the recipes were selected: We have tried to include in this book recipes for the most delectable and historically interesting dishes prepared in America from the time of its discovery to the beginning of this century. From old cookbooks, hand-written manuscripts, historic menus, and other original sources, these recipes were painstakingly collected. They were adapted for use in today's kitchen, to take full advantage of modern equipment and of current freezing, packaging, and transportation methods, and then tested by trained home economists. All the recipes, we hope, retain the flavor and charm of the originals.

Organization of recipes: To make selection easy, recipes are grouped by course—under Fish, Desserts, and similar headings. Each of these sections contains regional recipes and foreign dishes that became American favorites, as well as traditional recipes enjoyed in all parts of the country. When a recipe is of more than usual historical interest, a note explaining its background appears in brown type. We have also included, in their original form, a few old recipes we found irresistible (the Birds-Nest Salad on page 135 is an example), but since these are just for fun and not something the average cook is likely to prepare, they are also printed in brown ink. The rule of thumb for using the recipe pages, then, is this: practical information for cooking appears in *black* type; historical notes and other comments intended solely for extra reading pleasure appear in *brown*.

Whenever there has been a choice of names for dishes, we tended to favor the old over the new. In some cases, this helps to place the recipe's origins; sometimes not (as with those curious desserts called grunts, fools, and slumps, whose beginnings no one seems certain about). Nomenclature aside, we wish that space permitted inclusion of all the fine old recipes enjoyed by Americans.

Thirty historic menus: On pages 216 to 245 are thirty historical and useful menus, assembled by Mrs. Helen Duprey Bullock, who also contributed a number of recipes to the book. Some of these menus—the Nellie Grant wedding breakfast, for example—were taken from accounts published at the time. Others, such as the Christmas dinner at Mount Vernon, were compiled by Mrs. Bullock after extensive research into writings by and about the persons involved; they are not so much a menu for one specific historical meal as they are a composite, based on expert knowledge of the tastes of the individuals and of the foods available in that time and place. *Asterisks (*) appear beside those dishes in the menus for which recipes are provided in the recipe section.*

RECIPES

SOUPS

PHILADELPHIA PEPPER POT

During the relentlessly harsh winter of 1777-78, morale was low at Valley Forge, and desertions frequent. According to legend, Washington ordered a good meal to cheer his troops one night—only to be told by his harried cook that there was nothing but tripe, some peppercorns, and useless scraps. Still, an order was an order, and the cook improvised a soup which he called, ex post facto, Philadelphia (in honor of his home town) Pepper Pot. It is said that some Philadelphians still attribute the success of the Revolution to Philadelphia Pepper Pot soup.

3 pounds tripe	1 teaspoon whole allspice
1 knuckle of veal with meat left on	6 whole cloves
2 pounds marrowbone, cracked	4 potatoes, diced fine
2 large onions, sliced	2 teaspoons dried marjoram
Soup bouquet: several sprigs parsley;	2 tablespoons chopped parsley
1 bay leaf; 2 sprigs thyme or ½ teaspoon	Salt
dried thyme; 1 carrot, cut in chunks	Pepper
½ teaspoon crushed red pepper	Dumplings (recipe below)

Wash the tripe, put into a kettle with 4 quarts of water, and bring to a boil. Reduce heat, cover, and cook over a low heat for 6 to 7 hours or until the tripe is very soft. Cool in the broth. When cool enough to handle, cut into very small pieces. Pour broth into a container. While tripe is coooking, put veal knuckle in a second kettle with 2 quarts of water. Remove the marrow from marrowbone with a knife or spoon and heat in a saucepan. Toss in onions and sauté until tender. Now combine with the veal knuckle and the de-marrowed bone. Add the soup bouquet, red pepper, allspice, and cloves and cook over a low heat for about 5 hours or until very tender. Cool veal in broth until meat can be handled comfortably, then chop veal in small pieces (discard bones), and add to chopped tripe. Pour broth into a separate container and refrigerate both the meat and the two broths overnight. Next day, remove and discard fat from tripe and veal broth. Combine the two broths and add the chopped tripe and veal, diced potatoes, marjoram, and salt and pepper to taste. Cook over a low heat for about 45 minutes. Add parsley, drop dumplings in broth, and cook as directed. Serves 12.

Dumplings:	¼ teaspoon salt
1 cup sifted all-purpose flour	1 tablespoon shortening
2 teaspoons baking powder	6 tablespoons milk (about)

Sift flour, baking powder, and salt together. Add shortening and pinch it in with your fingers until it is well distributed. Gradually stir in milk with a fork—just enough to make a soft dough. Drop by tablespoons into simmering soup, cover tightly, and cook 15 minutes. Serves 6. The dumplings are limited to 6 servings because your kettle will not accommodate more and they must be cooked, all at one time, in the simmering soup. You can make a second batch of dumplings when you serve the soup on the second day.

CORN CHOWDER

This chowder originated in Massachusetts, but it is also made in the South with tomatoes added to the ingredients below.

3 slices salt pork, cubed
1 large onion, sliced
4 large potatoes, sliced
2 cups water
6 large soda crackers

1 cup milk
2 cups corn (fresh, canned whole kernel, or frozen, thawed)
1 teaspoon salt
Dash of paprika

Fry salt pork in a saucepan until crisp and lightly browned. Stir in onion and cook until golden, then add potatoes and water. Continue cooking until potatoes are tender. Crumble soda crackers into a bowl, pour in milk, and soak. Add to the cooked potatoes, then add corn, salt, and paprika. Simmer over a low heat for 8 to 10 minutes. Serves 4.

CHICKEN CORN SOUP

Chicken Corn Soup was a favorite in Lancaster County, Pennsylvania, where it was often served on picnics during the summer.

A 4-pound stewing chicken
1 onion, chopped
4 quarts water
Salt
Pepper
10 ears fresh corn
½ cup chopped celery with leaves

2 hard-cooked eggs, chopped
Rivels:
1 cup flour
Pinch of salt
1 egg
Milk

Cut chicken into pieces and place in a soup kettle. Add onion, water, salt, and pepper. Bring to a boil, then reduce heat, cover, and simmer gently until chicken is tender. Remove chicken from stock and, when cool enough to handle, strip meat from bones. Discard bones and skin, and cut into bite-sized pieces. Return chicken to stock, add corn (cut kernels from cob) and celery. Continue simmering for 30 minutes and prepare *rivels*.

To make the rivels: Combine flour, salt, egg, and enough milk to make a crumbly mixture. Mix with a fork or with your finger tips until crumbs are the size of small peas. Drop *rivels* and chopped eggs into soup. Cook 15 minutes, then season to taste. Serves 6.

PEANUT SOUP

½ cup roasted peanuts
3 cups beef broth
1 cup half-and-half (milk and cream)

½ teaspoon chili powder
½ teaspoon salt

Blend peanuts with *1 cup of the broth* in an electric blender until smooth. Pour into a saucepan and add all remaining ingredients. Bring to a boil, reduce heat to simmer, and cook slowly for 15 minutes. Serve hot with a dab of whipped cream on top, or cold, garnished with thin slices of cucumber or radishes. Serves 4.

BLACK BEAN SOUP

2 cups dried black beans
Ham bone with meat, or ham hock
2 medium onions, chopped
2 carrots, chopped
3 stalks celery, chopped
4 to 5 sprigs parsley
3 whole cloves
Pinch mace or allspice

Pinch thyme
2 bay leaves
1 teaspoon dry mustard
1 tablespoon Worcestershire sauce
¼ cup sherry
2 eggs, hard cooked
Lemon

Soak beans overnight in enough cold water to cover. Drain, add 2 quarts water, ham bone, onions, carrots, celery, parsley, cloves, mace, thyme, bay leaves, dry mustard, and Worcestershire sauce. Bring to a boil, then reduce heat, and simmer gently for 2 to 3 hours or until beans are very tender. Remove ham and bone, cutting any meat into small pieces. Work soup through a sieve or blend in an electric blender. Add diced ham and sherry and season to taste. If soup is too thick (it should look like heavy cream), stir in a little water. Reheat and serve with sliced hard-cooked eggs and thin lemon slices on top. Serves 6.

PUMPKIN SOUP

We have pumpkins at morning, and pumpkins at noon,
If it were not for pumpkins we should be undone.
> —From an anonymous poem, circa 1630

Cut half a small pumpkin into wedges, remove seeds and outer skin. Chop pulp into pieces and cook in boiling, salted water until tender when tested with a fork. Drain and work through a sieve. Combine 2 cups pumpkin purée with 3 tablespoons butter, 1 teaspoon sugar, 1 teaspoon salt, and ¼ teaspoon white pepper. Cook over a low heat about 10 minutes. Stir in 3 cups hot milk, a little at a time, and simmer gently for several minutes. Serve with croutons. Serves 4.

SOPA DE ALBONDIGAS
(Meatball Soup)

3 quarts beef broth
¼ cup olive oil
1 small onion, chopped
1 clove garlic, crushed
1 can (8 ounces) tomato sauce
¾ pound beef, ground

¾ pound lean pork, ground
⅓ cup uncooked rice
1 egg, beaten
1½ teaspoons salt
½ teaspoon chili pepper
¼ cup chopped parsley

Use a good rich beef broth, preferably homemade. Heat oil in a soup kettle, stir in chopped onion and garlic, and cook until light gold in color. Stir in tomato sauce and beef broth. Combine ground beef and pork with rice, egg, salt, and chili pepper. Shape into balls the size of a walnut. When broth is boiling briskly, drop in the meatballs, cover, and cook over a moderate heat for 30 minutes. Serve with chopped parsley strewn on top. Serves 4 to 6.

OLD-FASHIONED VEGETABLE SOUP

A 1½-pound shin bone of beef with meat
1½ pounds lean brisket, cubed
3 stalks celery
3 large carrots
2 medium onions
1 can (1 pound, 13 ounce size) tomatoes
½ teaspoon dried basil
½ teaspoon dried thyme

½ teaspoon dried marjoram
½ cup chopped parsley
1½ tablespoons salt
½ teaspoon pepper
½ pound green Lima beans, shelled
½ pound green peas, shelled
3 ears fresh corn

Put the shin bone and the cubed brisket in a large kettle and add enough water to cover them. Cook to the boiling point, then add chopped celery, carrots, and onions. Stir in tomatoes, basil, thyme, marjoram, parsley, salt, and pepper. Cover and cook over a low heat for 2 to 3 hours (timing is not important in vegetable soup—some cooks let it simmer all day long). Thirty minutes or so before serving, add Lima beans, peas, and corn cut off the cob. Before dishing up, skim off all excess fat. Serves 6.

SORREL SOUP

1 pound fresh sorrel
1 medium onion, chopped
¼ cup butter
1 cup light cream

2 egg yolks, beaten
3 cups chicken broth
Salt
Pepper

Chop well-washed and dried sorrel leaves very fine. Cook onion in heated butter until limp, but do not brown. Stir in sorrel and cook over a low heat until wilted—takes about 5 minutes. Blend cream and egg yolks together. Heat chicken broth to a boil, then stir a little into yolk mixture, beating hard. Pour back into broth and heat. Beat constantly and do not allow it to boil. Add sorrel mixture and salt and pepper to taste. Serve hot or refrigerate and serve icy cold. If you like a smoother mixture, blend in the electric blender. Serves 4 to 6.

SPLIT PEA SOUP

1½ cups split peas
Ham bone
1 onion, stuck with 2 cloves
2 or 3 stalks of celery

1 bay leaf
3 or 4 carrots
½ cup heavy cream

Cover the split peas with water and soak overnight or use the quick-cooking variety. Place ham bone, peeled onion stuck with 2 cloves, celery, bay leaf, carrots, and drained split peas in a large kettle. Add 2 to 3 quarts of water, or enough to cover, and bring to a boil. Then lower the heat and simmer gently until the peas are soft and mushy. Lift the ham bone out of the kettle and purée the soup in an electric blender or push through a sieve. Cut off any meat on the bone and cut in slivers. Set aside. Pour soup back into kettle, add cream, and taste for seasoning. Then add slivered ham and bring to a boil, but do not cook further. Serve with a sturdy, crusty bread or croutons. Serves 6.

AN ONION SOUP CALL'D THE KING'S SOUP

This recipe is adapted from *The Lady's Companion*, a cookbook published in 1753, which was owned by Martha Washington.

2 large Bermuda onions, thinly sliced	1½ teaspoons salt
1 quart milk	1 egg yolk
½ teaspoon mace blades	Chopped parsley
½ cup (1 stick) butter	Croutons

Place onions, milk, mace, butter, and salt in a saucepan. Bring to a boil, then reduce heat, and cook slowly for 30 to 40 minutes or until onions are very tender. Pick out mace blades and discard. Beat egg yolk in a small bowl, then add a little of the hot soup, beating constantly. Pour egg mixture into soup and cook a minute or two to thicken slightly. Sprinkle each serving with finely chopped parsley, then add a few croutons. Serves 4.

To make toasted croutons: Toast old firm bread, then cut into tiny squares.

Hot soup at table is very vulgar; it either leads to an unseemly mode of taking it, or keeps people waiting too long whilst it cools. Soup should be brought to table only moderately warm.
　　　　　　　　　　　　　　　　　—Charles Day, *Hints on Etiquette*, 1844

CRÈME VICHYSSOISE GLACÉ

In 1910, when the roof garden was opened at the Ritz-Carlton on 46th Street and Madison Avenue, chef Louis Diat celebrated by presenting Manhattan society with a new soup. It was one his mother had made— the traditional hot leek-and-potato peasant soup of France, cooled with rich, sweet milk. It was refined by *le maître*, named Vichyssoise after the fashionable French watering spot, Vichy, and was served for the first time to Charles Schwab, the steel magnate.

4 leeks	1 tablespoon salt
1 onion, sliced	2 cups milk
2 tablespoons butter	1 cup light cream
6 medium potatoes, sliced	1 cup heavy cream
1 quart chicken broth or water or combination of both	Chives, chopped fine

Wash leeks very carefully and discard green stalks. Slice the white part, combine with onion, and cook in melted butter until limp but not brown. Add potato slices, chicken broth, and salt. Bring to a boil and boil 35 minutes. Rub through a fine strainer or purée in an electric blender, return to heat, and add milk and light cream. Season to taste and bring to a boil. Do not cook further. Finally, add the heavy cream and chill thoroughly in the refrigerator. Serve in cups with a sprinkling of finely chopped chives on top. Serves 8.

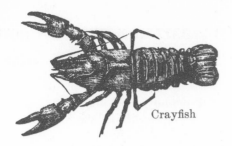

Crayfish

BISQUE D'ÉCREVISSE
(*Crayfish Bisque*)

8 quarts live crayfish
1 tablespoon vinegar
Leaves from 1 bunch celery
4 tablespoons butter
2 large onions
4 cloves garlic
1 cup fine dry bread crumbs
2 tablespoons chopped parsley
1 tablespoon lemon juice
Cayenne
Tabasco
Salt
2 eggs

¾ cup flour
2 carrots, chopped fine
1 parsnip, chopped fine
6 ripe tomatoes, skinned and chopped, or
   1 can (1 pound, 3 ounces) solid-
   pack tomatoes
3 sprigs parsley
2 sprigs (¼ teaspoon dried) thyme
2 sprigs (¼ teaspoon dried) basil
1 bay leaf
Hot steamed rice
4 shallots, chopped fine

Wash the crayfish thoroughly under running water. If the bellies are silty, scrub with a stiff brush. Place in a very large deep kettle, cover with cold water, add 2 or 3 tablespoons of salt, and let stand about an hour. Drain, cover with fresh water, add vinegar and celery leaves. Cover, and cook over a low heat until water boils, then simmer gently for 5 minutes. Strain and reserve the liquid. Crack the tender shell of the tails, pick out the meat, and place in a bowl. Shake the fat from the bodies (or heads) into a second bowl by gently tapping the bottom of the heads. Save about 30 of the largest heads to stuff.

To make the stuffing: Heat *2 tablespoons of the butter* in a saucepan. Toss in *1 onion* and *2 cloves of garlic,* both chopped fine. Cook over a low heat until straw colored. Add half the crayfish fat and all the crayfish tails, coarsely chopped. Cook, stirring constantly, for several minutes. Mix in crumbs, 1 cup of strained liquid in which crayfish cooked, chopped parsley, lemon juice, cayenne, Tabasco, and salt to taste. Continue cooking for about 15 minutes. Remove from heat, beat in eggs thoroughly, and stuff the crayfish heads generously. Save any leftover stuffing. Place stuffed heads on a tray or in a shallow baking dish, dot with butter, and set aside.

To make the bisque: Put flour into a skillet and cook over a moderate heat, stirring constantly, until light brown in color. Cook remaining onion and garlic, both chopped fine, in a large soup kettle with 2 tablespoons of butter and remainder of the crayfish fat until limp. Stir in browned flour until smooth, then add 2 quarts of the strained crayfish liquid, carrots, parsnip, tomatoes, any leftover stuffing, parsley, thyme, basil, bay leaf, additional salt, cayenne, and Tabasco—enough to give a slight bite to the bisque. Simmer over a low heat, without a cover, for 1½ hours, stirring occasionally. Thirty minutes before bisque has finished cooking, bake stuffed crayfish heads in a preheated 350° oven for 15 minutes. Place carefully in the bisque and continue simmering for the final 15 minutes. Serve over steamed rice with a sprinkling of shallots on top. Serves 8.

NEW ENGLAND CLAM CHOWDER

Several centuries ago, in the coastal villages of France, when a fishing fleet came home each man threw a share of his catch into a huge copper pot—*la chaudière*—and the community shared in a feast celebrating the safe return of the fishermen. The tradition found its way to Canada, then drifted down the coast to New England, where *la chaudière* became "chowder"—any concoction made of fish or shellfish or both. The most famous of the American chowders is Clam Chowder, with its two essential ingredients: clams and salt pork or bacon. But "essential" is a prickly word. Every New Englander worth his salty independence has his own version of what is essential to Clam Chowder. The most notable heresy is Manhattan Clam Chowder which calls for water rather than milk—and tomatoes! Down Easters are so nettled over the Tomato Question that the Maine legislature once introduced a bill to outlaw forever the mixing of clams and tomatoes.

1 quart clams with liquor	3 tablespoons butter
3 cups water	1¾ cups half-and-half (milk and cream)
2 slices salt pork, chopped	1 tablespoon salt
1 medium onion, sliced	Dash of pepper
3 medium potatoes, cut in small cubes	

Combine clams, liquor, and water and cook to a boil. Drain, reserving the broth. Mince the necks and the coarse membranes, chop the rest. Set all aside. Fry the salt pork until lightly browned, stir in onion, and cook until limp but not brown. Add the clam broth and potatoes and cook until potatoes are tender. Then stir in butter, half-and-half, salt, pepper, and clams. Heat but do not boil, pour immediately into large, warmed soup bowls. Serve with crackers. Serves 6 to 8.

MANHATTAN CLAM CHOWDER

½ pound bacon, chopped fine	1 pint clams in liquor
4 medium onions, chopped fine	2 teaspoons salt
4 carrots, chopped fine	¼ teaspoon freshly ground pepper
2 stalks celery, chopped fine	1½ teaspoons dried thyme
2 tablespoons chopped parsley	1 bay leaf
1 can (1 pound, 13 ounce size) tomatoes	3 medium potatoes, diced fine

Fry bacon in a large saucepan or kettle until almost crisp. Toss in onions and cook until they take on color. Next, stir in carrots, celery, and parsley and cook over a low heat for about 8 minutes. Drain tomatoes, putting liquid into a measuring cup. Add tomato pulp to saucepan. Drain clams, mixing the liquor with the tomato liquid. Add enough water to make 1½ quarts of liquid and pour into saucepan. Season with salt, pepper, thyme, bay leaf, and cook to a boil. Reduce heat and simmer gently for 40 minutes. Add potatoes, cover, and cook about 20 minutes. Finally, add the clams, chopped, and simmer 15 minutes longer. Serves 6 generously.

CODFISH CHOWDER

4 pounds fresh cod
2-inch cube of salt pork
1 onion, sliced
6 cups thinly sliced potatoes
4 cups milk

1 tablespoon salt
¼ teaspoon pepper, freshly ground
3 tablespoons butter
8 common crackers, split in half

Have your fish dealer clean and skin the fish. Be sure to ask for the head, tail, backbone, and other trimmings. Cut the cod into 2-inch pieces and set aside. Put head, tail, and all the trimmings in a saucepan with 2 cups of water. Heat to the boiling point, then reduce heat, and cook slowly about 20 minutes. Cut salt pork in small chunks and fry over a low heat until crisp. Stir in onion slices and cook until limp. Parboil potato slices for 5 minutes (use enough boiling water to cover). Drain. Add the potatoes and 2 cups of boiling water to salt-pork mixture. Cook 5 minutes. Add liquid drained from fish bones, then add the cod. Cover and simmer for 10 minutes. Scald milk, pour into fish mixture, and add salt, pepper, butter, and crackers. Heat until piping hot. Serves 6 to 8.

Four tablespoonfuls of onions, fried with pork. One quart of boiled potatoes, well mashed. One and a half pounds sea-biscuit, broken. One teaspoonful of thyme, mixed with one of summer savory. Half-bottle of mushroom catsup. One bottle of port or claret. Half of a nutmeg, grated. A few cloves, mace, and allspice. Six pounds of fish, sea-bass or cod, cut in slices. Twenty-five oysters, a little black pepper, and a few slices of lemon. The whole put in a pot and covered with an inch of water, boiled for an hour, and gently stirred.
—Daniel Webster's chowder recipe, from *The Cook*, 1885

MULLIGATAWNY SOUP

A 3-pound chicken, cut in pieces
¼ cup butter
½ cup chopped carrots
½ cup chopped green pepper
2 greening apples, cored and chopped
1 tablespoon flour
2 teaspoons curry powder

2 quarts chicken broth
2 whole cloves
Pinch mace
Few sprigs parsley, chopped
1 tablespoon sugar
¼ teaspoon pepper
1 tablespoon salt

Sauté chicken pieces in heated butter until well browned. Stir in carrots, green pepper, and apples, and continue cooking, stirring frequently, until mixture is brown. Sprinkle in flour and curry powder. Add broth, a little at a time. Season with all remaining ingredients. Cook to a boil, then reduce heat, cover, and simmer gently until chicken is very tender. Remove chicken from soup and cool until it can be handled comfortably. Strain the soup, working vegetables through a sieve, then return to kettle, and heat. Strip chicken from bones (discard bones and skin) and add to soup. Serve hot with steamed rice. Serves 6 to 8.

BREADS

ANADAMA BREAD

One story that was repeated in Massachusetts in the nineteenth century was of the fisherman who became enraged with his wife. All she gave him for dinner was corn meal and molasses—day after day. One night, when he could no longer control his anger, he tossed flour and yeast into the corn meal and molasses, put it all in the oven, and sat down later to eat a loaf of bread that had no name, mumbling, "Anna, damn her!"

½ cup corn meal
3 tablespoons shortening
¼ cup molasses
2 teaspoons salt
¾ cup boiling water

1 package active dry yeast or
  1 cake compressed
¼ cup warm water
1 egg, beaten
3 cups sifted all-purpose flour

Combine corn meal, shortening, molasses, salt, and boiling water in a large bowl. Let stand until lukewarm. Sprinkle yeast over warm water to dissolve, then stir yeast, egg, and *half of the flour* into corn-meal mixture. Beat vigorously. Stir in remaining flour and mix thoroughly until dough forms a soft ball. Use your hand if it seems easier. Transfer to a greased loaf pan, cover with a cloth, and set in a warm place until dough reaches 1 inch above the pan. Sprinkle top with a little corn meal and salt. Bake in a preheated 350° oven for 50 to 55 minutes. Cool before slicing.

SAFFRON BREAD

¼ teaspoon saffron
2 cups milk
½ cup melted butter or shortening
1 package active dry yeast or 1 cake
  compressed
1 cup sugar

½ teaspoon salt
½ teaspoon nutmeg
6 to 7 cups sifted all-purpose flour
½ cup candied lemon peel, chopped
2 cups currants

Steep saffron in ½ cup boiling water for at least 30 minutes, then strain, saving the saffron liquid. Scald milk, pour into a large mixing bowl, add saffron liquid, and stir in melted shortening. Dissolve yeast in 2 tablespoons warm water and stir into warm (not hot) milk. Add sugar, salt, and nutmeg, then sift in the flour. Add candied lemon peel and currants. Mix thoroughly. Dough should be quite stiff. Cover with a tea towel and let stand in a warm place, away from drafts, until double in size. This takes about 1½ hours. Now punch the dough down with your fist and knead on a floured board until smooth. Divide in half, shape into loaves, and place in 2 greased loaf pans. Let rise a second time until double in size. Bake in a preheated 350° oven about 1 hour. Remove from oven and brush tops of loaves with melted butter. Cool in pans about 10 minutes before turning out. Do not slice until bread has cooled completely. Cut in thin slices and toast, if you wish. Serve with sweet butter.

SHAKER DAILY LOAF

½ package active dry yeast or
  ½ cake compressed
2 tablespoons warm water
1 cup milk

1 tablespoon butter
1 tablespoon sugar
1 teaspoon salt
3½ cups sifted all-purpose flour

Sprinkle yeast over warm water and stir until dissolved. Combine milk, butter, sugar, and salt and heat. Skim off the film and cool to lukewarm, then stir in the yeast. Mix in flour as thoroughly as possible, brush surface with a little melted butter, cover with a tea towel, and set in a warm place until double in size. Transfer to a lightly floured board and knead until satiny smooth. Shape into a loaf and place in a greased loaf pan. Again brush the top with melted butter and let rise a second time until double in size. Bake in a preheated 350° oven for 50 minutes.

SWEDISH RYE BREAD

⅓ cup molasses
1¼ cups water
⅓ cup brown sugar, firmly packed
½ tablespoon aniseed
1 teaspoon salt
1 teaspoon grated orange or lemon rind

1 tablespoon shortening
1 package active dry yeast or
  1 cake compressed
2 cups sifted rye flour
3½ cups sifted all-purpose flour

Combine molasses, water, brown sugar, aniseed, salt, orange or lemon rind, and shortening in a saucepan. Heat to boiling point, then boil 5 minutes. Cool to lukewarm, then stir in yeast until dissolved. Beat in rye flour, cover with a tea towel, and let rise in a warm spot for 4 to 6 hours or overnight. Beat in white flour and knead until thoroughly blended. Let rise in a warm place until double in size. Divide in half, shape into 2 round flat loaves, and place in well-greased 9-inch pie pans. Let rise a third time for 1½ hours. Bake in a preheated 300° oven for 1 hour. Brush crust with melted butter, then cool before cutting.

BOSTON BROWN BREAD

"It was a common saying among the Puritans," Matthew Henry reported in his *Commentaries*, published in the early eighteenth century, " 'Brown bread and the Gospel is good fare.' "

1 cup rye flour
1 cup corn meal
1 cup Graham flour
¾ teaspoon baking soda

1 teaspoon salt
¾ cup molasses
2 cups buttermilk
1 cup chopped raisins (optional)

Sift all dry ingredients together, add molasses, buttermilk, raisins. Divide batter and place in 2 buttered 1-quart pudding molds or 3 buttered 1-pound coffee cans, filling them about ¾ full. Molds must be covered tightly, with buttered lids tied and taped so the bread won't force the cover off on rising. Place molds in a pan filled with enough boiling water to reach halfway up the mold and steam for 3 hours, keeping water at the halfway mark. Serve piping hot with butter and Boston Baked Beans (page 111).

SOURDOUGH BREAD

Sourdough may be the oldest of all breads, dating as far back as 4,000 B.C., but—according to one theory—it was unknown in America until Columbus landed with a sourdough starter in the hold of his ship. Sourdough starter is simply a self-perpetuating yeast mixture, made by combining flour, sugar, and water. The bread became identified with America because of the Alaskan sourdoughs—prospectors who carried sourdough starter pots strapped to their packs so that they could make a batch of bread whenever they felt the need, without walking fifty miles to the nearest town for a bit of yeast.

1 cup sourdough starter
1 package active dry yeast or
  1 cake compressed
1½ cups warm water

6 cups unsifted all-purpose flour
2 teaspoons salt
2 teaspoons sugar
½ teaspoon baking soda

To make sourdough starter: Mix together 1 cup flour, 1 cup water, and 1 tablespoon sugar and let the mixture stand in a warm place 2 to 3 days or until fermented. Sourdough starter may also be purchased.

Sprinkle yeast over warm water to dissolve. Stir in the sourdough starter, *4 cups of the flour,* salt, and sugar. Stir vigorously for 3 minutes. Transfer to a large greased bowl, cover with a tea towel, and let rise in a warm place until double in size. This takes about 2 hours. Mix baking soda with *1 cup of the remaining flour* and stir into dough. Turn dough onto a floured board and knead in remaining cup of flour (even a little more, if necessary) until dough is smooth and not sticky. Shape it into one large round loaf or 2 oblong loaves and place on a lightly greased cooky sheet. Cover and let rise in a warm place until nearly double in size. Before baking, brush surface with water and score or slash the top diagonally with a sharp knife. Before putting bread in the oven to bake, place a shallow pan of hot water in the bottom of the oven. Bake bread in a preheated 400° oven for 45 to 50 minutes.

OATMEAL BREAD

¾ cup milk
1 package active dry yeast or
  1 cake compressed
1 cup quick-cooking oatmeal
1¼ cups boiling water

1½ teaspoons salt
½ cup dark molasses
1 tablespoon butter
5 cups sifted all-purpose flour

Heat milk until a film forms. Skim surface. Remove from heat and, when lukewarm, stir in the yeast. Put oatmeal in a large bowl. Stir in boiling water, salt, molasses, and butter. Cool to lukewarm, then mix in flour and milk thoroughly. Use your hands because the dough is very heavy. Cover bowl with a clean tea towel and set in a warm spot away from drafts until dough doubles in size (about 1½ hours). Turn out on a floured board and knead lightly for about 3 minutes. Divide in half, shape into 2 loaves, and place in greased loaf pans. Let bread rise a second time until double in size. Bake in a preheated 350° oven for about 1 hour. Remove from oven and brush crust with melted butter. Cool slightly, then remove from pans, and cool completely on a rack. A delicious bread that keeps well.

SALT RISING BREAD

Sometimes called lightnin' bread, Salt Rising Bread was popular at a time when homemade yeasts were unreliable. Today's cooks may find this type of bread difficult to prepare.

2 cups milk
2 cups white corn meal
1 tablespoon sugar
1 teaspoon salt

½ teaspoon baking soda
8-10 cups sifted all-purpose flour
2 tablespoons shortening

Scald milk, remove from heat, and stir in corn meal, sugar, and salt until smooth. Cover with a tea towel and set in a warm place overnight. The following morning, add 1 cup warm water mixed with baking soda and *about 2½ cups flour* (enough to make a rather stiff batter). Set the bowl of batter in a pan of warm water, cover, and let stand until it foams up (this can take from 2 hours to half a day). Try to keep the water at an even temperature all the time —not too hot, not too cold. If it seems as though the batter is not rising, give it a stir to help it along. Some people object to the odor during this period but, as *Practical Housekeeping* explained, this is "the result of acetous [or sour] fermentation, but the more of that the more sure you are of having sweet bread when baked." When the batter has risen, knead in shortening and more flour (it may take as many as 8 cups) to make a stiff bread dough. Shape into 2 loaves, set in greased loaf pans, and let rise until double in bulk. Bake in a preheated 350° oven for about 1 hour or until light brown in color.

A RISE IN BREAD-STUFFS!—EFFECTS OF EATING AËRATED BREAD.

Magazine cartoon, 1860

MORAVIAN SUGAR CAKE

2 medium potatoes	1 teaspoon salt
1 package active dry yeast or	2 eggs, well beaten
1 cake compressed	4 cups sifted all-purpose flour (about)
½ cup warm water	Butter
¼ cup soft butter	Brown Sugar
½ cup shortening	Cinnamon
1 cup sugar	

Pare potatoes and cook in boiling water until tender. Drain (reserve 1 cup of the water) and mash potatoes until smooth. Sprinkle yeast over warm water to dissolve. Combine hot mashed potatoes with butter, shortening, sugar, and salt. Mix thoroughly and, when cooled to lukewarm, stir in 1 cup of potato water and the dissolved yeast. Cover with a tea towel and place in a warm spot until spongy-looking. Beat the mixture with eggs and enough flour to make a soft dough. Cover again and let rise in a warm place until double in size. Divide dough in half and make an even layer in 2 greased 11¼ x 7½ x 1½-inch baking pans. Let rise the third time until light, then with your finger poke holes in the dough, filling the holes with generous amounts of butter and brown sugar. Sprinkle top with cinnamon and bake in a preheated 375° oven for 20 to 30 minutes. Cool and cut into squares to serve.

PHILADELPHIA STICKY BUNS

In the nineteenth century, Sticky Buns—a Philadelphia specialty—were sold fresh every day and were eaten at breakfast, teatime, and dinner.

1 package active dry yeast or	6 tablespoons sugar
1 cake compressed	2 egg yolks, well beaten
¼ cup lukewarm water	1 teaspoon salt
1 cup milk	Grated rind of 1 lemon
4½ cups sifted all-purpose flour	1 teaspoon cinnamon
½ cup plus 2 tablespoons butter,	½ cup currants
melted	¾ cup brown sugar

Sprinkle yeast over lukewarm water to dissolve. Scald milk, remove from heat, and cool to lukewarm. Combine milk, yeast, and *1½ cups of the flour* and beat vigorously until smooth. Cover with a tea towel and let stand in a warm place, away from drafts, until light or until mixture has big dimples on the surface. Now add *4 tablespoons of melted butter, 4 table-spoons sugar*, egg yolks, salt, grated lemon, and the remaining 3 cups of flour. Knead the mixture, right in the bowl, until smooth and springy. Cover with a tea towel and let rise in a warm place until double in size—this takes several hours. Transfer dough to a floured board and roll about ¾ of an inch thick in a long rectangular shape (dough is elastic and springs back, but persevere). Brush the surface with *2 tablespoons of melted butter* and sprinkle with remaining 2 tablespoons of sugar, the cinnamon, and currants. Roll tightly and cut in 1-inch slices. Work brown sugar with remaining butter, spreading it over the bottom of a heavy skillet. Place the swirls of dough on top of sugar mixture, spacing them evenly, and let rise again, in a warm place, until double in size. Bake in a preheated 350° oven for 30 minutes or until well browned on top. Invert skillet over cooling rack. Makes 12.

SALLY LUNN

There are several old accounts of the origin of the name "Sally Lunn." One of the more appealing is about an English girl who sold bread on the streets, crying "Solet Lune!" to advertise the buns. The sun and the moon—*soleil-lune*, as it is in French—were the images evoked to describe the golden tops and white bottoms of the buns. By the time *soleil-lune* reached America it had become Sally Lunn and, rather than a bun, was a bread baked in a Turk's-head mold.

1 cup milk
1 package active dry yeast or
  1 cake compressed
½ cup (1 stick) butter

⅓ cup sugar
3 eggs
4 cups sifted all-purpose flour
1 teaspoon salt

Heat milk until a film forms. Skim. Cool until lukewarm, then sprinkle in the yeast to dissolve. Meanwhile, work the butter until soft, then add the sugar gradually, and continue working until creamy. Beat the eggs in very hard. Sift flour and salt together. Beat in the flour and the milk mixture alternately. Cover dough with a tea towel and set in a warm place until it doubles in size. Beat very hard and pour into a greased Turk's-head or *gugelhupf* mold or a 10-inch tube pan. Let rise again until double in size, then bake in a preheated 350° oven for 45 to 50 minutes or until nicely browned on top.

PANETTONE

1 cup milk
⅓ cup butter
1 cup sugar
4 eggs
1 package active dry yeast or
  1 cake compressed
1 tablespoon sugar

4 cups all-purpose flour
1 teaspoon salt
1 cup currants
2 tablespoons brandy
½ cup thinly sliced citron
1 teaspoon almond extract
Sliced almonds

Scald milk. Remove from heat and cool to lukewarm. While milk cools, work butter until soft, then work in sugar, a little at a time, as thoroughly as possible. Beat in *3 whole eggs and 1 egg yolk* (set aside remaining white to use later). Sprinkle yeast over lukewarm milk, add 1 tablespoon sugar, and stir until well blended. Add to butter mixture, alternating with flour that has been sifted with salt. Beat vigorously. Soak currants in brandy and stir into dough. Add citron and almond extract. Cover bowl with a tea towel and place in a warm spot about 2 to 3 hours or until double in size. Punch down with your fist, turn out on a board sprinkled with ½ cup flour, and knead gently. Place in a greased 10-inch tube pan or Turk's-head mold, patting down the dough. Beat the egg white until it stands in peaks and brush over surface of the dough. Press a layer of thinly sliced almonds on top, cover with a tea towel, and let rise again in a warm place about 1 hour or until double in size. Bake in a preheated 350° oven for 30 to 40 minutes. *Panettone* may be made in two 6-inch molds or in four 1-pound coffee tins, all well greased. When smaller containers are used, reduce the baking time slightly.

PARKER HOUSE ROLLS

The Parker House, established in 1855, is one of Boston's newer institutions. It is also the home of Parker House Rolls, long considered the patrician of American dinner rolls.

1 package active dry yeast or
  1 cake compressed
¼ cup warm water
2 cups milk
2 tablespoons sugar

1 teaspoon salt
3 tablespoons butter
6½ to 7 cups sifted all-purpose flour
1 egg, well beaten

Dissolve yeast in warm water. Combine milk, sugar, salt, and butter in a saucepan, scald, then cool to lukewarm. Stir in yeast and *3 cups of the flour,* beating very hard. Cover with a tea towel and place in a warm spot. Let rise until light and bubbly, then mix in egg and enough of the remaining flour to make a kneadable dough. Knead well, cover again, and let stand in a warm place until double in size. Roll dough about ⅓ inch thick on a lightly floured board (dough will spring back at first). Cut with a 3-inch round cutter. Brush each circle with a little melted butter, crease center with the back of a floured knife, and fold over, pinching the edges together. Place rolls 1 inch apart on ungreased cooky sheets. Let rise again until almost double in size, then bake in a preheated 450° oven for 12 to 15 minutes. Makes about 30.

Butter molds and stamp

MORAVIAN LOVE FEAST BUNS

1 large potato
1 package active dry yeast or
  1 cake compressed
¼ cup warm water
½ cup butter, melted

1 cup sugar
1 teaspoon salt
2 eggs, well beaten
4 cups sifted all-purpose flour (about)

Pare the potato, cut in chunks, and cook in boiling water until tender. Drain, saving ½ cup of the potato water. Mash potatoes until smooth and measure out ½ cup of them. Sprinkle yeast over warm water to dissolve. Combine mashed potato, ½ cup of the reserved potato water, butter, sugar, salt, and eggs. When mixture is lukewarm, stir in yeast. Cover with a tea towel and set bowl in a warm place until mixture is spongy-looking. Then mix in the flour thoroughly. (At this point you should have a soft dough—add more flour, if needed.) Cover and let rise in a warm spot until double in size. Punch dough down and knead on a floured board until smooth. Pinch off pieces of the dough and shape into buns about 3 inches in diameter. Place on a greased cooky sheet and let rise a third time until almost double in size. Bake in a preheated 375° oven for 25 to 30 minutes. When buns begin to turn golden brown, brush tops with cream or melted butter. Cool before serving. Makes 12.

SWEET POTATO ROLLS

1 large yam	3 tablespoons sugar
1 package active dry yeast or	1 tablespoon butter
1 cake compressed	1 cup milk
1 teaspoon salt	3½ to 4½ cups sifted all-purpose flour

Pare yam and cut in several pieces. Add enough water to cover and cook until tender. Drain, saving ¼ cup of the water in which yam was cooked. Cool yam water to lukewarm and dissolve the yeast in it. Mash yam, then beat in salt, sugar, and butter vigorously. Heat milk until a film shines on top, skim, stir into yam mixture, and cool to lukewarm. When right temperature has been reached, add the softened yeast. Stir in flour, a cupful at a time, until dough is thick enough to knead. Lift onto a floured board and knead until smooth and elastic. Place in a greased bowl, cover with a tea towel, and let rise in a warm place until double in size. Punch dough down with your fist. Pinch off pieces the size of a golf ball and put into greased muffin pans. Let rise again until double in size. Bake in a preheated 425° oven for 13 to 15 minutes. Makes about 20.

KOLACHES

When the Bohemians arrived in Nebraska in the 1860's, they brought *kolaches*, often made with prune, apricot, or other fruit filling.

6 tablespoons milk	4 cups sifted all-purpose flour
2 packages active dry yeast or	*Prune Filling:*
2 cakes compressed	1 pound prunes
1 teaspoon salt	1 tablespoon sugar
2 tablespoons sugar	1 tablespoon butter
½ cup soft butter	½ teaspoon cinnamon
4 whole eggs	½ teaspoon vanilla
4 egg yolks	

Heat milk until lukewarm, add yeast, and let stand several minutes to dissolve. Stir in salt and sugar. Put butter in a large mixing bowl, add *1 whole egg and 1 egg yolk,* beating very hard. Continue adding *1 whole egg and additional yolk,* followed each time by hard beating. When all the eggs have been used, mix in yeast and then flour, beating hard. Cover with a tea towel and place in a warm spot until double in size. Pinch off pieces of dough and shape into smooth balls the size of a large walnut. Place 2 inches apart on a buttered baking sheet, cover, and let rise in a warm place for 30 minutes. Press a hollow in the center of each with your thumb and fill the cavity with marmalade, jam, or prune filling. Bake in a preheated 350° oven for 20 minutes. Remove from oven and, when cool, sprinkle tops generously with confectioners' sugar.

To make prune filling: Cook prunes according to package directions. When tender, drain, discard pits, and chop coarsely. Stir in sugar, softened butter, cinnamon, and vanilla. Taste and add sugar if necessary.

QUICK BREADS

Quick breads have one distinctive ingredient—baking powder. Until the end of the eighteenth century, lightness in baked goods could be achieved only by laboriously beating air into dough along with eggs, or by adding yeast or spirits. In the 1790's, pearlash—a refined form of potash that produces carbon dioxide in baking dough—was discovered in America. Pearlash transformed baking methods: 8,000 tons of it were exported to Europe in 1792. Amelia Simmons published several recipes in her *American Cookery* (1796) calling for pearlash.

It was not until the 1850's that baking powder (which worked in the same way as pearlash or saleratus, except that it was new and improved) was commercially produced, first by Preston and Merrill of Boston. In 1857, Professor E. N. Horsford of Harvard developed a formula for phosphate baking powder which moved *Practical Housekeeping* to declare, "Horsford's Bread Preparation saves time, simplifies the whole process of bread-making, saves labor, and reduces the chances of failure to the minimum . . . It is certain that for rolls, biscuits, griddle-cakes, and the whole list of 'Breakfast and Tea Cakes,' the 'Bread Preparation' is superior to yeast or soda."

PECAN BREAD

2½ cups sifted all-purpose flour
1 cup sugar
1 teaspoon salt
2 teaspoons baking powder

2 cups (two 3-ounce cans) pecans, chopped
2 eggs
1 cup milk

Sift the flour, sugar, salt, and baking powder together in a mixing bowl and stir in the pecans. Beat eggs vigorously in a separate bowl until very thick, add the milk, and stir into the flour-nut mixture. Pour into a greased loaf pan and bake in a preheated 350° oven for 1 hour. Turn out of the pan onto a cake rack and cool. Keeps well, wrapped in foil.

BLACK WALNUT BREAD

3 cups sifted all-purpose flour
4½ teaspoons baking powder
½ cup sugar
1 teaspoon salt

1 cup chopped black walnuts
2 eggs
1 cup milk
¼ cup butter, melted

Sift flour, baking powder, sugar, and salt together into a mixing bowl, then stir in the nuts. Beat the eggs, milk, and melted butter, add to flour mixture, and stir until thoroughly blended. Don't attempt to beat out all the lumps. Spoon into a greased loaf pan and bake in a preheated 350° oven for 1 hour. Turn out of pan and cool before serving.

BANANA BREAD

1½ cups sifted all-purpose flour
½ teaspoon baking soda
½ teaspoon baking powder
¼ teaspoon salt
½ cup butter
1 cup sugar
2 eggs

1 teaspoon vanilla
Grated rind of half a lemon
¾ cup mashed ripe bananas
2 tablespoons commercial sour cream
½ cup chopped walnuts or
    Macadamia nuts

Sift together flour, baking soda, baking powder, and salt. Set aside. Work butter until soft, then work in sugar, a little at a time, until smooth. Beat in eggs, one at a time, add the vanilla, grated lemon rind, and bananas. Stir in flour mixture alternately with sour cream. Last of all, mix in the nuts. Pour into a greased loaf pan and bake in a preheated 350° oven for 1 hour or until a toothpick tested in the center comes out dry. Remove from pan and cool on a rack. Cut in thin slices to serve.

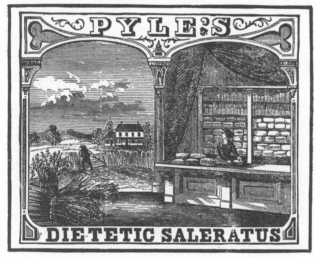

1867 label

CINNAMON FLOP

Topping:
1 cup brown sugar
4 tablespoons softened butter
½ teaspoon cinnamon
Dough:
2 cups sifted all-purpose flour

2 teaspoons baking powder
¼ teaspoon salt
1½ cups sugar
2 tablespoons softened butter
1 egg, well beaten
1 cup milk

Make topping first: Work brown sugar and butter together with your finger tips until well mixed. Then work in cinnamon.

To make dough: Sift flour, baking powder, and salt together and set aside. Mix sugar and butter with your finger tips until butter is well dispersed. Stir in beaten egg thoroughly, then add flour and milk alternately, beginning and ending with flour. Pour into a greased 8-inch square pan, sprinkle the topping over the surface, and bake in a preheated 425° oven for 30 to 35 minutes. Served warm, it makes a delicious breakfast bread.

BISCUITS

The Marquis de Chastellux, traveling through North America in the early 1780's, wrote of a meal he had at the Bullion Tavern in Basking Ridge, New Jersey: "Our supper was very good: only bread was lacking; but inquiring of us what sort we wanted, in an hour's time they served us what we had asked for. This speed will appear less extraordinary if one knows that in America little cakes (*galettes*), which are easily kneaded and baked in half an hour often take the place of bread. Possibly one might . . . tire of them, but I always found them to my taste whenever I met with them." M. Chastellux was describing what Americans commonly call biscuits, which, though rare in most parts of the world, have always been an indispensable ingredient in American cuisine. Recipes for some of the most popular American biscuits, including a few for the cocktail hour, follow.

RICH SHORT BISCUITS

2 cups all-purpose flour or pastry flour
4 teaspoons baking powder
Dash of salt

½ cup (1 stick) butter
Milk

Sift flour, baking powder, and salt into a bowl. Add butter (straight from the refrigerator) cut into 4 or 5 pieces, and work into flour mixture with a pastry blender or two knives until butter is about the size of peas. Add cold milk, a little at a time, stirring it in with a fork. Use only enough milk to hold the dough together. The less you use, the better your biscuits. Now work the dough together with your hands until you've made a ball and all the flour is worked in. Roll dough about ½ inch thick on a lightly floured board, cut with very small biscuit cutter, and place on an ungreased cooky sheet. If you have the time, refrigerate the biscuits for an hour or longer. Bake in a preheated 450° oven for 10 to 12 minutes or until biscuits are lightly browned. Serve hot with fresh, sweet butter. Excellent with cold salads or served with thin slices of Smithfield ham as a cocktail accompaniment. Makes about 20.

CORN MEAL BISCUITS

¾ cup milk
1 cup corn meal
2 tablespoons shortening

¾ teaspoon salt
¾ cup sifted all-purpose flour
4 teaspoons baking powder

Scald milk. Combine corn meal, shortening, and salt in a mixing bowl, then stir in the hot milk until mixture is smooth and shortening has melted. Cool. Sift flour and baking powder together and stir into cold corn-meal mixture. Dump onto a lightly floured board and roll about ¾ inch thick. Cut with a small biscuit cutter, place on ungreased cooky sheet, and bake in a preheated 425° oven for 15 to 20 minutes. The biscuits have a crunchy "bite" to them. Serve hot with butter and, perhaps, maple syrup or honey. Makes about 15.

CREAM BISCUITS

2 cups sifted all-purpose flour
½ teaspoon salt

3 teaspoons baking powder
1 cup heavy cream

Sift flour, salt, and baking powder together in a bowl. In a second bowl, whip the cream until stiff enough to hold a shape. Combine cream and flour mixture with a fork. Place dough on a lightly floured board and knead for about one minute. Pat dough ½ inch thick and cut with a biscuit cutter. Bake in a preheated 450° oven for about 12 minutes. Serve piping hot with plenty of butter. Makes about a dozen medium-sized biscuits.

BUTTERMILK BISCUITS

2 cups sifted all-purpose flour
1 teaspoon baking soda
1 teaspoon baking powder

1 teaspoon salt
1 cup buttermilk or commercial sour cream

Sift flour, baking soda, baking powder, and salt together into a bowl. Add buttermilk or sour cream and blend with a fork until you have a soft dough. Place on a lightly floured board and roll ½ inch thick. Cut with a small biscuit cutter, place on a cooky sheet, and bake in a preheated 425° oven for 12 to 15 minutes or until tipped with gold. Serve piping hot with butter and with honey or strawberry preserves on the side. Makes 12 to 15.

Buttermilk vendor

BENNE SEED COCKTAIL BISCUITS

½ cup benne (sesame) seeds
2 cups sifted all-purpose flour
½ teaspoon salt
1 teaspoon baking powder

½ cup shortening
¼ cup milk (about)
Coarse salt

While you make the dough, toast the benne seeds in a shallow pan in a preheated 350° oven. Sift together flour, salt, and baking powder. Cream shortening until soft, then add the flour mixture, working it in with your hand until it is well combined. Work in the benne seeds. Gradually add milk, stirring with a fork, until dough holds together and has the "feel" of pastry. Roll paper-thin on a lightly floured board and cut with a very small biscuit cutter. Place on a cooky sheet and bake in a 350° oven for 10 to 12 minutes. Sprinkle with coarse salt while they are still hot. Makes about 40 or even more, depending on size of cutter.

BEATEN BISCUITS

In her *New Cookery Book* (1857), Eliza Leslie slighted a southern tradition almost as sanctified as southern belles—Beaten Biscuits. "This is the most laborious of cakes," Miss Leslie said, "and also the most unwholesome, even when made in the best manner. We do not recommend it; but there is no accounting for tastes. Children should not eat these biscuits—nor grown persons either, if they can get any other sort of bread. When living in a town where there are bakers, there is no excuse for making Maryland biscuit. Believe nobody that says they are not unwholesome. . . . Better to live on Indian cakes."

In 1885, Mary Stuart Smith, in her *Virginia Cookery-Book*, replied, "In the Virginia of the olden time no breakfast or tea-table was thought to be properly furnished without a plate of these indispensable biscuits. . . . Let one spend the night at some gentleman-farmer's home, and the first sound heard in the morning, after the crowing of the cock, was the heavy, regular fall of the cook's axe, as she beat and beat her biscuit dough. . . . Nowadays beaten biscuits are a rarity, found here and there, but soda and modern institutions have caused them to be sadly out of vogue."

2 cups flour	1½ teaspoons sugar
½ teaspoon salt	2 tablespoons lard
½ teaspoon baking powder	⅓ to ½ cup water and milk, mixed

Sift dry ingredients together, then cut in lard until mixture appears mealy. Add liquid, a little at a time, to make a stiff dough. Knead thoroughly, then beat with a heavy mallet for half an hour or run several times through the coarse chopper of a meat grinder until dough is elastic. Roll ½ inch thick and cut with small biscuit cutter. Prick tops with fork tines and bake on a cooky sheet in a 325° oven for 35 to 45 minutes or until lightly browned. Makes about 2 dozen.

LOG CABIN CHEESE STRAWS

¼ cup soft butter	Dash cayenne
1 cup grated Cheddar cheese	¾ cup sifted all-purpose flour
¼ cup milk	1½ cups fine soft bread crumbs
¼ teaspoon salt	*Topping:* coarse salt, grated Parmesan
Dash Tabasco	cheese, poppy seeds, or sesame seeds
Dash paprika	

Work butter until creamy, then blend in cheese, milk, salt, Tabasco, paprika, and cayenne. Add flour and bread crumbs, combining thoroughly. Divide mixture in half and refrigerate for several hours or overnight. Roll one portion of the dough at a time, between 2 sheets of wax paper, until quite thin. Work quickly because this very rich pastry will readily soften. With a pastry wheel (called a jagger in old recipes) or knife cut pastry into strips about 5 inches long and ¾ inch wide. Place on a cooky sheet, sprinkle with any one of the suggested toppings, and bake in a preheated 350° oven for 12 to 15 minutes or until delicately browned. Pile log-cabin style on platter. Serve with cocktails or salad. Makes about 40.

CHEDDAR BISCUITS

1 cup sifted all-purpose flour
¼ teaspoon salt

⅓ cup butter
1 cup grated Cheddar cheese

Sift flour and salt together into a bowl. Cut in butter with a pastry blender or two knives, then mix in cheese. Mix lightly with your hand until dough holds together. Roll about ½ inch thick on a lightly floured board. Cut with a small biscuit cutter and prick tops with fork tines. Place on an ungreased cooky sheet and bake in a preheated 350° oven for 12 to 15 minutes. Properly baked, the biscuits should be a rich Cheddar color, not brown. These biscuits taste best cold. Serve with cocktails or as a companion to a simple green salad. They keep well. Makes 22 to 24 biscuits.

Making butter curls

FLASH UN KAS

Flash un Kas is a Pennsylvania Dutch corruption of the German *Fleisch und Käse,* meaning meat and cheese.

2 cups all-purpose flour
Pinch of salt

1 cup (2 sticks) butter
1 package (8-ounce size) cream cheese

Sift flour and salt together in a bowl, then cut in butter and cream cheese with a pastry blender or two knives until mixture appears mealy. Gather into a ball and chill several hours or overnight. Pinch off bits of the pastry and roll as thin as possible on a lightly floured board. Work fast. Cut with a 2-inch round cooky cutter and place on a baking sheet. Spread with any of these fillings: canned liver *pâté* seasoned with a little Worcestershire sauce; ground Smithfield ham highly seasoned with steak sauce and a little ketchup; anchovy paste; caviar. Fold the circles to make a half moon, press edges together, and bake in a preheated 400° oven until delicately browned. Traditionally served with cold beer. Makes 12 to 15.

HOMEMADE CRACKERS

4 cups all-purpose flour
2 tablespoons sugar
1 teaspoon salt

¼ cup butter
1 cup milk

Sift together flour, sugar, and salt. Cut in butter with a pastry blender or two knives until mixture looks mealy. Stir in enough milk to make a stiff dough. Roll about ¼ inch thick on a lightly floured board and cut with a large round cooky cutter. Prick surface in many places with fork tines and brush lightly with milk. Place on an ungreased baking sheet and bake in a 425° oven for 15 to 18 minutes or until light gold in color. Makes several dozen.

POPOVERS

1 cup sifted all-purpose flour
½ teaspoon salt
2 eggs

1 cup milk
1 tablespoon vegetable oil

Grease aluminum or iron popover pans and set them aside or, if custard cups are used, heat in the oven and grease just before filling with batter. Combine all ingredients in a bowl and beat until smooth. Fill pans or cups slightly less than half-full. Bake in a preheated 425° oven about 35 minutes (do not open oven door during baking). Serve immediately to 6.

BLUEBERRY MUFFINS

In 1894, recalling a breakfast in Boston he had had some years earlier with Oliver Wendell Holmes's publisher, James T. Fields, William Dean Howells wrote, "I remember his burlesque pretence that morning of an inextinguishable grief when I owned that I had never eaten blueberry cake before, and how he kept returning to the pathos of the fact that there should be a region of the earth where blueberry cake was unknown." There are those—though Mr. Howells apparently did not share this confusion—who think they have eaten blueberry muffins when, in fact, they have eaten huckleberry muffins. Though the difference is slight, it is one Howells' friend Holmes would have seized upon: the blueberry is a *Vaccinium*, and the huckleberry a *Gaylussacia;* the blueberry has many small seeds, and the huckleberry has ten hard, quite noticeable seeds.

1½ cups sifted all-purpose flour
1½ teaspoons baking powder
¼ teaspoon salt
5 tablespoons softened butter

½ cup sugar
1 egg
½ cup milk
1 cup fresh blueberries

Sift together flour, baking powder, and salt. Set aside. Cream butter, add sugar a little at a time, and continue creaming until mixture is smooth and fluffy. Beat in the egg vigorously. Then stir in flour combination and milk, alternating them and beginning and ending with flour. Fold in blueberries and spoon into a well-greased muffin tin. Bake in a preheated 400° oven for 25 to 30 minutes. Makes 12.

SQUASH GEMS

1½ cups sifted all-purpose flour
¼ teaspoon salt
½ cup sugar
2 teaspoons baking powder

1 egg
¾ cup milk
½ cup frozen squash, thawed
1 tablespoon butter, melted

Sift together flour, salt, sugar, and baking powder. Beat egg vigorously and stir in milk, squash, and butter. Stir into dry ingredients, using as few strokes as possible. Pour into a well-greased muffin tin and bake in a preheated 425° oven for 25 to 30 minutes. Makes 12.

GRAHAM GEMS

1 cup sifted all-purpose flour
¾ teaspoon salt
2 tablespoons brown sugar
3 teaspoons baking powder

1 cup Graham or whole-wheat flour
1 egg
1 cup milk
3 tablespoons shortening, melted

Sift together flour, salt, brown sugar, and baking powder. Stir in Graham or whole-wheat flour thoroughly. Beat egg vigorously in a separate bowl, then stir in milk and melted shortening. Stir into flour mixture until blended—don't attempt to beat out the lumps. Pour into a greased muffin tin and bake in a preheated 400° oven for 15 to 20 minutes or until a toothpick tested in the center comes out dry. Serve warm with butter. Makes 12.

CRANBERRY MUFFINS

2 cups sifted all-purpose flour
2 teaspoons baking powder
3 tablespoons sugar
½ teaspoon salt
1 cup fresh cranberries

½ cup confectioners' sugar
1 egg
1 cup milk
3 tablespoons melted butter

Sift together flour, baking powder, sugar, and salt and set aside. Cut cranberries in half and mix with confectioners' sugar. Beat egg vigorously, then stir in milk, flour combination, and butter. Stir as little as possible—the batter should be lumpy. Fold in the cranberries, spoon into greased muffin tins, and bake in a preheated 400° oven for 20 to 25 minutes or until a toothpick tested in the center comes out dry. Makes 12 to 15.

LAPLANDS

Presenting this recipe for Laplands in her *Virginia Cookery-Book,* Mary Stuart Smith declared, "Nothing in the shape of bread can be more delicate or tempting."

1 cup sifted all-purpose flour
¼ teaspoon salt

3 eggs
1 cup heavy cream

Grease a muffin tin very thoroughly. Sift flour and salt together. Separate eggs and beat the yolks in a small bowl until very thick and creamy. Whip cream until it holds a shape when you lift the beater. Now add the flour and whipped cream to egg yolks alternately, beginning and ending with flour. Finally, whip the egg whites until they stand in peaks. Dump egg batter on top of whites and mix with your hands until all white patches have disappeared. Work quickly. Spoon into muffin tin, filling half-full. Bake in a preheated 375° oven for 20 to 25 minutes. You can prepare the mixture, except for the egg whites, ahead of time. Serve hot with sweet butter. Makes 12.

SPOON BREAD

One of the most famous southern dishes, Spoon Bread traces its origin to the Indian porridge, *suppawn*, and still retains the consistency of a porridge or pudding.

5 tablespoons butter	2 cups boiling water
1 cup water-ground corn meal	1 cup cold milk
1 teaspoon salt	4 eggs

Heat oven to 425°. Put butter in a medium-sized earthenware or glass baking dish and place in oven to melt while you prepare the batter. Combine corn meal and salt in a mixing bowl and stir in boiling water until smooth. Let stand several minutes, then stir in milk. Add the eggs, one at a time, beating hard after each addition. Stir in melted butter last of all. Pour batter into the hot baking dish and bake 25 to 30 minutes. Serve hot, right from the baking dish, with plenty of extra butter. Serves 4.

HOMINY BREAD

½ cup uncooked hominy grits	½ cup white corn meal
1 tablespoon butter	½ teaspoon salt
3 eggs, separated	2 teaspoons baking powder

Stir grits into 2½ cups of boiling, salted water, cover, and cook over a low heat for 30 minutes. Measure out 2 cups of the hot grits and spoon into a mixing bowl. Stir in butter until melted, then add the egg yolks, thoroughly beaten. Sift the corn meal, salt, and baking powder together into the mixture and stir in thoroughly. Beat the egg whites until they stand in peaks and fold into the batter. Pour into a buttered 1½-quart baking dish. Bake in a preheated 350° oven for 1 hour. Serve piping hot with lots of sweet butter. Like Spoon Bread, Hominy Bread is served with meats. Serves 4 to 6.

CRACKLIN' BREAD

Originally Cracklin' Bread was made with cracklings (the crisp bits of pork left after lard has been rendered), salt, corn meal, and water. However, like many old recipes this one has been refined, and now contains eggs and buttermilk.

¾ cup finely diced salt pork	1 teaspoon salt
2 cups corn meal	2 eggs, well beaten
1½ teaspoons baking powder	1 cup buttermilk
½ teaspoon baking soda	2 tablespoons salt-pork drippings

Fry salt pork over a low heat until nicely browned. Drain fat, saving both drippings and cracklings. Sift together corn meal, baking powder, baking soda, and salt. Combine eggs, buttermilk, and drippings. Stir into corn-meal mixture, together with cracklings. Spread dough in a greased 11 x 7 x 1½-inch baking pan and bake in a preheated 400° oven for 25 to 30 minutes.

SPIDER CORNCAKE

Spider Corncake is named for the "spider," an old iron frying pan with legs, which was set right over the hot coals.

1½ cups white corn meal,
    preferably water-ground
1 tablespoon sugar
1 teaspoon salt

1 teaspoon baking soda
2 eggs, well beaten
2 cups buttermilk
1½ tablespoons melted butter

Start your oven at 450° and put in a 12-inch iron skillet or spider to heat. Sift together corn meal, sugar, salt, and baking soda into a bowl. Combine eggs and buttermilk and stir into corn-meal mixture, keeping it smooth. Last of all, stir in butter. Pour into the hot spider, well greased, and bake (at this same high temperature) for 30 minutes.

"Spider" frying pan and hanging skillet

RHODE ISLAND JOHNNYCAKES

Johnnycakes, originally an Indian food, may first have been known as Shawnee cakes. (Another theory is that they were called journey cakes, since travelers often took packages of them on long trips.) Whatever its origin, the name was gradually battered into "Johnny," and the recipes were jounced through frontier country until no one can agree on the "authentic" ingredients. Today, purists insist that they should not be made with sugar. In Richard Henry Dana's novel *Two Years Before the Mast*, published in 1840, the captain tells his unruly crew, "I'm Frank Thompson, all the way from 'down east.' I've been through the mill, ground, and bolted, and come out a *regular-built down-east johnny-cake*, when it's hot, damned good; but when it's cold, damned sour and indigestible;—and you'll find me so."

1 cup stone-ground white corn meal
1 teaspoon salt

1 teaspoon sugar (optional)
1¼ cups boiling water

Combine corn meal, salt, and sugar. Stir in water until mixture is smooth (batter will be very thick). Drop by tablespoons onto a well-greased griddle and fry over moderate heat for 6 minutes. Turn and cook the second side for 5 minutes. Makes 8 to 10.

VARIATION: If you want thin Johnnycakes, as Rhode Islanders say they should be, thin the batter with ½ cup milk or water. Serve buttered and, if you like, with maple syrup.

CREAM WAFFLES

The Dutch introduced waffles to America. It was their custom, when they settled in New York, to give a new bride a waffle iron with her initials and the date of her wedding carved into it.

1 cup sifted all-purpose flour
4 teaspoons baking powder
¼ teaspoon salt

3 eggs, separated
1 cup heavy cream

Sift together flour, baking powder, and salt. Set aside. Beat yolks vigorously, then add cream, and continue beating hard. Stir in flour combination and beat with a rotary or electric beater until smooth. Fold in stiffly beaten egg whites thoroughly and refrigerate for half an hour. Bake in a preheated waffle iron until crisp and delicately browned. Serve with butter and warm honey or maple syrup. The number of waffles depends on the size of your waffle iron.

STRINGS OF FLATS

Stacks of these griddlecakes were consumed in the old lumbering camps, where they were known both as Flannel Cakes (possibly in honor of the layers of flannel shirts worn by the lumberjacks or because the griddlecakes tasted like flannel) and as Strings of Flats, or Flatcars, presumably for the railroad flatcars that took the lumber to market.

1 cup sifted all-purpose flour
1 tablespoon baking powder
½ teaspoon salt
2 tablespoons sugar

2 eggs
1 cup milk
2 tablespoons melted butter

Sift flour, baking powder, salt, and sugar into a mixing bowl. In a separate container, beat eggs until light, then stir in milk and melted butter. With as few strokes as possible blend egg mixture in with the dry ingredients. Pour batter onto a hot, greased griddle (griddle is hot enough when a few drops of water tested on it sizzle) and cook until both sides are nicely browned. Serve at once with butter and warm maple syrup or honey.

BUTTERMILK PANCAKES

1½ cups all-purpose flour
½ tablespoon baking powder
¼ teaspoon salt
½ tablespoon sugar

1 egg
1¼ cups buttermilk
2 tablespoons melted butter

Sift together flour, baking powder, salt, and sugar. Beat egg vigorously, then stir in buttermilk and butter. Combine with flour combination, using as few strokes as possible—overbeating toughens pancakes. Mixture will be lumpy. Drop batter by spoonfuls onto a hot, greased griddle (griddle is right temperature when a few drops of water sprinkled on it sizzle). When large bubbles appear and begin to burst, turn pancakes, then brown on second side. Serve at once.

BUCKWHEAT CAKES

A popular breakfast staple in America's Northwest, Buckwheat Cakes were made famous in London, too, by James McNeill Whistler, who served them at his sophisticated literary breakfasts.

½ package active dry yeast or
  ½ cake compressed
¼ cup lukewarm water
2 cups milk

2 cups buckwheat flour
½ teaspoon salt
1 tablespoon molasses
1 scant teaspoon baking soda

Dissolve yeast in lukewarm water. Scald milk, then cool to lukewarm. Blend together yeast, milk, buckwheat, and salt, beating hard for 2 minutes. Cover with a tea towel and let stand at room temperature overnight. Next day, mix in molasses, baking soda, and ¼ cup warm water. Pour onto a hot greased griddle (griddle is hot enough when several drops of water tested on it sizzle). Brown on both sides. Serve immediately with butter and warm maple syrup.

Label for sacks of buckwheat flour

NEW ORLEANS PAIN PERDU

This recipe for "lost bread," similar to French toast, is adapted from *La Cuisine Creole*. *Pain perdu* was originally flavored with orange-flower water.

Combine 2 eggs with 1 tablespoon confectioners' sugar, a pinch of salt, and ¾ cup milk and beat thoroughly. Stir in grated rind of half a lemon. Dip slices of bread, not too fresh, in the mixture, then fry in plenty of heated butter until crisp and golden brown on both sides. Serve immediately with maple syrup, honey, or a mixture of sugar and cinnamon. This makes enough batter for about 6 slices.

FISH

BAKED SHAD WITH ROE SOUFFLÉ

Shad were so plentiful in colonial days that they were altogether unfashionable. Edward Eggleston wrote in *Century Magazine* in 1885, "Shad were too plentiful; incredible stories are told of three thousand taken at a haul; they sold for from one to two cents apiece of our present money, and were held so cheap that the salmon were sometimes picked out of a net and the shad rejected. Well-to-do people only ate shad on the sly, lest they should be suspected of not having a good supply of pork." In spite of the commonness of shad, it was the excuse for a number of parties in Washington—in the early days of the republic, senators and representatives sailed down the Potomac nearly every Saturday on parties organized for the sole purpose of eating shad and having a few drinks. George Washington had several fishing stations on the Potomac where shad were caught, and Baked Shad was one of Washington's favorite dishes.

A 5- to 6-pound roe shad	Few sprigs parsley
Flour	¼ cup butter
Salt	1 medium onion, chopped fine
Paprika	½ cup flour
Lemon juice	1 cup milk
Butter	1 cup parsley, chopped
Topping:	¼ cup white wine
1 extra roe	3 eggs, separated
1 tablespoon vinegar	1 teaspoon salt
½ teaspoon salt	Juice of 1 lemon
1 bay leaf	

Buy shad split and boned, but *not* cut in half. Set roe aside. Oil skin and place fish, skin down, on a piece of foil. Spread the shad flat, sprinkle with a little flour, salt, paprika, and lemon juice, and dot with butter. Bake in a 350° oven about 1 hour (12 minutes per pound). While shad bakes, prepare topping.

To make the topping: Cover the two shad roe with water. Add vinegar, salt, bay leaf, and parsley. Cook over a low heat about 10 minutes or until the roe is firm. Drain, remove membrane, and separate the eggs with a fork. Melt butter in a saucepan, stir in onion, and cook until limp. Add roe and cook until well coated with butter. Stir in flour until smooth, then add milk, and cook, stirring constantly, until sauce is thick and bubbly. Remove from heat, stir in chopped parsley and wine. Beat egg yolks slightly, stir in some of the hot sauce gradually, then combine with remaining sauce. Season with 1 teaspoon salt and the lemon juice. Beat egg whites until they stand in peaks, then fold into yolk mixture gently. Remove fish from oven and spread roe mixture over the entire shad. Dot with butter and sprinkle with paprika. Return to oven and bake 10 minutes. Place under broiler for a few minutes or until "soufflé" top is delicately browned. Serve at once to 10 or 12.

PLANKED STUFFED SHAD

Shad was known as *elft*, the eleven fish, to the early Dutch settlers in New York. It was on the eleventh of March each year that the first shad were caught and cooked on a plank—a method learned from the Indians.

Buy a 4-pound shad, split and boned, with head, tail, and fins left on. Wash the fish, then rub, inside and out, with sherry, and sprinkle lightly with a mixture of salt, pepper, a little dried thyme, and nutmeg. Stuff with this dressing:

1 cup cooked finnan haddie	1½ teaspoons grated onion
2 cups fresh bread crumbs	Salt
3 tablespoons melted butter	Pepper
¼ cup chopped parsley	Pinch each of nutmeg, thyme, and mace
¼ cup chopped celery leaves	Dry white wine

Prepare the plank by oiling well, then place in a cold oven, and bring the heat up to 400°. Cook finnan haddie as for Creamed Finnan Haddie (page 46).Work through a food grinder. Combine with all ingredients and enough wine to hold the mixture together lightly. Stuff fish and sew the opening together. Reduce heat to 375°. Place shad on the hot plank and bake, allowing 10 to 15 minutes per pound. Baste frequently with melted butter. Shortly before the fish is done, remove the plank from the oven. With a pastry tube, pipe a border of Potatoes Duchesse (page 113) around the edge of the plank. Brush the potatoes with butter, return the plank to the oven, and bake until the fish is done and the potatoes delicately browned. Before serving the planked shad, inside the border of potatoes arrange small bouquets of hot cooked vegetables, such as French green beans, glazed small white onions, asparagus tips with Hollandaise Sauce (page 126), or broiled mushroom caps. Serve with lemon wedges. Serves 6 to 8.

BAKED COD

Cod was once one of the main sources of food for New England. As early as 1640, the cod fishing industry had reached such proportions that in one year New Englanders prepared 300,000 dried codfish for market. So important was the fish—dietarily and economically—for Massachusetts that on March 17, 1784, according to the Journal of the Massachusetts House of Representatives: "Mr. John Rowe moved the House that leave might be given to hang up the representation of a Cod Fish in the room where the House sit, as a memorial of the importance of the Cod Fishery to the welfare of this Commonwealth." In 1798, the four-foot-eleven-inch codfish, called the Sacred Cod, was moved to the new State House and, in 1895, to its present location in the House chamber, opposite the speaker's desk.

Place fillets of cod in a well-oiled baking dish. Sprinkle with salt, pepper, lemon juice, and a little paprika. Dot with butter or cover with buttered crumbs. Bake in a preheated 400° oven until fish flakes easily when tested with a fork. Baking time varies from 12 to 30 minutes, depending on the thickness of the fillets.

LOUISIANA BAKED BLUEFISH

A 4- to 4½-pound bluefish
Salad oil
Salt
Pepper
1 tablespoon finely chopped onion

¾ cup tomato juice
Creole Sauce (page 129)
¾ cup fine fresh bread crumbs
2 tablespoons melted butter

Have fish cleaned, leaving head and tail intact. Lay fish in a shallow, well-oiled baking pan, rub the skin with oil, and sprinkle with salt and pepper. Scatter onion over the fish, then add tomato juice to pan. Bake in a preheated 350° oven for 30 minutes, basting occasionally with the tomato juice. Remove from oven and pour Creole Sauce over fish. Mix bread crumbs with melted butter and sprinkle on top. Slide fish under a preheated broiler, 4 inches from tip of flame, and broil until browned. Serves 6.

FRIED CATFISH

Father Dollier and Father Galinée, members of the American expedition of La Salle, reported on a journey through the Northwest in 1669-70, "Fishing is pretty good. . . . We had only to throw a line in the water to catch forty or fifty fish of the kind called here *barbue* [catfish]. There is none like it in France. Travelers and poor people live on it very comfortably, for it can be eaten, and is very good cooked in water without sauce."

Dip skinned fish (whole or in chunks) in beaten egg yolk. Then coat with dry bread crumbs, cracker crumbs, or corn meal. Preheat deep fat to 370° on a deep-fat thermometer or until a 1-inch cube of bread browns in 60 seconds. Fry fish until crisp and nicely browned. This takes about 3 to 5 minutes, depending on the size of the fish. Drain on paper towels and season to taste with salt and pepper. Serve with Hush Puppies (page 117), Coleslaw (page 132), and pickles.

BROILED SALT ROE HERRING

Herring was the staple fish on the Potomac during the time Washington lived at Mount Vernon. The General had several fishing stations on the river, and one of the managers of his estate recorded, "excellent herring were caught . . . which, when salted, proved an important article of food to the poor. For their accommodation he [Washington] appropriated a station—one of the best he had—and furnished it with all the necessary apparatus for taking herring."

Soak the fish (1 to 2 salt roe herring per person) for 24 hours in enough water to cover. Change the water several times. Place herring, roe side up, on a broiling pan or tray, sprinkle with lemon juice, dot generously with butter, and broil under a low heat for 15 minutes. Serve hot with Corn Sticks (page 33), Spoon Bread (page 34), or hominy grits.

NEW ENGLAND BROILED SCROD

Scrod (a young filleted cod) is strictly a New England dish, and it seems to be always available there. Describing an outing, Benjamin Franklin once wrote: "Being becalm'd off Block Island, our people set about catching cod, and hauled up a great many. Hitherto I had stuck to my resolution of not eating animal food [he had been a vegetarian], and on this occasion I consider'd . . . the taking of every fish as a kind of unprovoked murder . . . But I had formerly been a great lover of fish, and, when this came hot out of the frying-pan, it smelt admirably well. I balanc'd some time between principle and inclination, till I recollected that, when the fish were opened, I saw smaller fish taken out of their stomachs; then thought I, 'If you eat one another, I don't see why we mayn't eat you.' So I din'd upon cod very heartily . . . So convenient a thing it is to be a *reasonable creature*, since it enables one to find or make a reason for every thing one has a mind to do."

Arrange 4 scrod fillets on a well-buttered broiling pan. Sprinkle generously with lemon juice, pour a little melted butter over each fillet, season with salt and a light dusting of paprika. Broil about 4 inches from broiling unit for 6 to 8 minutes or until scrod flakes easily with a fork. Remove to a heated platter with a broad spatula. Serve with Lemon Butter (page 127) and boiled potatoes. Makes 4 servings.

GRILLED TROUT

1 large, freshly caught trout	Pepper
Salt	Melted butter

Cut the cleaned trout so that it will lie flat when opened and remove the backbone. Place, skin side down, in a well-oiled broiling pan. Sprinkle with salt and pepper and brush generously with butter. Broil 3 inches from tip of unit in a preheated 450° broiler 8 to 10 minutes or until fish flakes easily when tested with a fork. Do not overcook.

To grill over hot coals: Use a hinged grill so the fish will stay in place. Make certain grill is hot enough to mark or score the fish. Before grilling, coat fish with flour, then brush thoroughly with oil. During the grilling, brush several times with more oil. For a 4- to 5-pound trout, allow 6 to 8 minutes per side.

FILLET OF FLOUNDER, AMERICAN STYLE

6 fillets of flounder	Corn meal
Flour	Fat for deep-fat frying
2 eggs	Salt
½ cup milk	Pepper

Beat eggs and milk together. Dust fillets with flour, dip in milk mixture, then coat with corn meal. Fry in deep fat preheated to 365° on deep-fat thermometer or until a 1-inch cube of bread browns in 60 seconds. When fillets are crisp and brown, drain on paper towels and season to taste. Serve with Lemon Butter (page 127) or Tartare Sauce (page 127). Serves 4 to 6.

STUFFED BAKED FILLETS CREOLE

4 tablespoons butter
2 tablespoons chopped onion
4 tablespoons chopped celery
2 tablespoons chopped green pepper
2 tablespoons flour
½ cup milk
½ cup fine dry bread crumbs
Pinch each of dried thyme,
   rosemary, and marjoram
1 cup cooked crab meat

1 cup cooked shrimp, cut in pieces
½ cup chopped parsley
¼ teaspoon salt
Dash pepper
1½ teaspoons Worcestershire sauce
Dash Tabasco
4 to 8 fillets of sole or flounder
   (depending on size)
Paprika
Creole Sauce (page 129)

Melt butter in a saucepan. Stir in onion, celery, green pepper and cook until tender. Stir in flour, keeping mixture as smooth as possible. Add milk and cook until thickened. Remove from heat and stir in all remaining ingredients, *except the fillets.* Make a mound of the filling on each of the fillets, roll up ends, and attach with a toothpick. Place in a shallow baking pan, leaving space between fillets. Brush with melted butter and sprinkle with salt and paprika. Bake in a preheated 350° oven for 15 minutes. Then pour Creole Sauce over fish, reduce heat to 325°, and bake 30 minutes longer. Serves 6 to 8.

Fish server

FILLET OF SOLE MARGUERY À LA DIAMOND JIM

2 flounder, filleted
1 pound halibut or cod
½ cup sliced carrots
1 leek, sliced
3 sprigs parsley
10 peppercorns
1 small bay leaf
1 sprig thyme

1½ quarts water
Salt
Pepper
12 oysters, poached
12 boiled shrimp, shelled
¼ cup dry white wine
½ cup (1 stick) butter
4 egg yolks

Ask the fish dealer to give you the heads, tails, and skin from the flounder. Place these trimmings and small chunks of the halibut or cod in a saucepan. Toss in carrots, leek, parsley, peppercorns, bay leaf, and thyme. Add water and cook to a boil, then reduce heat, and simmer gently until liquid is reduced to about 1 pint. Strain through a fine cheesecloth, saving the stock. Arrange fillets in a buttered baking dish and sprinkle with salt and pepper. Add 1 cup of the fish stock and bake in a preheated 325° oven for 15 to 20 minutes. With a broad spatula, carefully transfer fillets to a hot ovenproof serving platter. Arrange oysters and shrimp on top. Set aside. Pour remaining cup of fish stock into pan in which fillets baked. Cook until stock is reduced to about ¼ cup. Strain into top of double boiler, add white wine and butter. Cook over hot water, stirring until butter is melted. Beat egg yolks vigorously, then stir in the butter mixture a little at a time. Pour egg mixture into top of double boiler and cook, stirring constantly, until sauce is the consistency of a medium cream sauce. Pour over fish. Broil in a preheated broiler until golden brown. Serves 4.

NEW ORLEANS BOUILLABAISSE

Bouillabaisse (its name deriving from the instruction, *"Quand ça commence à bouillir—baisse!"*) is one of the most famous of New Orleans dishes. Thackeray, in his *Roundabout Papers* (1891), recalled this New Orleans stew: "At that comfortable tavern on Pontchartrain we had a *bouillabaisse* than which a better was never eaten at Marseilles; and not the least headache in the morning, I give you my word; on the contrary, you only wake with a sweet refreshing thirst for claret and water."

Court bouillon:
Head of a red snapper
1½ quarts boiling water
Bunch of herbs (thyme, parsley, bay leaf)
1 onion, sliced
Bouillabaisse:
6 slices red snapper
6 slices redfish
Salt
Pepper
Cayenne
3 cloves garlic, minced
3 sprigs thyme, chopped, or
  1 teaspoon dried thyme

3 sprigs parsley, chopped
3 bay leaves, crushed
1 teaspoon allspice
2 tablespoons olive oil
3 mild onions, chopped
2 cups dry white wine
6 large ripe tomatoes,
  canned or fresh
½ lemon, thinly sliced
¼ teaspoon saffron
12 slices French bread
½ cup (1 stick) butter

To make the court bouillon: Place the red snapper head in boiling water with the bunch of herbs and the sliced onion. Cook over a low heat, uncovered, until liquid is reduced to about 1 pint. Strain and set liquid aside.

To make the Bouillabaisse: Sprinkle the slices of red snapper and redfish with salt, pepper, and cayenne. Combine garlic, thyme, parsley, bay leaves, allspice and sprinkle over fish slices. Let stand about 30 minutes for flavor to permeate the fish. Heat olive oil in a large heavy kettle, add chopped onions, and cook over a low heat until limp. Lay fish slices on top (do not overlap), cover, and cook slowly for 5 minutes. Turn the slices and cook another 5 minutes. Carefully transfer fish to a platter. Add wine to kettle, then add the tomatoes (sliced, if fresh ones are used), lemon slices, and court bouillon previously set aside. Cook, uncovered, until liquid is reduced by half. Return fish slices to the liquid and simmer gently for 5 minutes. Meanwhile, dissolve the saffron in a little of the hot liquid from the kettle. Set aside. Sauté slices of French bread in melted butter and place on a large deep serving dish. Put a slice of fish on top of each piece of bread and spread the saffron mixture over the fish. Pour the hot broth over all and serve immediately. Serves 12.

VARIATION: To the simmering court bouillon, add ½ pound large uncooked shrimp (in their shells) and 1 pound lobster tails. Cook 5 minutes, then remove from liquid. Shell and clean shrimp (add the shells to the court bouillon). Set shrimp aside. Do the same with the lobster tails. When cooked, cut the lobster meat into small pieces and set aside with the cooked shrimp. In a separate pan, steam open 1 dozen cherry stone clams and ½ pound mussels. Before serving Bouillabaisse, add shrimp and lobster pieces to liquid. Place clams and mussels in the serving dish with the slices of sautéed bread.

POACHED HALIBUT WITH HOLLANDAISE SAUCE

Halibut was at one time so plentiful on the eastern coast that the cod fishermen considered it a nuisance. This recipe was quite common on the menus of nineteenth-century hotels and inns in the East.

Place 4 halibut steaks, 1½ to 2 inches thick and each weighing about half a pound, in a large skillet. Cover almost completely with cold water and season with lemon juice, bay leaf, and salt. Bring to a boil, reduce heat, and simmer for 10 minutes or until fish flakes easily. Do not overcook. Drain thoroughly on a napkin. Place on a hot serving platter, spoon Hollandaise Sauce (page 126) over the fish (or serve the sauce in a warm sauceboat), and garnish with parsley. Serves 4.

POMPANO EN PAPILLOTE

Pompano, which is native to the waters bordering the southern states, is one of the most highly prized fish in the South. This recipe comes from the famous restaurant Antoine's, in New Orleans. The dish was created in honor of a famous balloonist who was visiting New Orleans, and the paper bag—although its main purpose is to retain the flavor of the fish while it cooks—was fashioned to resemble an inflated balloon.

3 medium pompano, filleted, and trimmings	2 tablespoons flour
1 teaspoon salt	3 shallots, chopped
3 cups water	2 cups cooked shrimp, chopped
1 stalk celery, sliced	2 cups cooked crab meat
1 onion, sliced	1 clove garlic, minced
2 cups dry white wine	1 bay leaf, crumbled
6 tablespoons butter	Pinch of dried thyme
	Dash of Tabasco

Have the fish filleted and ask for the trimmings. Place the trimmings (heads and bones) in a kettle, add salt, water, celery, and onion. Bring to a boil, then reduce heat, and continue cooking slowly for 30 minutes. Strain and set aside 1 cup of the stock. Pour remaining stock into a skillet and add ½ cup of the wine. Sprinkle fillets with a little salt and pepper and fold in half. Place in the stock and wine mixture and simmer gently for 8 minutes. Remove from heat and allow fish to cool in the stock. When cool, lift out fillets and drain well. Set aside while you make the sauce.

To make the fish sauce: Melt *2 tablespoons of the butter* in a saucepan, stir in flour until smooth, and cook several minutes. Stir in the cup of fish stock and cook, stirring constantly, until sauce bubbles. Set aside.

Sauté shallots in remaining butter for 5 minutes. Stir in shrimp, crab meat, garlic, bay leaf, thyme, and Tabasco thoroughly. Add remaining wine and cook for 15 minutes, stirring frequently. Blend with the fish sauce and cool. Cut 6 hearts, about 8 inches long and 12 inches wide, from parchment paper. Brush the paper with oil. Place a spoonful of sauce on one side of each heart, then a pompano fillet, and cover with a little sauce. Fold paper hearts over and double fold all surrounding edges to seal securely. Arrange on an oiled baking sheet and bake in a preheated 425° oven for 15 minutes. Serve in the paper to 6.

SHRIMP-STUFFED POMPANO

"We had dinner on a ground-veranda over the water," Mark Twain wrote in *Life on the Mississippi*. "The chief dish [was] the renowned fish called the pompano, delicious as the less criminal forms of sin."

4 pompano (about 1 pound each)	Dash of pepper
1 pound cooked shrimp	3 tablespoons sherry
1 egg, well beaten	1 cup heavy cream
½ teaspoon salt	

Split the cleaned pompano, leaving head and tail intact. Place in an oiled, shallow baking pan. Work shrimp through a food grinder, then combine with egg, salt, pepper, sherry, and *half the cream*. When well blended, stuff fish cavities with the mixture. Pour remaining cream over all and bake in a preheated 350° oven for 40 minutes. Baste occasionally. Serves 4.

―――――――――

NEW ENGLAND POACHED SALMON WITH EGG SAUCE

From the earliest days it has been a tradition all through New England to serve Poached Salmon with Egg Sauce, along with the first new potatoes and early peas, on the Fourth of July. The eastern salmon began to "run" about this time, and the new vegetables were just coming in.

To poach salmon: Take a whole salmon or a 4- to 6-pound piece cut from center of the fish. Wrap the washed, cleaned salmon securely in a piece of cheesecloth, leaving long ends to expedite removing it from the broth when it is cooked. Bring to a boil 2 to 3 quarts of salted water (the amount depends on the amount of fish) containing 3 or 4 peppercorns, a bay leaf, and a couple of slices of lemon. Boil for at least 15 minutes. Reduce heat until liquid is simmering, add the salmon. Turn up the heat until it boils again, then reduce to simmer (it should be barely bubbling) until salmon is cooked. Figure on 6 to 8 minutes per pound. It is cooked perfectly when it flakes easily. Take care not to overcook it. When the salmon is done, lift from the broth and remove the cheesecloth. Place on a hot serving platter and skin very carefully. Garnish with lemon and parsley. While salmon is cooking, make the Egg Sauce.

Sauce:

1 cup milk	3 tablespoons butter
1 cup light cream	3 tablespoons flour
2 small onions, sliced thin	1 teaspoon salt
½ bay leaf	Dash white pepper
1 whole clove	2 hard-cooked eggs

Heat milk and cream together with the onion slices, bay leaf, and whole clove until a film forms. Skim the surface. Melt butter in a saucepan, stir in flour, keeping it smooth, and cook over a very low heat for a few minutes. Pour in scalded milk mixture and cook over a low heat, stirring constantly, until mixture bubbles. Remove from heat, season with salt and pepper, and strain into a saucepan. Add eggs, coarsely chopped, and heat through. Do not cook any further. If the sauce seems too thick, add a little more light cream. Serve separately in a warm sauceboat.

COLD SALMON MOUSSE

1 can (1 pound) red salmon or
   2 cups cooked fresh salmon
2½ tablespoons fresh lemon juice
1 teaspoon salt
Dash cayenne

1 envelope unflavored gelatin
½ cup cold water
3 tablespoons mayonnaise
¼ cup heavy cream

Drain salmon, discard any bones, and mash as smooth as possible with a fork. Combine salmon with lemon juice, salt, and cayenne. Sprinkle gelatin over cold water to soften. Put in a pan of boiling water and stir until gelatin is dissolved. Add to salmon mixture, then add the mayonnaise and the cream, which has been whipped until it holds a shape. Pour into a 1-quart mold and chill until firm. Unmold on a cold platter and garnish with watercress and deviled eggs. Serves 4.

CREAMED FINNAN HADDIE

Finnan Haddie is a Scottish dish, named for Findon, a fishing village in Scotland renowned for its cured haddock. The recipe became common in New England as fishermen began to take haddock off the coast.

1½ pounds finnan haddie
2 tablespoons butter
1 tablespoon flour

1 cup half-and-half (milk and cream)
Dash cayenne

Cut finnan haddie into 1-inch cubes. Cover with boiling water and let stand about 5 minutes. Drain very thoroughly. Heat butter in a saucepan, stir in flour until smooth, then add half-and-half. Season with cayenne and cook, stirring constantly, until smooth. Let the mixture bubble 1 or 2 minutes; stir in finnan haddie. Heat through; do not cook any further. Serves 4.

GEFILTE FISH

5 pounds fish fillets (equal amounts of
   whitefish and pike, and some carp)
   plus trimmings
4 onions, sliced
1 stalk celery, sliced

3 carrots, sliced
Salt
Pepper
3 eggs, well beaten
2 tablespoons matzo meal

Work fish fillets through the finest blade of a food grinder and set aside. Put fish heads, bones, and trimmings in a large kettle along with *3 onions*, celery, carrots, salt, pepper, and enough water to cover. Cook to the boiling point, then simmer. Grate the remaining onion very fine and combine with eggs. Mix thoroughly with the ground fish, adding the matzo meal, a little more salt and pepper, and 4 tablespoons of water. Shape into balls and drop into the simmering fish broth. Make certain broth is barely bubbling, then cover, and cook 2 hours. Cool right in the broth, then transfer to a serving platter. Use the cooked carrots for garnish. Strain the broth and refrigerate until jellied. Serve Gefilte Fish with the jellied broth and horse-radish. Makes 15 to 20 balls.

SCANDINAVIAN FISH PUDDING

1 pound raw ground pike, cod, or haddock	4 eggs, separated
½ cup softened butter	3 tablespoons flour
1 tablespoon anchovy paste	1 cup light cream
1 teaspoon salt	1 cup heavy cream
¼ teaspoon white pepper	

Mix the ground fish, butter, anchovy paste, salt, and pepper together. In a separate bowl, beat egg yolks, flour, and light cream vigorously, then beat into fish mixture. Whip the heavy cream until it holds a shape; beat the egg whites until they stand in peaks. Fold or mix both of these into the fish pudding very gently. Pour into a 2-quart baking dish, buttered and dusted with dry bread crumbs, and bake in a preheated 325° oven for 1 to 1¼ hours or until cake tester (or toothpick) inserted in the center comes out clean. Remove from oven, let stand several minutes, then invert and unmold on warm serving platter. Serve with Hollandaise Sauce (page 126) or Mushroom Sauce (page 128). Serves 6.

CODFISH CAKES

1 box (1.6 ounces dehydrated) codfish	1 egg, well beaten
3 medium potatoes	Fat for deep-fat frying

Cover dried codfish with cold water and soak for about 1 hour. Squeeze out as much water as possible and put fish and potatoes (pared and cut in quarters) in a saucepan with enough cold water to almost cover. Cook over a moderate heat until potatoes are tender. Drain thoroughly and mash as smooth as possible. Beat in the egg and drop by tablespoons into hot fat (375° on deep-fat thermometer or until fat browns a 1-inch cube of bread in 60 seconds). Drain on paper towels. Serve with tomato sauce or applesauce. Makes 4 servings.

CIOPPINO

1½ pounds sea bass	1 green pepper, chopped
1 pound uncooked shrimp in shells	4 ripe tomatoes, skinned and chopped
1 live lobster	½ cup tomato purée
1 quart clams or mussels	2 cups red wine
½ cup olive oil	½ cup parsley, chopped
1 large onion, chopped	1 teaspoon salt
2 cloves garlic, chopped	¼ teaspoon pepper

Cut fish into serving pieces, shell shrimp and remove veins. Sever spinal cord of lobster by inserting a knife where tail and body meet, and cut into pieces. Do not remove shells. Scrub the clams or mussels thoroughly and leave in the shells. Arrange fish, shrimp, and lobster in layers in a large kettle. Heat oil in a saucepan, then toss in onion, garlic, and green pepper, and cook about 5 minutes. Now add tomatoes, tomato purée, wine, *half the parsley,* and seasonings. Cover and cook over a low heat for 15 minutes. Pour sauce over layers of fish and shellfish. Cover and simmer slowly for 30 minutes or until bass is tender when tested with a fork. Add the clams or mussels and continue cooking until the shells open. Sprinkle remaining parsley on top and serve with hot garlic bread. Serves 6.

LOBSTER NEWBURG

In the early 1890's, Delmonico's honored one of its best customers, Ben Wenberg, by naming a dish after him: Lobster Wenberg. Shortly thereafter, however, Mr. Wenberg and Mr. Delmonico had a falling-out, and the name of the creation was changed to Lobster Newburg.

1½ cups cooked lobster meat
4 tablespoons butter
Salt
Cayenne

1 cup heavy cream
¼ cup Madeira or sherry
3 egg yolks, lightly beaten

Cut lobster meat in large chunks. Heat butter in a heavy saucepan, add lobster, season with a little salt and cayenne, and cook for a few minutes. Pour in cream and bring to a boil, then add Madeira or sherry. Pour some of the hot liquid into the egg yolks, a little at a time, beating hard. Pour back into lobster mixture and cook over a very low heat (or in a double boiler), stirring constantly, until slightly thickened. Do not boil. Serve in patty shells or on toast or rice. Serves 2.

BOILED LOBSTER

"Now that we are on marine matters," Captain Frederick Marryat wrote in 1839, "I must notice the prodigious size of the lobsters off Boston coast: they could stow a dozen common English lobsters under their coats of mail. My very much respected friend Sir Isaac Coffin [the Coffins were among the first settlers of Nantucket Island],...once laid a wager that he would produce a lobster weighing thirty pounds. The bet was accepted, and the admiral despatched people to the proper quarter to procure one; but they were not then in season, and could not be had. The admiral, not liking to lose his money, brought up, instead of the lobster, the affidavits of certain people that they had often seen lobsters of that size and weight....The case was referred to arbitration, and the admiral was cast with the following pithy reply, 'Depositions are not lobsters.'"

A 1- to 1½-pound lobster serves one person. To cook 4 lobsters, bring 4 quarts water to a rolling boil (if sea water is not available, add 4 tablespoons salt to fresh water). Drop live lobsters into the water and bring to a boil again, then cover, reduce heat, and simmer 5 minutes for the first pound, 3 minutes for each additional pound. If overcooked, lobsters will be dry and tough. Remove lobsters immediately from water, lay them on their backs, and split them in half, from end to end, using a large, heavy knife. Remove and discard stomach and intestinal vein. The green liver, or tomalley, is eaten. Hen lobsters yield coral, a pink roe also considered a delicacy. Serve hot with melted butter and lemon wedges or at room temperature with mayonnaise.

To cook lobster in a court bouillon: To 4 quarts water, add 1 cup white vinegar, 1 sliced carrot, 2 large onions (sliced), 6 stalks celery (sliced), 3 bay leaves, 1 teaspoon dried thyme, 1 teaspoon crushed peppercorns, 4 tablespoons salt, and a pinch of caraway. Bring all ingredients to a boil, add lobsters, then cook according to directions above. Cool the lobsters in the court bouillon.

STEAMED CLAMS

In *Cape Cod,* Henry Thoreau speaks of walking with a friend along the shore of Cape Cod after a storm. "We found some large clams... which the storm had torn up from the bottom, and cast ashore. I selected one of the largest, about six inches in length, and carried it along.... We took our nooning under a sand-hill, covered with beach-grass... I kindled a fire with a match and some paper, and cooked my clam on the embers for my dinner.... Though it was very tough, I found it sweet and savory, and ate *the whole* with a relish. Indeed, with the addition of a cracker or two, it would have been a bountiful dinner."

Scrub steamers with a stiff brush and wash several times until free from sand. Place clams (about 20 per person) in a large, deep kettle with about a half inch of salted water in the bottom. Cover the kettle very tightly and steam over moderate heat until the clams open. This will take from 6 to 10 minutes depending on the size of the clams. Serve at once with melted butter and cups of the clam broth. Taste the broth first to see if it needs seasoning.

Implement for baking clams

CLAM FRITTERS

John Lawson, visiting the Carolinas in 1709, had a few remarks about "Man of Noses" (as soft clams, or maninose, were then called) : "Man of Noses are a Shell-Fish commonly found amongst us. They are valued for increasing Vigour in Men, and making barren Women fruitful; but I think they have no need of that Fish; for the Women in *Carolina* are fruitful enough without their Helps."

2 cups minced clams, fresh or canned
2 eggs, separated
1 cup fine bread crumbs, toasted
1 teaspoon salt
½ teaspoon pepper

½ tablespoon chopped parsley
½ tablespoon chopped chives
⅓ cup milk (about)
Butter or vegetable oil

Clams should be well drained and minced very fine. Beat egg yolks vigorously, then stir in clams, crumbs, seasonings, chopped parsley, and chives. Add enough milk to make a heavy batter. Fold in stiffly beaten egg whites. Drop batter from a tablespoon into a skillet containing heated butter or oil. Fry, turning once, until both sides are browned. Serves 4.

AGUACATES RELLENOS CON JAIBA
(Baked Avocado, Stuffed with Crab Meat)

3 firm avocados
Lemon or lime juice
1½ cups crab meat
1 cup thick Cream Sauce (page 542)
Salt

White pepper
Few drops of Tabasco
1 tablespoon capers, drained
6 tablespoons grated Cheddar cheese
  (optional)

Cut unpeeled avocados in half lengthwise and remove pits. Sprinkle surfaces generously with lemon or lime juice. Mix crab meat with Cream Sauce, seasonings, and capers. Spoon into avocados and sprinkle with cheese. Place in a shallow baking pan with ½ inch hot water and bake in a preheated 350° oven for 20 to 25 minutes. Serves 6.

MARYLAND DEVILED IMPERIAL CRAB

4 tablespoons butter
1 green pepper, chopped fine
1 small onion, minced
1 tablespoon prepared mustard
1 tablespoon dry mustard

½ teaspoon salt
2 tablespoons good brandy
½ cup Cream Sauce (page 126)
2 tablespoons fine bread crumbs
1 pound crab meat

Melt *2 tablespoons of the butter* in a saucepan, add the green pepper and onion, and cook over a low heat, stirring often, for 10 minutes. Stir in the 2 mustards, salt, brandy, Cream Sauce, and *1 tablespoon of the bread crumbs*. Then add the crab meat. Heat only for a few minutes, stirring gently and taking care not to break up the crab flakes. Spoon into 6 individual baking shells or into a small baking dish that can go to the table. Sprinkle on remaining bread crumbs and dot with remaining butter. Bake in a preheated 400° oven (shells will take about 10 minutes, the baking dish about 25 minutes). Slide under the broiler for a few minutes to brown the tops. Serves 6.

CRAB LOUIS

Crab Louis was created by the chef at the Olympic Club in Seattle, Washington. When the Metropolitan Opera Company played Seattle in 1904, Enrico Caruso kept ordering the salad until none was left in the kitchen.

Dressing:
1 cup mayonnaise
½ cup heavy cream, whipped
¼ cup chili sauce

2 tablespoons grated onion
2 tablespoons parsley, chopped fine
Dash of cayenne

Combine all ingredients and refrigerate. Shred lettuce, arrange on a platter, and heap 1½ pounds lump crab meat, picked over and flaked, on top. Garnish with hard-cooked eggs, fresh tomatoes (peeled and quartered), and slices of avocado or artichoke hearts. Pour the Louis dressing over all. Serves 4.

FRIED SOFT-SHELLED CRABS

Two to three soft-shelled crabs are the usual portion per person. Have them cleaned at the market. Dust lightly with flour, then dip in lightly beaten egg, and, last of all, in fine dry bread or cracker crumbs. Heat fat in a deep frying pan to 350° on deep-fat thermometer or until a 1-inch cube of bread browns in 60 seconds. Add a few crabs at a time and fry about 5 minutes or until golden. Drain on paper towels and sprinkle with salt and pepper. Serve with Tartare Sauce (page 127) or Sauce Remoulade (page 130).

CRAB STEW

2 tablespoons butter
1 small onion, grated
¼ pound mushrooms, sliced thin
2 ripe tomatoes, skinned and chopped
1 pound crab meat
1 teaspoon salt

Dash cayenne
1½ cups heavy cream
Few sprigs parsley, chopped
1 teaspoon chopped chives
¼ cup brandy

Melt butter, stir in grated onion, and cook over a moderate heat for a minute or two. Stir in mushroom slices and cook several minutes. Now add tomatoes and cook about 5 minutes. Stir in crab meat, salt, cayenne, and cream. Heat until mixture comes to a boil—but no longer. Add parsley, chives, and brandy. Serve in soup plates with a heaping tablespoon of cooked rice in the center. Serves 4 to 6.

MARYLAND CRAB CAKES

6 slices white bread
¾ cup olive oil
3 eggs, separated
¼ teaspoon dry mustard
½ teaspoon salt

2 teaspoons Worcestershire sauce
1½ pounds crab meat
Paprika
3 tablespoons butter

Trim crusts from bread and lay slices on a shallow platter. Pour oil over them and let stand until bread is thoroughly saturated. Use forks to break into small pieces. Combine egg yolks with mustard, salt, and Worcestershire sauce. Beat lightly. Stir in bread and crab meat, gently fold in stiffly beaten egg whites, and shape mixture into patties. Sprinkle with paprika and sauté in heated butter until golden on both sides. Serves 6.

FRIED SHRIMP

Remove shells from 1 pound of raw shrimp, leaving tails intact. Mix together 1 egg and 1 tablespoon cold water. Dip the shrimp in this, then coat with fine dry bread or cracker crumbs. Fry in deep fat heated to 350° on deep-fat thermometer (or until a 1-inch cube of bread browns in 60 seconds) until crisp and golden. Drain on paper towels, sprinkle with salt, and serve immediately with Dill and Mustard Sauce (page 127), Sauce Remoulade (page 130), or Tartare Sauce (page 127). Serves 4.

PICKLED SHRIMP

2 pounds raw shrimp
¼ cup mixed pickling spices
Celery leaves (about a handful)
1 cup salad oil
¾ cup white vinegar

1 teaspoon salt
¼ teaspoon black pepper
2 teaspoons celery seed
Few drops of Tabasco
1 large onion, chopped

Combine unshelled shrimp, pickling spices, and celery leaves in a saucepan and add enough water to cover. Cover tightly, bring to a boil, reduce heat, and simmer 3 to 5 minutes. Do not overcook. Cool shrimp in the liquid, then remove the shells. Mix together salad oil, vinegar, salt, pepper, celery seed, and Tabasco. Arrange layers of shrimp and chopped onion in a jar or bowl, add the oil-vinegar mixture, cover, and refrigerate overnight.

SHRIMP CREOLE

¼ cup butter
2 medium onions, chopped fine
1 clove garlic, chopped fine
3 green peppers, coarsely chopped
1 can (1 pound, 3 ounces) tomatoes

2 teaspoons salt
¼ teaspoon pepper
1 teaspoon paprika
1½ pounds raw shrimp
1 teaspoon gumbo filé

Melt butter in a large saucepan. Stir in onions, garlic, green peppers and cook over a low heat until tender. Stir frequently. Pour in the tomatoes and simmer gently for 25 to 30 minutes. Season with salt, pepper, and paprika. While tomato mixture cooks, remove shells and clean shrimp. Add to the sauce and cook 5 minutes longer. Stir in filé. Serve immediately with steamed rice. Serves 6.

SEAFOOD ROYALE

2 tablespoons butter
2 stalks celery, diced
3 medium onions, chopped
1 tablespoon flour
1 cup water
1 teaspoon salt
2 tablespoons chili powder
2 cups canned tomatoes

1 cup cooked peas
1 tablespoon vinegar
1 teaspoon sugar
2 cups cooked, cleaned shrimp
    or combination of shrimp, crab meat,
    scallops, or other shellfish
⅓ cup sherry
3 cups hot cooked rice

Melt butter in a saucepan. Add celery and onions and cook over a moderate heat until onions are limp. Stir in flour until smooth, then add water, salt, and chili powder. Cook, stirring constantly, until mixture thickens. Reduce heat and simmer for about 15 minutes. Then add tomatoes, peas, vinegar, sugar, and shrimp. Cook 10 minutes longer or until shrimp are heated through. Stir in sherry last of all. Serve with hot rice to 6.

OYSTERS

In the nineteenth century, oysters were very much a part of American life. The Lincolns, while they were living in Springfield, Illinois, were often hosts at oyster feasts—affairs at which oysters, and oysters exclusively, were served in every conceivable manner. A few of the variations were: broiled, boiled, deviled, curried, fricasseed, panned, scalloped, pickled, stewed, steamed, pies, omelettes, ketchups, and fritters.

Oysters were consumed in great quantity, by the dozens—a feat all the more remarkable because of the prodigious size of oysters in the nineteenth century. Today it is a rarity to find the enormous six- and eight-inch oysters that were common a hundred years ago. And there is no contemporary story to match that told by a companion of William Makepeace Thackeray, when the British writer visited Boston in 1852. Thackeray was presented with a half-dozen typically large American oysters. "He first selected the smallest one... and then bowed his head as though he were saying grace. Opening his mouth very wide, he struggled for a moment, after which all was over. I shall never forget the comic look of despair he cast upon the other five over-occupied shells. I asked him how he felt. 'Profoundly grateful,' he said, 'as if I had swallowed a small baby.' "

SCALLOPED OYSTERS

1 pint oysters
¼ cup oyster liquor
2 tablespoons light cream
½ cup day-old bread crumbs
1 cup cracker or rusk crumbs

½ cup (1 stick) butter, melted
Salt
Freshly ground pepper
Paprika

Drain oysters, reserving ¼ cup of the liquor. Combine oyster liquor and cream and set aside. Mix both kinds of crumbs together with the melted butter and sprinkle a thin layer on bottom of a buttered 1-quart casserole. Cover with *half of the oysters, half of the liquor and cream mixture,* and a light sprinkling of salt and pepper. Cover with a second layer of crumbs, remaining oysters, remaining liquor and cream, and more salt and pepper. Finish off the dish with the last of the crumbs and sprinkle with paprika. *Note:* Never make more than two layers of oysters in a scallop because the middle layer will remain uncooked. Bake in a preheated 425° oven for 30 minutes. Serves 4.

TO FATTEN OYSTERS

Mix one pint of salt with thirty pints of water. Put the oysters in a tub that will not leak, with their mouths upwards and feed them with the above, by dipping in a broom and frequently passing over their mouths. It is said that they will fatten still more by mixing fine meal with the water.

—From *Housekeeping in Old Virginia,* 1877

LA MEDIATRICE

The oyster loaf, popular throughout America in the nineteenth century, was known in the Vieux Carré of New Orleans as *la médiatrice*, or the mediator. It was the one thing a man felt might effectively stand between his enraged wife and himself when he came home after spending an evening carousing in the saloons of the French Quarter. A man bought his mediators for pennies, just before going home, in the French market.

Take small French rolls, cut off the tops, and scoop out most of the center. Brush the cut side of the tops and the hollowed-out center of the rolls with melted butter. Place both tops and rolls in a 425° oven until toasted to a very light brown. Meanwhile, sauté the oysters in hot butter until they plump up and the edges curl (takes 2 to 3 minutes). Add salt, pepper, 2 or 3 drops of Tabasco, and, if you like, a little hot cream. Fill the hot rolls and cover with crusty tops. Allow about 3 oysters to one roll. Serve hot.

OYSTER PAN ROAST

½ cup (1 stick) butter
1 pint of oysters
Salt
Freshly ground pepper

2 tablespoons ketchup
1 tablespoon Worcestershire sauce
Big squeeze of lemon juice

Melt butter in a skillet, then add the drained oysters, salt, pepper, and all remaining ingredients. Cook over a moderate heat, stirring constantly, until oysters plump up (1 to 2 minutes). Serve on toast. Makes 4 servings.

GRAND CENTRAL OYSTER STEW

One reassuring oasis of stability in the ever-changing city of New York is the Oyster Bar that opened in Grand Central Station on May 22, 1912, and continues to serve an Oyster Stew made according to its original recipe.

2 cups milk
2 cups light cream
1 quart oysters and liquor
2 tablespoons butter

Salt
Pepper
Celery salt
Paprika (optional)

This recipe is prepared quickly; heat soup bowls before you start. Scald milk and cream together but do not boil. Drain oyster liquor into a saucepan and bring to a boil. Heat oysters in a separate saucepan with 2 tablespoons of the oyster liquor and the butter until the oysters are plump and the edges begin to curl. Remove from heat immediately. Combine hot milk and cream, hot oysters, and hot oyster liquor. Add salt, pepper, and celery salt. Ladle into soup bowls, sprinkle with paprika, and serve with oyster crackers. Serves 6 to 8.

OYSTERS FARCIS

3 dozen oysters
½ cup (1 stick) butter
1 cup shallots, chopped fine
1 cup parsley, chopped fine
½ cup celery, chopped fine
1 tablespoon flour

¾ cup dry bread crumbs
Salt
Cayenne
1 egg, well beaten
6 large oyster shells

Heat oysters in their liquor until edges begin to curl. Drain and cut into small pieces. Set aside. Melt butter in a saucepan. Stir in shallots, parsley, and celery and cook over a low heat until limp. Blend in flour until smooth, then add *½ cup of the bread crumbs* and the chopped oysters. Remove from heat, season with salt and cayenne, and stir in the egg. Cool, then spoon into shells. Sprinkle with remaining crumbs and dot with additional butter. Just before serving, place in a preheated 450° oven 8 to 10 minutes or until brown. Serves 6.

OYSTERS ROCKEFELLER

Oysters Rockefeller originated in 1899 at Antoine's, the celebrated restaurant founded in New Orleans by M. Antoine Alciatore. The recipe was named, according to legend, when one of the customers tasted it and cried, "Why, this is as rich as Rockefeller!"

6 tablespoons butter
6 tablespoons raw spinach, chopped fine
3 tablespoons parsley, chopped fine
3 tablespoons celery, chopped fine
3 tablespoons onion, chopped fine
5 tablespoons fine dry bread crumbs

Few drops of Tabasco
½ teaspoon salt
½ teaspoon Pernod or anisette
36 oysters on the half shell
Rock salt

Melt butter in a saucepan and stir in all ingredients *except oysters and rock salt*. Cook over a low heat, stirring constantly, for 15 minutes. Work through a sieve or food mill and set aside. Make a layer of rock salt in pie tins and place oysters on top. Put a teaspoonful of the vegetable mixture on each oyster. Broil under a preheated 400° broiler 3 to 5 minutes or until topping begins to brown. Serve immediately in the pie tins. Serves 6.

DEVILED OYSTERS

1 tablespoon dry mustard
12 oysters
1 egg, beaten

1 cup fresh bread crumbs
2 tablespoons melted butter

Mix mustard and a little water to a smooth paste in a small saucepan. Add freshly opened oysters and cook for 2 minutes, stirring with a gentle hand. Oysters should be thoroughly coated with the mustard. Remove from stove and, when cool, dip them, one by one, in beaten egg, then coat with fresh bread crumbs. Place in a buttered pan, sprinkle tops with melted butter, and broil quickly in a preheated broiler to brown both sides. Serves 2.

POULTRY & GAME

CHICKEN À LA KING

There are innumerable stories about the origin of Chicken à la King—all of them equally authoritative. One version says it was created by Foxhall Keene, suggested to Delmonico's, and first served in that restaurant as Chicken à la Keene. Another authority insists that it was created by the chef at Claridge's Hotel in London in 1881 for the sportsman J. R. Keene (Foxhall's father), whose horse Foxhall had won the Grand Prix in Paris. There are other well-substantiated stories that the dish originated in Florida, on Long Island, and at the Waldorf.

4 tablespoons butter	Dash cayenne
1 cup fresh mushroom slices	4 egg yolks
1 green pepper, sliced thin	½ cup cream
½ cup dry sherry	3 cups boiled chicken, cut in large chunks
2 cups Cream Sauce (page 126)	1 tablespoon chopped pimiento
1 teaspoon salt	

Heat butter in a saucepan, add mushrooms, and sauté about 5 minutes or until lightly browned. Stir in green pepper and simmer a few more minutes. Add sherry, Cream Sauce, salt, and cayenne. Heat to a boil, stirring constantly. Combine egg yolks with cream, then stir into mushroom mixture. Add the chicken and heat through, but do not boil. Just before serving, add the pimiento. Serve on toast triangles with rice or in patty shells. Serves 6.

MARYLAND FRIED CHICKEN

6 strips bacon	¼ teaspoon pepper
Butter or vegetable oil	A 3- to 3½-pound frying chicken
¾ cup flour (about)	2 tablespoons flour
1 teaspoon salt	2 cups half-and-half (milk and cream)

Fry bacon in a large skillet until brown on both sides. Remove bacon, drain on paper towels, and set aside. Add enough butter or oil to bacon drippings to make 1 inch of fat in skillet. Dump ¾ cup flour, salt, and pepper into a paper bag and shake it well. Drop in the chicken pieces and shake to coat the chicken. When fat is bubbling hot (but not brown), add chicken pieces and fry until browned on all sides. Now cover skillet, reduce heat, and cook over a low heat for about 25 minutes or until tender when tested with a fork. Transfer chicken to a hot platter and keep warm. Pour off all but 4 tablespoons of the fat, stir in the 2 tablespoons of flour, and cook a few minutes. Then pour in the half-and-half. Cook, stirring constantly, until sauce is smooth and thick. Season to taste. Pour sauce over the hot chicken and garnish with bacon strips. Serves 4.

CAPITOLADE OF CHICKEN

Capitolade—a hash—was served at Monticello. Annette, a French governess for Jefferson's family, suggested, "This dish is for breakfast."

2 tablespoons chopped onion
2 tablespoons melted butter
1 tablespoon shallots, chopped fine
1 clove garlic, crushed
1 cup sliced mushrooms

1 tablespoon flour
⅓ cup white wine
1 cup stock or leftover chicken gravy
2 cups cooked chicken, diced
Chopped parsley

Cook onions in melted butter until limp. Stir in shallots, garlic, and mushrooms. Cook over a low heat about 5 minutes, then stir in flour until smooth. Add wine and stock. Cook until sauce bubbles, then reduce heat and simmer gently for 10 minutes. Stir in diced chicken and season to taste. Spoon into serving dish and sprinkle with chopped parsley.

CHICKEN HASH À LA RITZ

Created by Louis Diat, the chef at the old Ritz-Carlton in New York, Chicken Hash à la Ritz came into existence at about the time the Ritz opened in 1910.

Hash:
3 cups cooked chicken
1½ cups light cream
1½ tablespoons butter
1½ tablespoons flour
1½ teaspoons salt
¾ cup milk

Sauce:
1 cup milk
4 tablespoons butter
2 tablespoons flour
1 medium onion, sliced
¼ teaspoon salt
3 egg yolks
3 tablespoons grated Parmesan cheese

To make the hash: Mince chicken. Combine with cream and cook, over a very low heat, until cream is reduced to about half the original amount. Melt butter in a separate saucepan, add flour and salt, stir until smooth, and cook a minute or two. Add milk slowly and cook over a low heat, stirring constantly, until sauce bubbles. Stir into chicken mixture and pour into a shallow baking dish. Keep the hash hot while you make the sauce.

To make the sauce: Heat milk until a film appears. Skim surface. Do not boil. Melt *2 tablespoons of the butter* in a saucepan and stir in flour until smooth. Cook a minute or so. Gradually add the hot milk, stirring all the while. Add sliced onion and salt and cook over a low heat for about 15 minutes, stirring frequently. Beat egg yolks slightly, then add the hot sauce very slowly, stirring constantly. Mix in remaining 2 tablespoons butter and the cheese last of all. Spoon this mixture over the chicken and broil 4 to 5 inches from broiling unit, in a preheated broiler, until surface is golden. Serves 4.

This hash is usually served with a border of puréed peas, prepared as follows: Cook frozen peas according to package directions, drain thoroughly, and purée in an electric blender. Spoon the hot purée, seasoned with salt and pepper, around the edge of the baking dish after it comes from the broiler.

BURGOO

Burgoo apparently originated in the mid-eighteenth century as a thick porridge, one of the mainstays of a ship's mess. As developed in America, it came to be associated with Kentucky, and to be even thicker by virtue of including hens, squirrels, beef, hogs, lambs, and a wide assortment of vegetables and seasonings. It was made in enormous quantities (800 pounds of beef, 240 pounds of chicken, a ton of potatoes) and served at picnics, horse sales, church suppers, and on Derby Day.

5 tablespoons bacon fat or vegetable oil
2 pounds lean shin bones of beef with meat
1 pound shoulder of veal
2 medium-sized chickens, quartered
4 quarts water
1 tablespoon salt
4 cups onions, chopped
1 clove garlic, chopped
2 cups potatoes, diced
1 bunch celery with tops, diced
1 quart skinned ripe tomatoes or
   2 cans (1 pound, 3-ounce size) tomatoes
6 carrots, diced
2 large green peppers, chopped

1 pint fresh butter beans or
   1 package frozen butter beans
1 small pod red pepper or
   ¼ teaspoon crushed red pepper
1 small onion, stuck with 4 cloves
1 bay leaf
¼ cup dark brown sugar
½ teaspoon freshly ground pepper
2 cups okra, sliced, or 1 package frozen okra
6 ears corn (cut kernels from cob) or
   2 packages frozen corn
½ cup (1 stick) butter
1 cup flour
1 cup parsley, chopped

Heat *3 tablespoons bacon fat or oil* in a large kettle. Add beef and veal and brown well. Add chickens, water, and salt, and cook over a low heat, covered, until very tender. Remove meat and chicken to a tray and, when cool enough to handle, remove and discard all bones and the chicken skin. Cut meat and chicken into sizable pieces, then return to broth. Cook onions in remaining 2 tablespoons bacon fat or oil until limp. Add to broth, along with garlic, potatoes, celery, tomatoes, carrots, green peppers, butter beans, red pepper, onion stuck with cloves, bay leaf, brown sugar, and ground pepper. Cook slowly for about 2 hours, stirring occasionally. Then add okra and corn and cook 15 minutes longer. Before serving, combine butter and flour, working the mixture until well blended. Stir into Burgoo and cook, stirring constantly, until Burgoo has thickened slightly. Taste for seasoning. Before serving, sprinkle with chopped parsley. Serves 20, but recipe can successfully be cut in half.

CHICKEN CROQUETTES

1 cup thick Cream Sauce (page 126)
2 egg yolks, lightly beaten
2 cups cooked chicken, finely chopped
2 tablespoons chopped parsley
½ teaspoon nutmeg
¼ teaspoon grated onion

1 teaspoon Worcestershire sauce
Flour
1 egg, well beaten
Dry bread crumbs
Fat for deep-fat frying

While Cream Sauce is still hot, stir it, a little at a time, into the egg yolks. Add chicken, parsley, nutmeg, grated onion, and Worcestershire sauce and blend thoroughly. Chill in a shallow baking dish. Divide mixture into 12 sections and shape into balls. Dip into flour, then into beaten egg, and finally into dry bread crumbs. Preheat deep fat to 375° to 385° or until a 1-inch cube of bread browns in 60 seconds. Fry croquettes, a few at a time, for 2 to 3 minutes or until golden. Drain on paper towels. Serve with creamed peas or Mushroom Sauce (page 128). Serves 4 to 6.

VARIATION I: Dust 1 cup chicken livers with a mixture of flour, salt, and pepper. Sauté in heated butter until well browned. Place a chicken liver in the center of each croquette.

VARIATION II: Season 12 medium-sized mushrooms with salt and pepper. Sauté in heated butter for several minutes. Shape each croquette around a mushroom.

VARIATION III: Substitute 2 cups of chopped, cooked sweetbreads for cooked chicken.

VARIATION IV: Substitute 2 cups chopped leftover roast veal for cooked chicken.

BRUNSWICK STEW

Brunswick County, North Carolina, has for years been attempting to lay claim to Brunswick Stew. The best-documented case, however, is held by Brunswick County, Virginia, which argues that in 1828 Dr. Creed Haskins of Mount Donum, a member of the Virginia state legislature, wanted something special for a political rally he was sponsoring. Haskins had eaten a squirrel stew created by Jimmy Matthews, and he turned to Matthews for a new variation on that stew. Squirrels gradually disappeared from the recipe for Brunswick Stew, and chicken is now accepted as its major ingredient, but it remained for many years—in its original form—one of the principal attractions of political rallies conducted by the Whigs and Democrats, and of cockfights, family reunions, tobacco curings, and other Virginia gatherings.

Two 3-pound chickens, cut in pieces
2 pounds shin bone of beef or veal
1 ham bone from baked Virginia
  or country ham
1 squirrel, cut in pieces (optional)
3 quarts water
½ cup sugar
1 bay leaf
1 teaspoon basil
2 tablespoons parsley, chopped

2 onions, sliced
4 cups skinned tomatoes, chopped
2 cups celery with tops, chopped
2 cups butter beans or small green
  Lima beans (fresh or frozen)
4 cups corn (fresh or frozen)
½ cup (1 stick) butter
1 pod red pepper, crushed
1 teaspoon coarse black pepper
4 large potatoes, pared and boiled until tender

Put chickens, beef or veal bone, ham bone, squirrel, water, sugar, bay leaf, basil, and parsley in a large soup kettle. Cook over a low heat until meat is tender enough to fall from bones. Remove meat from broth and cool. To the broth add onions, tomatoes, celery, and beans. Continue cooking slowly until beans are tender. Stir frequently. Remove meat from bones and cut into pieces. Add to stew, then add corn. Simmer for 10 minutes, then stir in butter, red pepper pod, and black pepper. Add salt to taste. Work potatoes through a ricer or blend in an electric blender and stir into stew. Stir constantly for 15 minutes or until mixture is the consistency of mush. Serves 20.

CHICKEN FRICASSEE

A 4- to 5-pound chicken
1 cup water
1½ teaspoons salt
Dash pepper
¼ cup butter

½ pound mushrooms, sliced
1 cup cream
¼ teaspoon mace
Few sprigs parsley

Cut the chicken into serving pieces, place in a Dutch oven or heavy saucepan with a tight-fitting lid, add water, salt, and pepper, and cook to a boil. Lower the heat, cover tightly, and cook very slowly for about 1½ hours or until chicken is extremely tender when pierced with a fork. Melt butter in a saucepan, add mushrooms, and sauté for about 5 minutes. Combine with chicken, then add the cream and mace. Cook, still over low heat, for 10 to 15 minutes longer. Arrange chicken pieces on a hot serving platter, spoon sauce over the top, and sprinkle with finely chopped parsley. Serves 4.

A Dutch oven

CHICKEN PIE, COUNTRY STYLE

1 large chicken
1 carrot
1 onion, stuck with 2 cloves
1 stalk celery
Several sprigs parsley
Salt
Pepper
2 tablespoons butter
2 tablespoons chicken fat

5 tablespoons flour
½ cup cream
Pastry:
2 cups sifted all-purpose flour
½ teaspoon salt
4 teaspoons baking powder
5 tablespoons butter
4 tablespoons solid chicken fat
5 tablespoons milk (about)

To make the filling: Place chicken in a large kettle and pour in enough water to almost cover the bird. Add carrot, onion, celery, and parsley. Season with salt and pepper. Cook over a low heat for about 1½ hours or until the bird is very tender when tested with a fork. Let cool in the stock until the chicken can be handled comfortably. Discard skin and bones, leaving meat in large pieces. Strain the broth, skim off the fat, and refrigerate fat until firm. (You will need 3 cups of broth and 6 tablespoons of chicken fat to make the pie.) Pour 1½ cups of chicken broth over chicken pieces. Heat butter and 2 tablespoons of chicken fat in the top of a double boiler, stir in flour, keeping mixture smooth, and cook a minute or two. Add the remaining 1½ cups of chicken broth and cook, stirring constantly, until sauce is smooth and thick. Stir in cream last of all and taste for seasoning.

To make the pastry: Sift flour, salt, and baking powder together. Cut in butter and chicken fat with two knives or a pastry blender until mixture looks mealy. Add milk gradually (just enough to hold pastry together) and knead on a lightly floured board for half a minute. Refrigerate for 30 minutes. Divide pastry in half and roll one half into a large circle. Line bottom and sides of a round 1½-quart baking dish. (This is an exceptionally rich pastry, so if it breaks at any time, simply patch it.) Drain the chicken pieces, lay all of them in the baking dish, and add the cream sauce. Cover with remaining pastry, rolled thin and slashed in several places. Pinch edges together to seal securely and bake in a preheated 450° oven for 25 minutes or until top crust is golden. Serves 4 to 6.

CHICKEN POTPIE

A 4-pound chicken
1 stalk celery
1 carrot
1 onion, stuck with 2 cloves
1 tablespoon salt

2 cups sifted all-purpose flour
½ teaspoon salt
2 eggs
2 to 3 tablespoons water
4 medium potatoes, sliced
6 to 7 sprigs parsley, chopped

Cut chicken into serving pieces, place in kettle along with celery, carrot, clove-studded onion, salt, and enough cold water to cover. Bring to a boil, then reduce heat, cover, and cook over a low heat for about 40 minutes or until tender when tested with a fork. Remove vegetables and discard them.

To make the dough: Sift flour and salt into a bowl. Dig a small well in the center, drop in eggs, and blend the mixture to make a stiff dough. Add 2 to 3 tablespoons water if needed. Roll as thin as possible on a lightly floured board and cut into 1-inch squares with a pastry wheel or sharp knife. Drop potato slices and pastry potpies into the boiling broth, cover, and cook over a moderate heat for 20 minutes. Sprinkle in the chopped parsley and serve in hot soup plates to 6.

COUNTRY CAPTAIN

According to Miss Eliza Leslie's *New Cookery Book,* Country Captain is an East Indian dish that was probably first introduced to the British by a captain of the sepoys, the native East Indian troops. Miss Leslie's story notwithstanding, Georgians claim this dish as their own, insisting that the mysterious captain drifted into Savannah via the spice trade and entrusted his recipe to southern friends. The recipe is, in any case, flavored with Indian spices.

A 2½-pound chicken (broiler or fryer)
¼ cup flour
1 teaspoon salt
¼ teaspoon pepper
4 to 5 tablespoons butter
⅓ cup onion, chopped fine
⅓ cup green pepper, chopped fine

1 clove garlic, crushed
1½ teaspoons curry powder
½ teaspoon dried thyme
1 can (1 pound) stewed tomatoes
3 tablespoons dried currants
Blanched, toasted almonds
Chutney

Mix together flour, salt, and pepper. Cut chicken in serving pieces and coat. Heat *4 tablespoons of the butter* in a large, heavy skillet until very hot. Add chicken and brown well on both sides. If all the fat is absorbed before chicken is browned, add remaining tablespoon of butter. Remove chicken and set aside. Add onion, green pepper, garlic, curry powder, and thyme to skillet and cook for a few minutes over a low heat, stirring in all the brown particles. Then add the stewed tomatoes. Put the chicken, skin side up, back into the skillet, cover, and cook slowly for 20 to 30 minutes or until tender when pierced with a fork. Last of all, stir in the currants. Serve to 4 with almonds and chutney on the side.

PLYMOUTH SUCCOTASH

Plymouth Succotash is distinguished from the more familiar form by the addition of meats. It was served in a number of Plymouth households once a year, on December 21, in celebration of the date on which the Pilgrims landed.

1 pint pea beans	4 quarts water
A 3-pound chicken	3 cooked potatoes, sliced
2½ pounds corned beef	1 small yellow turnip, cooked and cubed
½ pound salt pork	1½ quarts whole hominy

Soak beans overnight. Drain, cover with fresh water, and cook about 2 hours or until very tender. Drain and work through a sieve or blend in an electric blender. While the beans are cooking, put chicken (cut into serving pieces), corned beef, salt pork, and water in a large kettle. Cook about 2 to 2½ hours or until beef is tender. Stir in bean purée, sliced potatoes, diced turnips, and hominy. Serves 10.

POACHED STUFFED CHICKEN WITH LEMON SAUCE

A 5- to 5½-pound chicken	1 onion, stuck with 2 cloves
3½ cups bread, crumbled fine	1 large bay leaf
Salt	Few sprigs parsley
Pepper	1½ teaspoons salt
1 generous teaspoon thyme	4 peppercorns, crushed
4 to 5 tablespoons butter, melted	*Sauce:*
Giblets and neck	1 cup chicken broth
2 carrots, cut in chunks	2 egg yolks
3 stalks celery with tops, sliced	Juice and rind of ½ lemon

Prepare the stuffing by crumbling enough old bread to make about 3½ cups. Mix in salt and pepper to taste, and the thyme. Then mix in the melted butter until it is well distributed. Stuff the cavity of the bird with mixture. So that liquid will not seep into stuffing, place a small piece of foil inside the bird just above the tail. Lap the loose skin over the foil and skewer securely. Pull the tail up, push inside the bird, and skewer. Truss the legs with soft string and fold the tips of the wings under the chicken. Place stuffed chicken in a large, deep kettle with all the remaining ingredients, add enough cold water to cover, and bring slowly to a boil. Reduce heat to simmer, cover, and poach until chicken is tender, about 1 hour. Take care not to overcook or the bird will lose its shape. Lift chicken from broth, remove all strings, skewers, and foil. Tuck a feather of celery tops or parsley in its tail, place on warm serving platter, and keep it warm while you make the sauce. Serves 4 to 5.

To make the sauce: Strain the broth into a heavy saucepan. Beat egg yolks until very thick and light. Add a little of the hot broth to the beaten eggs, then combine the two. Add the lemon juice and cook over a very low heat, stirring constantly, until sauce is somewhat thicker than heavy cream. Watch carefully because overcooking will curdle the sauce. Just before pouring into a warm sauceboat, add the grated lemon rind. Small white onions steamed in butter go well with this unusually flavored chicken. Use the strained broth for soup, or bottle and refrigerate it to use later.

CHICKEN SALAD

There are innumerable ways to prepare and serve Chicken Salad. Essentially, it is cold chicken (either poached or the remains of roast chicken) usually combined with chopped celery and moistened with either boiled dressing or mayonnaise.

VARIATION I: To make Breast of Chicken Salad, poach 4 chicken breasts in stock until tender when pierced with a fork. When cool enough to handle, remove skin, bone, and all gristle. Cut the meat into ¾-inch chunks, sprinkle with fresh lemon juice, then combine with enough Virginia Boiled Dressing (page 127) or mayonnaise to bind lightly. Arrange on salad greens, garnish with capers and the yolks of 2 hard-cooked eggs forced through a sieve. Serves 4 to 6.

VARIATION II: To make Breast of Chicken Salad with grapes, add ½ to ¾ cup of green seedless grapes to above recipe and eliminate both capers and hard-cooked eggs. Serves 4.

VARIATION III: To make Chicken Salad with celery, add to every 2½ cups cooked chicken, cut in large chunks, 1 cup chopped raw celery. Blend with Virginia Boiled Dressing or mayonnaise to taste. Arrange on a bed of lettuce and garnish with any or all of the following: quartered tomatoes, capers, pimiento strips, stuffed olives. Serves 4.

VARIATION IV: To make Chicken Salad with toasted nuts, follow directions above, replacing celery with same amount of chopped toasted almonds, walnuts, filberts, or pecans. Serves 4.

CHICKEN PUDDING

This recipe is from the family cookbook of President James Monroe.

A 4- to 4½-pound chicken
½ cup flour
1 teaspoon salt
¼ teaspoon pepper
⅓ cup butter

Batter topping:
1¼ cups sifted all-purpose flour
½ teaspoon salt
3 eggs
1 cup milk
2 tablespoons melted butter

Cut chicken into serving pieces. Put the neck, giblets, and backbone in a pan, pour in enough water to cover, and add 1 onion (cut in half), 1 stalk of celery (cut in chunks), a few sprigs of parsley, 1 teaspoon salt, ¼ teaspoon pepper, and ½ teaspoon dried thyme. Cook over a low heat about 45 minutes. Strain and reserve the broth. Combine flour, salt, and pepper in a paper bag. Drop in pieces of chicken and shake until evenly coated. Heat butter in a skillet (one with a tight-fitting lid), add chicken, and sauté until nicely browned on all sides. Add broth, cook to a boil, cover tightly, and simmer gently for 1 to 1¼ hours or until chicken is tender when tested with a fork. Transfer chicken to an 8-inch square baking dish that can be used for serving. Reserve the broth.

To prepare the batter topping: Sift together flour and salt. Set aside. Beat eggs soundly, pour in milk and butter. Stir in flour mixture until smooth. Pour over the chicken, covering it evenly with the batter. Bake in a preheated 450° oven for 15 minutes. Reduce oven temperature to 350° and continue baking 20 to 25 minutes. Topping will puff up and brown around the edges like Yorkshire Pudding.

While the pudding bakes, make a smooth paste with 1 or 2 tablespoons of flour and water. Stir into chicken broth and cook, stirring constantly, until slightly thickened. Serve immediately, with the gravy in a separate dish. Serves 4 to 6.

CHICKEN WITH SMITHFIELD HAM

A 3½- to 4-pound chicken
1 teaspoon salt
1 onion, stuck with 2 cloves
Few sprigs of parsley
2 stalks celery
Sauce:
2 tablespoons butter
2 tablespoons flour
2 cups light cream
¼ teaspoon salt

Dash of nutmeg
Stuffing:
2 cups fresh bread crumbs, finely crumbled
1 small onion, minced
2 tablespoons parsley, chopped
1 teaspoon dried summer savory
¼ teaspoon salt
Dash of pepper
6 thin slices Smithfield ham

To prepare the chicken: Cut chicken in quarters and place in a large saucepan. Toss in salt, onion stuck with cloves, parsley, celery, and enough water to almost cover. Bring to a boil, cover tightly with a lid, and simmer for an hour or two or until tender. Cool in the broth until comfortable to handle, then strip meat from bones in sizable pieces, and discard bones and skin. Arrange chicken pieces in a medium-sized baking dish. Strain broth and save.

To make the sauce: Melt butter in a saucepan, stir in flour until smooth, and cook a minute or two. Pour in cream and cook, stirring constantly, until slightly thickened. Season with salt and nutmeg and pour over chicken.

To make the stuffing: Combine bread crumbs, onion, chopped parsley, summer savory, salt, and pepper in a bowl. Mix in just enough broth to hold stuffing together. Place some stuffing in the center of each slice of ham and roll ham around it (save about two tablespoons of stuffing to use later). Arrange the ham rolls around the chicken in the baking dish, then sprinkle the top with remaining stuffing. Bake in a preheated 350° oven for 30 minutes.

Potato masher

ROAST GOOSE WITH POTATO STUFFING

Although Catharine Beecher suggested this potato stuffing for roast goose in her *Domestic Receipt-Book,* it is also appropriate to use an oyster or chestnut stuffing, or wild rice.

Potato Stuffing:
2 cups hot mashed potatoes
1½ cups bread crumbs
1 medium onion, chopped fine
2 eggs, lightly beaten

1½ teaspoons salt
1 teaspoon sage
½ cup chopped celery leaves
¼ cup chopped parsley

Combine mashed potatoes with all remaining ingredients. Singe and remove all pinfeathers from an 8- to 9-pound goose. Rub the cavity and skin with a cut lemon and salt. Stuff and truss the goose. Place on a rack in a roasting pan (breast side up), toss a cut clove of garlic and a stalk of celery with leaves into the pan, and roast in a preheated 350° oven for 18 to 20 minutes per pound. Prick the skin, around the wings and legs, with a fork to release the fat. Baste occasionally with pan drippings. When goose is tender and the skin brown and crisp, place on a heated platter and garnish with watercress. Serve with applesauce.

TO DRESS DUCKS WITH ORANGE

This recipe for roast duck with orange sauce is adapted from Mary Randolph's *Virginia Housewife*.

1 large duck
Salt
Pepper
½ cup sugar
1 tablespoon red wine vinegar
Juice of 2 oranges

¼ cup orange liqueur
Grated rind of 1 orange
¼ cup orange peel, cut in thin strips
Fresh lemon juice (optional)
Parsley

Rub cavity of cleaned duck with salt and pepper, then truss securely. Prick the skin around the thighs, back, and lower breast to allow fat to escape. Place in a 350° oven and roast for 1 hour and 40 minutes. Do not baste. When the leg moves easily or the flesh of the leg feels soft when pressed, the duck is done. While the duck roasts, remove excess fat with a baster. When duck is properly roasted, remove trussing strings, place duck on a hot platter, and keep it warm. Sprinkle lightly with salt. Skim off excess fat from roasting pan. Cook sugar and vinegar in a heavy pan over a moderately high heat until mixture has caramelized. Remove from heat, add orange juice, orange liqueur, and the grated orange rind. Put back on the stove and simmer, stirring constantly, until caramel has dissolved completely. Add this to juices left in roasting pan, bring to a boil, and cook for a few minutes, stirring constantly, scraping down the sides of the pan to incorporate all the rich brown particles. Next add the orange peel, then taste. If the sauce seems to lack sharpness, add a squeeze of fresh lemon juice. Pour sauce over duck, arrange orange sections along the backbone down the full length of the duck, and tuck a bouquet of parsley into the tail. Serves 4.

ROAST DUCK

1 large duck
Pinch mace
Few celery leaves
3 sprigs parsley
1 small onion, chopped
½ teaspoon dried sage
½ teaspoon salt
½ teaspoon pepper

Sauce:
1 medium onion, chopped
1 tablespoon butter
1½ cups giblet broth
1 teaspoon arrowroot or cornstarch
1 teaspoon grated lemon rind
1 tablespoon sweet pickles, chopped

Cook duck giblets and neck with 2 cups water, mace, celery leaves, parsley, and a pinch of salt until tender. Strain (save broth). Chop giblets extremely fine and set aside. Combine onion, sage, salt, and pepper and stuff into duck cavity. Place bird on a rack in roasting pan and roast in a preheated 350° oven for 1¼ to 1½ hours. To serve, cut into quarters with kitchen shears, place on platter, and keep duck warm while you make sauce. Serves 2 to 3.

To make the sauce: Chop onion very fine and sauté in heated butter until golden. Pour in almost all of the giblet broth (if there isn't enough to make 1½ cups, add dry red wine). Stir enough of the broth into the arrowroot or cornstarch to make a smooth paste and add to the giblet mixture. Cook over a moderate heat, stirring constantly, until sauce bubbles and thickens. Add lemon rind, sweet pickles, and, last of all, the chopped giblets. Bring to a boil again and pour into gravy boat.

PÂTÉ

2 tablespoons butter
½ pound chicken livers
2 hard-cooked eggs
2 packages (3-ounce size) cream cheese
2 or 3 truffles, coarsely chopped

¾ teaspoon salt
Dash freshly ground pepper
Cognac to taste (about 3 tablespoons)
Canned jellied consommé

Melt butter in a saucepan. Add chicken livers and cook, stirring frequently, until tender (about 8 to 10 minutes). Work liver and eggs through a food grinder or blend in an electric blender. If you use the latter method, do a small quantity at a time. Work the cream cheese until soft, then combine with the ground liver mixture. If you have a blender, put it all back in the container and give it another whirl to make it as smooth as possible. Then stir in truffles, salt, pepper, and cognac. Makes 1½ cups.

To prepare Pâté en Bellevue: Line a small mold (2-cup size) with jellied consommé or aspic, decorate with strips of truffles and the whites of hard-cooked eggs. Cover these with a second layer of consommé. Chill thoroughly. Fill center with the chicken liver *pâté* and cover with another layer of consommé. Chill thoroughly again. Unmold and serve with toast.

THE TURKEY

In *The Physiology of Taste*, Brillat-Savarin—gastronomy's Marquis of Queensbury—wrote: "The turkey is surely one of the noblest gifts which the Old World has received from the New. Superlatively knowing persons maintain that the *Romans* were addicted to the turkey, that it was served at *Charlemagne's* wedding-feast, and that therefore it is false to praise the Jesuits for this most savoury of imports. Let us silence such dealers in paradox with a twofold refutation: 1) The French name of the bird, which, being *coq d'Inde*, clearly betrays its origin; for at first *America* was always known as the *Western Indies;* 2) The appearance of the bird, which is clearly outlandish. A scholar could make no mistake about it."

The origin of the name "turkey" has been variously explained; among the most reasonable speculations is that the word is a corruption of *furkee*, an Indian name for the bird. Americans, of course, rarely think of turkey without thinking of the first Thanksgiving, which the Pilgrims shared with Massasoit and his tribe. As Edward Winslow described that occasion in 1621: "Our harvest being gotten in, our governor sent four men on fowling, that so we might, after a special manner, rejoice together after we had gathered the fruit of our labors. They four in one day killed as much fowl as, with a little help beside, served the company almost a week."

Benjamin Franklin once wrote his daughter, Sarah Bache: "I wish the Bald Eagle had not been chosen as the Representation of our Country; he is a Bird of bad moral Character, like those among men who live by sharpening and robbing, he is generally poor and often very lousy.... The turkey is...a much more respectable bird, and withal a true original Native of America."

DIRECTIONS FOR ROASTING TURKEY

Wash the turkey thoroughly, remove any pinfeathers, and singe any hairs along the edges of the wings and around the legs. Rub the cavity with the cut side of a half lemon and stuff the bird lightly with any of the suggested stuffings (pages 70–71). Close the opening by skewering or sewing it and truss the bird well. Rub the turkey with butter and season with salt and pepper. Place in a large roasting pan and cover with several layers of cheesecloth soaked in butter. Do not add water to the pan. Roast in a preheated 325° oven. Baste several times during roasting period, right through the cheesecloth. Remove the cheesecloth during the last half hour of cooking to allow the turkey to brown. To test whether it is done, move the leg joint up and down—it should give readily—or take several layers of paper towels and squeeze the fleshy part of the drumstick—if properly cooked, it should feel soft. To roast an 8- to 10-pound stuffed turkey, allow 4 to 4½ hours; for a 12- to 14-pound stuffed turkey, allow 5 to 5¼ hours; and for a large stuffed turkey, 18 to 20 pounds, allow 6½ to 7½ hours.

TO PREPARE A TURKEY FOR CHRISTMAS DINNER

The turkey should be cooped up and fed some time before Christmas. Three days before it is slaughtered, it should have an English walnut forced down its throat three times a day, and a glass of sherry once a day. The meat will be deliciously tender, and have a fine nutty flavor.
—Mrs. Stephen J. Field,
Statesmen's Dishes and How to Cook Them, 1890

TURKEY GIBLET GRAVY

Cover the giblets and the neck with water and dry white wine (2 parts of water to 1 of wine). Add a teaspoon of salt, 3 or 4 peppercorns, a sprig of parsley, 1 onion stuck with 2 cloves, and 1 carrot. Bring to a boil and boil for 1 minute. Skim, cover the pan, and lower the heat. Cook gently for 1 hour. Strain the broth, cook it down to 1 cup, and season to taste. Chop giblets and set aside. When the turkey is done, add the juices from the roasting pan to the giblet broth. If you wish a slightly thicker sauce, stir in a little arrowroot, or knead together about 2 tablespoons of butter with the same amount of flour and drop in little balls into the hot liquid. Stir the sauce until thick and well blended. Add chopped giblets before serving.

DEVILED TURKEY

Blend, according to taste, a marinade of cayenne, salt, dry mustard, grated lemon rind, lemon juice, sherry, and Worcestershire sauce. Carve nice slices of cold, cooked turkey and spread each slice with a light coating of softened butter. Arrange in a large, flat baking dish and cover with the marinade. Let stand for about 1 hour. Then bake in a preheated 300° oven for 20 minutes or until hot.

BRAISED GUINEA HEN

The guinea hen, a native of West Africa, was introduced to Europe in the sixteenth century and became popular in colonial America.

1 guinea hen
2 tablespoons butter
1 tablespoon vinegar
1 teaspoon salt
¼ teaspoon pepper

¼ teaspoon dry mustard
1 clove garlic, crushed
Dash cayenne
½ cup chicken broth

Cut the guinea hen into quarters and sauté in heated butter on all sides until nicely browned. Mix together all remaining ingredients, pour over bird, cover, and simmer for 30 minutes or until almost tender. Remove cover, turn up the heat, and continue cooking until liquid is almost evaporated. Wild rice is an excellent accompaniment. Serves 4.

To roast guinea hen: Have the butcher wrap the breasts in large pieces of salt pork and tie them securely (like pheasant, which it resembles in flavor, guinea hen is inclined to be dry). Stuff as you would a chicken (cook the giblets and use them in the stuffing). Roast in a preheated 400° oven for 40 minutes, basting occasionally. Then remove the pork from the breasts, return to oven, and roast 10 minutes, at same temperature, to brown.

Quail

Guinea hen

PHEASANT IN CASSEROLE

The pheasant came to America by way of England from China and the shores of the Black Sea. Richard Bache, an Englishman who married Benjamin Franklin's only daughter, was the first to attempt to raise pheasants in this country—on his estate in New Jersey.

A 2½- to 3-pound pheasant
Salt
2 strips larding pork
6 tablespoons butter

2 medium-sized truffles, sliced
1 can (7½ ounces) beef gravy
¾ cup Madeira wine
¼ cup cognac

Truss legs and wings of pheasant close to the body and rub skin with a little salt. Cover breast of bird with strips of larding pork, since pheasant is inclined to be dry. Place in a roasting pan along with *4 tablespoons of the butter* and roast in a preheated 425° oven for 45 minutes. A few minutes before the bird is done, heat the remaining 2 tablespoons butter in a heavy casserole with a tight-fitting lid. Add truffles and sauté for a few minutes. Remove pheasant from oven, discard pork, and cut off cord. Place bird in casserole. Skim fat from pan and discard. Add the gravy and Madeira to remaining pan juices. Bring to a boil, stirring constantly until smooth. Then stir in cognac. Pour this sauce over the pheasant, cover, return to oven, and continue roasting at the same high temperature 15 minutes. Serves 2 to 3.

ROAST WILD DUCK

In the Gay Nineties, an entree of wild duck was almost *de rigueur* at any fashionable dinner. "The Canvasback is superior in flavor to any other species of wild duck, and is much esteemed..." Mary Ronald wrote in *The Century Cook Book* in 1895. "Wild ducks should be very rare and served very hot, on hot plates."

Rub the cavity of the dressed, cleaned duck with salt, then insert one of the following: a few sprigs of parsley; a few juniper berries; apples (pared, cored, and quartered); 2 or 3 small peeled onions; or 1 or 2 teaspoons of currant jelly. Skewer the opening. Place duck or ducks on a rack, breast side up, and rub generously with soft butter. For rare duck, roast the bird in a preheated 500° oven for 18 to 20 minutes, basting every few minutes with melted butter. For well-done duck, roast in a preheated 350° oven, allowing 15 minutes per pound. Baste frequently with melted butter. Serve with fried hominy or wild rice, currant jelly, and a bottle of dry red wine.

SMALL GAME BIRDS, ROASTED

4 small game birds	Beef broth or sherry
2 slices dry firm bread	Salt
4 tablespoons butter	Pepper
¼ cup pecans, chopped	

Clean birds and set aside. Crumble bread into fine crumbs and cook in *2 tablespoons of the butter* for a minute or two. Combine with pecans, adding just enough broth or sherry to moisten. Season with salt and pepper. Stuff birds until plump, then close the cavities with small skewers or toothpicks. Truss legs and wings close to the bodies with string and place in shallow baking pan. Add just enough boiling water to cover bottom of pan. Brush birds with remaining butter, melted, and bake in a preheated 425° oven for 30 minutes. Baste frequently with melted butter. Serve birds immediately on buttered croutons. Serves 4.

SQUAB IN COMPOTE

This French recipe, a favorite of Jefferson's, is taken from his records at Monticello.

6 plump squabs	½ teaspoon salt
2 tablespoons butter	2 slices bacon, diced
1 cup onion, chopped fine	¼ pound mushrooms, sliced
1 carrot, diced fine	⅓ cup sherry or Madeira

Ask your butcher to truss the squabs. Melt butter in a casserole (one with a tight-fitting lid), add squabs along with onion, carrot, and salt. Sauté until delicately browned on all sides, turning the birds frequently. Next add the bacon, mushrooms, and sherry or Madeira. Cover tightly and simmer gently for 40 to 45 minutes or until tender when tested with a fork. Take care not to overcook or they will fall apart. To serve, place on large croutons (traditionally used as a "mount" for small game birds) and spoon some of the sauce around.

FORCEMEATS

Forcemeats, as they were generally called in old cookbooks, are nothing more than seasoned mixtures used to stuff meats, fish, and fowl. Forcemeat derives from the French *farcir*, "to stuff." Today, they are generally called stuffings or dressings. The stuffings given here are taken from seventeenth- and eighteenth-century cookbooks.

CHESTNUT STUFFING

2 pounds chestnuts
1½ cups (3 sticks) butter
2 cups onion, chopped fine
2 cups thinly sliced celery
9 cups fine dry bread crumbs

2 teaspoons salt
1 teaspoon dried thyme
1 teaspoon dried marjoram
1 teaspoon dried savory

Make a gash in the flat side of each chestnut, place them in a saucepan with boiling water to cover, and simmer for about 5 minutes. While nuts are still hot, remove shells and inner brown skins. Cover chestnuts with more boiling water and cook slowly for 20 to 30 minutes or until tender. Drain and chop coarsely. Melt butter in a saucepan, add onions and celery, and sauté until limp. Add bread crumbs to vegetable-butter combination and mix thoroughly. Then add salt, thyme, marjoram, and savory, mixing them in well. Add the chestnuts. This is enough stuffing for a 12- to 15-pound turkey.

CORN BREAD STUFFING

1½ cups corn meal
2 cups all-purpose flour
2 tablespoons sugar
1 teaspoon salt
4 teaspoons baking powder
2 eggs
2 cups milk
4 tablespoons bacon drippings

1 pound sausage meat
4 medium onions, chopped fine
4 stalks celery, chopped fine
½ teaspoon dried sage
½ teaspoon dried thyme
1 teaspoon salt
Dash pepper

To make the corn bread: Grease two 9-inch square pans. Sift the corn meal, flour, sugar, salt, and baking powder together into a mixing bowl, then stir in lightly beaten eggs, milk, and bacon drippings until well mixed. Spread in baking pans and bake in a preheated 450° oven for 30 minutes. Cool, then crumble.

To make the stuffing: Fry the sausage meat over a low heat until lightly browned, then break it in pieces with a fork. Add the crumbled corn bread and mix together. Remove from heat. Cook the chopped onions in a little bacon fat until limp. Add to the mixture, then add the chopped celery and all remaining ingredients, mixing well. Makes enough stuffing for a 12- to 15-pound turkey.

ALMOND STUFFING

2 cans (4½-ounce size) blanched almonds
6 eggs, separated
1 cup light cream
¼ teaspoon nutmeg (freshly ground, if possible)

1½ pounds (about 1½ loaves) white bread, crumbled fine
½ cup (1 stick) butter, melted
Salt
Pepper

Chop almonds quite fine and toast in a preheated 300° oven until golden, stirring occasionally to brown them evenly. Set aside. In a large bowl beat egg yolks with cream and nutmeg. Add bread crumbs, almonds, butter, and a little salt and pepper. In a separate bowl beat egg whites until they stand in peaks. Spoon on top of the crumb mixture and mix together lightly with your hand. Makes enough stuffing for a 12- to 15-pound turkey.

OYSTER STUFFING

1 pound loaf firm white bread
1 cup (2 sticks) butter
1 large onion, chopped
1 stalk celery, chopped

¼ cup parsley, chopped
2 teaspoons salt
¼ teaspoon pepper
1 pint oysters in liquor

Crumble the bread quite fine. Melt butter in a saucepan, add onion and celery, and cook until onions take on a gold color. Stir into bread crumbs, then add parsley, salt, and pepper. Drain liquor from oysters and heat the liquor to the boiling point. Cut oysters in half, add to hot liquid, and cook until the edges begin to curl. Drain and stir oysters into stuffing. Makes enough stuffing for a 12- to 15-pound turkey.

PECAN STUFFING

1 turkey liver
½ cup (1 stick) butter
1 onion, minced
Toasted bread (enough to make 9 cups)
½ pound fresh mushrooms, chopped fine
1 teaspoon salt
½ teaspoon pepper
1 teaspoon celery seed

1 teaspoon dried thyme
1 tablespoon chopped parsley
½ nutmeg, grated
¼ teaspoon mace
6 eggs, hard-cooked
2 cups salted pecans, coarsely chopped
½ cup dry sherry

Cook the liver in boiling, salted water until tender, then mince. Melt *2 tablespoons of the butter*, add minced onion, and cook until soft. Add the turkey liver and sauté until lightly browned. Toss in the mushrooms and cook very briefly. Crush the toast into fine crumbs (it must be well toasted and dry), combine with the remainder of the butter (melted), the salt, pepper, celery seed, thyme, parsley, nutmeg, and mace. Put the hard-cooked eggs through a ricer and mix in thoroughly. Finally, combine the liver and herb mixtures, and add the pecans and sherry. Makes enough stuffing for a 12- to 15-pound turkey.

TO ROAST STANDING RIBS OF BEEF

This recipe is taken from Mary Ronald's Century Cook Book (1895).

"To roast beef on a spit before the fire is unquestionably the best method of cooking it; but as few kitchens are equipped for roasting meats, baking them in the oven is generally practised, and has come to be called roasting. Beef should be well streaked with fat, and have a bright-red color. Place the meat to be baked on a rack which will raise it a little above the bottom of the pan. Dredge the whole, top and sides, with flour. Place in a corner of the pan a half teaspoonful of salt and a quarter teaspoonful of pepper. Do not let them touch the raw meat, as they draw out the juices. Put into the pan also two tablespoonfuls of drippings. Place it in a very hot oven for fifteen or twenty minutes, or until the meat is browned; then shut off the drafts and lower the temperature of the oven, and cook slowly until done; baste frequently; do not put water in the pan, as it makes steam, and prevents browning. A roast has a better appearance if the ribs are not too long."

By suggesting that you start the roast at a high temperature, and then lower it, the author follows the French, or searing, method of roasting. Preheat the oven to 450°, then lower it to 325°. The beef should be brought to room temperature before roasting. To cook a rib roast rare, allow 16 to 18 minutes per pound; medium rare, 18 to 22 minutes per pound; well done, 23 to 28 minutes per pound. Do not baste. Salt and pepper the meat after it has finished roasting and stand on a warm platter 10 to 15 minutes before carving. This helps the juices to settle and makes the meat easier to carve.

Thermometer method of roasting: Insert thermometer in the fleshiest part of the roast, making sure it does not touch the bone. Place roast in a preheated 325° oven and roast, without basting, until thermometer reaches 140° for rare; 160° for medium; 170° for well done.

To roast rolled ribs of beef: Place the roast, fat side up, on a rack in the roasting pan and roast as you would a standing rib. Allow an additional 5 to 10 minutes per pound since the bone in a standing rib roast transmits heat and, consequently, the meat roasts more quickly.

YORKSHIRE PUDDING

2 eggs	Salt
1 cup milk	Beef drippings
1 cup flour (scant)	

Heat an 8 x 10-inch baking pan in the oven, then pour in ¼ cup beef drippings. Move the pan back and forth until the bottom is well covered. Beat the eggs until very light and fluffy, then beat in the milk and flour, a little at a time. Add a generous pinch of salt and 2 tablespoons beef drippings. Pour the egg mixture into the prepared baking pan and bake in a preheated 450° oven for 10 minutes. Reduce heat to 350°, and bake 10 to 15 minutes longer or until pudding is puffy and delicately browned. Serve immediately to 4.

WESTERN POT ROAST

A 4-pound pot roast
2 teaspoons salt
¼ teaspoon pepper
Dash ginger
3 tablespoons shortening or oil
2 cloves garlic, chopped fine

3 onions, chopped fine
1½ cups prunes
1 cup pitted ripe olives
1 can (6-ounce size) mushrooms or
   1 cup sliced fresh mushrooms

Rub the pot roast with a mixture of salt, pepper, and ginger. Rub it in well. Heat shortening or oil in a Dutch oven, add beef, and brown on all sides. When nicely browned, add garlic, onions, and ½ cup water. Cover tightly and cook over a low heat for about 1½ hours, turning the roast occasionally. As roast is cooking, soak prunes in 1½ cups water. At the end of the cooking period, add prunes and liquid to meat, then add sliced olives and mushrooms (if canned, drain well). Cover and cook gently for another hour or until pot roast is very tender when pierced with a fork. To serve, place beef in the center of a hot serving platter and surround with the fruit mixture. Serves 6 to 8.

One day we were at dinner at head-quarters; an Indian entered the room, walked round the table, and then stretching forth his long tattooed arm seized a large joint of hot roast beef in his thumb and fingers, took it to the door, and began to eat it. We were all much surprised, but General Washington gave orders that he was not to be interfered with, saying laughingly, that it was apparently the dinner hour of this Mutius Scaevola of the New World.

—Chevalier de Pontigibaud,
A French Volunteer of the War of Independence, 1898

BOEUF BOUILLI

This recipe for boiled beef is adapted from one prepared by Étienne Lemaire, Jefferson's steward in Washington.

4 to 5 pounds lean beef (first cut brisket,
   bottom round, or plate beef)
1 large onion, stuck with 6 cloves
3 carrots, cut in chunks
3 to 4 stalks celery with leaves

1 white turnip, quartered
1 parsnip, cut in chunks (optional)
Parsley
4 to 5 peppercorns
1 tablespoon salt

Place the meat in a heavy kettle, then add all the ingredients *except the salt*. Cover with water, bring to a boil, and boil for 5 minutes. Skim off froth, then add salt. Cover, lower the heat, and simmer 2 to 2½ hours or until meat is very tender when pierced with a fork. Potatoes and cabbage are especially compatible with boiled beef and may be cooked separately or added to the meat for the last hour. When meat is tender, lift from the broth, place on warm platter, and surround with cooked vegetables. Serve *Boeuf Bouilli* with Horse-radish Sauce (page 130) or tomato sauce with horse-radish added to taste. Serves 6.

BREAKFAST STEW OF BEEF

This breakfast stew, when presented in slightly different form by Marion Harland in her *Common Sense in the Household,* was one of a number of recipes marked by a cross. Miss Harland noted: "I do not claim for these greater merit than should of right be accorded to many others. I merely wish to call the attention of the novice to them as certainly safe, and for the most part simple. . . . Most of them are in frequent, some in daily, use, in my own family."

2 tablespoons butter
1 medium onion, chopped
2 pounds lean beef, cubed
2 tablespoons flour
1 cup beef broth
¾ teaspoon salt
¼ teaspoon pepper

½ teaspoon savory
½ teaspoon marjoram
1 teaspoon Worcestershire sauce
1 teaspoon prepared mustard
Juice of ½ lemon
Few sprigs parsley, chopped

Melt butter in a saucepan, add onion, and cook until wilted. Dust beef cubes with flour, add them to the onion, and sauté until well browned on all sides. Stir in broth, salt, pepper, savory, and marjoram. Cover and cook over a low heat for about 1½ hours or until very tender. Before serving, stir in remaining ingredients. Serve over toast, hot grits, steamed rice, or with boiled potatoes. Serves 4.

Meat broiler

SWISS CREAM STEAK

2 pounds round steak
Salt
Pepper
½ teaspoon dried marjoram
Flour
¼ cup butter

2 medium onions, thinly sliced
½ cup beef broth or 1 beef bouillon cube
    dissolved in ½ cup boiling water
½ cup commercial sour cream
2 tablespoons grated Parmesan cheese

Sprinkle both sides of steak with salt, pepper, marjoram, and flour. Pound in, using the rim of a heavy plate. Heat butter in a large skillet (one with a tight-fitting lid), toss in onion slices, and cook until straw colored. Lift out onions with a slotted spoon and set aside. Add steak to hot fat and fry on both sides, over a brisk heat, until well browned. Add beef broth mixed with the sour cream, grated cheese, and cooked onions. Cover tightly and cook over a very low heat for about one and one half hours or until meat is tender when tested with a fork. Serves 6.

SHAKER FLANK STEAK

3 pounds flank steak
2 tablespoons flour
2 tablespoons butter
1 teaspoon salt
¼ teaspoon pepper
1 stalk celery, chopped

1 carrot, chopped fine
½ green pepper, chopped fine
2 medium onions, chopped fine
Juice of ½ lemon
½ cup ketchup

Cut or score both sides of the steak diagonally and dust with flour. Sauté in heated butter until well browned on both sides. Season with salt and pepper, then add all the chopped vegetables. Last of all, add lemon juice and ketchup. Cover tightly and simmer very gently for 1 to 1½ hours or until the steak is tender when tested with a fork. The vegetables cook down to a rich sauce to be served with the meat. Serves 6.

PAN-FRIED STEAK

One of Mark Twain's favorite foods was porterhouse steak with mushrooms, pan fried as in the recipe below.

Choose a porterhouse steak at least 1½ inches thick. Score the fat so the steak will not curl during cooking. If there is sufficient fat or suet on the steak, cut off a few bits and melt in a large heavy frying pan. In lieu of sufficient fat, use about a tablespoon of butter. Place over a high heat and cook 5 minutes on each side. Make an incision near the bone with a sharp knife. If it is too rare, cook a bit longer. Salt and pepper lightly and serve with lemon wedges. Serve, with Mushrooms in Cream (page 104), to 4 or 6.

FILET MIGNON

4 *filets mignons* (about ⅓ pound each)
2 tablespoons melted butter
Salt
Pepper

Small piece of salt pork or bacon
8 large mushrooms
1 cup tiny peas

Have the butcher lard the *filets*. Bring to room temperature before cooking. Brush with butter and sprinkle with salt and pepper. Place the salt pork or bacon in the bottom of a small roasting pan. Arrange a rack on top and place *filets* on the rack. Bake in a preheated 500° oven for 20 to 30 minutes. Transfer meat to hot serving platter. Sauté mushroom caps in a little butter for 5 minutes, then fill with hot, drained, and buttered peas. Remove salt pork or bacon from pan and discard. Stir in the finely chopped stems of the mushrooms and sauté over a brisk heat for a minute or two. Pour in a little water (about ¼ cup) and boil rapidly to concentrate the flavors. Pour over beef. Garnish the platter with the mushrooms, grilled tomatoes, Potatoes Duchesse (page 113), and watercress. Serves 4.

HAMBURGERS

The name for the hamburger sandwich is derived from Hamburg, Germany, a city that once enjoyed prosperous commerce with the Baltic Provinces in Russia, where shredded raw meat (we now know it as steak tartare) comprised a large part of the cuisine. It is from them that Hamburg developed an appreciation of "hamburger," though it was left to Americans to place the meat in a bun and create what is now considered an American specialty. Americans have eaten hamburger without buns, of course. Salisbury steak came into being at the turn of the century, promoted by the physician and food faddist J. H. Salisbury, who recommended eating ground steak three times a day for the relief of colitis, pernicious anemia, asthma, bronchitis, rheumatism, tuberculosis, gout, and hardening of the arteries.

SWEDISH MEATBALLS

2 pounds round or chuck steak, ground
1 pound lean pork, ground
2 eggs, well beaten
1 cup mashed potatoes
1 cup dry bread crumbs
1 teaspoon brown sugar
1 teaspoon freshly ground pepper
2 teaspoons salt

½ teaspoon ground ginger
½ teaspoon ground cloves
½ teaspoon allspice
1 cup milk
Flour
¼ cup shortening
2 cups light cream

Mix together, in a very large bowl, ground beef and pork, eggs, mashed potatoes, bread crumbs, brown sugar, all the seasonings and spices, and the milk. Blend thoroughly and shape into balls the size of a large walnut. The mixture should be soft. Coat the meatballs with flour. Heat the shortening, add a few meatballs at a time, and brown on all sides over a moderate heat. Do not crowd the pan. Transfer the browned meatballs to a large casserole, pour cream over them, and bake in a preheated 325° oven for 40 minutes. Serves 8.

INDIAN CORN STEW

2 tablespoons butter
1 pound beef, ground
1 onion, chopped fine
1 clove garlic, chopped fine
1 green pepper, coarsely chopped
3 cups corn, fresh or frozen

3 ripe tomatoes, skinned and coarsely
    chopped
1 tablespoon Worcestershire sauce
2 teaspoons sugar
1½ teaspoons salt

Melt butter in a large skillet, add beef, and sauté over a high heat until brown. Stir in onion, garlic, green pepper, and cook about 5 minutes. Add corn, tomatoes, and seasonings. Cover and simmer gently for about 30 minutes. Serves 4 to 6.

STEAK TARTARE

Ask the butcher for beef that is free of fat. As a main dish, about 1¼ pounds ground meat will be needed for two people. If served as a first course, allow about ¼ pound per person. Make a mound of the meat on individual plates. In the center of the mound make a small well and drop in the yolk of one egg. Take great care not to break the yolk. To serve, mix the yolk into the meat with one or more of the following: fine-chopped onions, fine-chopped parsley, drained capers, salt, freshly ground pepper. Serve with sweet butter and pumpernickel bread.

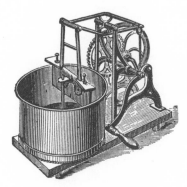

Meat chopper

HAMBURGER ROLL WITH MUSHROOM SAUCE

To prepare meat:
2 pounds lean beef, ground
Grated rind of 1 lemon
1 egg
2 tablespoons melted butter
Few sprigs parsley
1 teaspoon salt
¼ teaspoon pepper
½ teaspoon onion juice
Dash nutmeg

Sauce:
1 can (6-ounce size) mushrooms or
    1 cup fresh mushrooms
¼ cup butter
1½ teaspoons lemon juice
¼ cup flour
1½ cups beef broth
½ teaspoon salt
Dash pepper

Mix ground beef thoroughly with grated lemon rind, egg, melted butter, parsley (chopped fine), salt, pepper, onion juice, and nutmeg. Shape into a neat roll about 10 inches long and 2 inches thick. Wrap the roll in brown paper, brush the paper with melted fat, and tie securely with a cord to keep the roll in shape. Place on a rack in baking pan. Bake in a preheated 350° oven for 30 minutes, basting several times, right through the paper, with a mixture of ¼ cup butter melted in 1 cup boiling water. Remove from oven, pull paper off the roll with care, and return meat to oven for 10 minutes more. Serves 6.

To make the Mushroom Sauce: Drain canned mushrooms well and discard liquid, or wash fresh mushrooms in cold water, wipe dry, and cut in quarters (stem and all). Melt butter in a saucepan, add mushrooms and lemon juice, and cook about 5 minutes or until nicely browned. Stir in flour, keeping it as smooth as possible. Remove from heat. Measure drippings from roasting pan and add enough beef broth to make 2 cups. Pour into mushroom mixture and cook over a low heat, stirring frequently, until bubbly. Season with salt and pepper. To serve, slice hamburger roll and spoon sauce over slices. Garnish with parsley.

CHILI CON CARNE

Among the lesser disputes that have raged along the Rio Grande is the one over chili. Mexicans claim it as Mexican; Texans claim it as Texan.

4 cans (1 pound, 4 ounce size) kidney beans
  or 1 pound dried red or pinto beans
1 onion, chopped
2 pounds round (top or bottom) of beef
2 tablespoons shortening
2 tablespoons flour

2 cloves garlic, crushed
1 teaspoon dried oregano
¼ teaspoon ground cumin
1 tablespoon salt
1 tablespoon chili powder

If you use dried beans, soak them overnight, then cook several hours until tender. Brown onion in heated shortening. Add meat, cut into very small cubes, and cook until well browned. Stir in flour, cook a minute or two, then add canned, undrained kidney beans (or home-cooked red beans plus 2 cups of the liquid in which they cooked) and all remaining ingredients. Cook over a low heat, stirring frequently, for about 1 hour or until beef is tender. Taste and add more chili if you wish. Serves 8.

NEW ENGLAND BOILED DINNER

Americans have often gone to great lengths to "dress up" their menus by giving French names to American dishes. One of the more outlandish examples of this tendency comes from Grover Cleveland's administration. He told a friend that while he was dining in the White House on refined dishes, he smelled the odor of corned beef and cabbage coming from the servants' quarters and asked to trade his dinner for that of the servants. Cleveland dined on the traditional New England Boiled Dinner and then exclaimed that it was "the best dinner I had had for months...this *Boeuf corné au cabeau!*"

4 to 5 pounds corned beef
6 carrots
6 medium potatoes

1 medium yellow turnip
1 small head green cabbage
1 small crookneck or butternut squash

Place beef in a large kettle and cover with cold water. Bring to a boil, then reduce heat, and simmer gently for 3 to 4 hours or until tender when pierced with a fork. While beef simmers, scrape carrots and leave whole; pare potatoes and leave them whole, too; pare turnip and cut in sixths; cut cabbage head in sixths; peel squash, remove seeds and membrane, and cut in large, even chunks. The trick to cooking a good boiled dinner is to have all the vegetables done at the same time. Carrots, potatoes, and turnips take about 30 to 35 minutes to cook. The cabbage and squash will cook in 15 to 20 minutes. As you drop each batch of vegetables into the liquid, increase the heat so the broth continues to bubble. To serve, place the beef in the center of a large heated platter and surround it with all the vegetables. Traditional accompaniments are freshly cooked beets dressed with vinegar, and johnnycake, with apple pie for dessert.

THE HOT DOG

The hot dog reputedly came to America from Frankfurt, Germany. It is said that Antoine Feuchtwanger, a Bavarian, introduced it to St. Louis in the 1880's. He sold hot "franks," along with cotton gloves to prevent customers from burning their fingers. In *Happy Days*, H. L. Mencken intimates that the frankfurter's American debut may date even earlier. "I devoured hot-dogs in Baltimore 'way back in 1886," Mencken said, "and they were then very far from new-fangled . . . They contained precisely the same rubbery, indigestible pseudo-sausages that millions of Americans now eat, and they leaked the same flabby, puerile mustard. Their single point of difference lay in the fact that their covers were honest German *Wecke* made of wheat-flour baked to crispness, and not the soggy rolls prevailing today, of ground acorns, plaster-of-Paris, flecks of bath-sponge, and atmospheric air all compact."

Whoever may have introduced hot dogs to America, it was Harry M. Stevens, a concessionaire at the Polo Grounds in New York, who popularized them, telling his vendors to get out in the stands one cold day and yell, "Red hots! Red hots!" Still, they were not known as hot dogs until T. A. "Tad" Dorgan, a cartoonist, characterized the "red hot" as an elongated bun containing a dachshund.

———————

TAMALE PIE

Many Mexican dishes are not Spanish so much as Indian. The Aztecs served *tamalli* to Cortes when he arrived in Tenochtitlán (Mexico City). Long before they became part of American cookery in the Southwest, they had worked their way toward the Northeast. In 1612, Captain John Smith described them as they were made by Indians in Virginia: "Their corne they rost in the eare greene, and bruising it in a morter of wood with a Polt, lappe it in rowles in the leaves of their corne, and so boyle it for a daintie."

3½ teaspoons salt
1 cup corn meal
3 tablespoons shortening
1 medium onion, chopped

1 small green pepper, chopped
1 pound chuck steak, ground
½ teaspoon chili powder
4 medium tomatoes

Bring 3 cups of water and *1½ teaspoons of the salt* to the boiling point. Then slowly add corn meal in a steady stream, stirring constantly. Cook over a low heat, stirring frequently, for 10 minutes. Remove from heat. Melt shortening in a frying pan, add onion and green pepper, and cook over a low heat until limp but not brown. Add the ground chuck and keep cooking until it is brown. Stir in chili powder and remaining salt. Remove from stove. Cut tomatoes in slices. Spread half the cooked corn meal over the bottom of a medium-sized casserole, cover with a layer of tomatoes, then all the meat mixture. Add a second layer of corn meal and top that with the remaining tomato slices. Bake in a preheated 375° oven for 25 minutes. Serves 4.

DAUBE GLACÉ

This Creole recipe is based, in part, on one found in *La Cuisine Creole*, thought to have been written by Lafcadio Hearn.

4½- to 5-pound beef round
2 bay leaves, crushed
¼ teaspoon sage
1 clove garlic, crushed
½ teaspoon thyme
½ teaspoon marjoram

6 slices bacon
1½ teaspoons salt
¼ teaspoon pepper
3 tablespoons shortening
1 small onion, chopped

Cut 6 deep slits in beef. Combine bay leaves, sage, garlic, thyme, and marjoram and sprinkle equal amounts of the mixture over each slice of bacon. Roll the bacon into small, tight rolls and stuff one in each of the slits. Place the beef in a large deep bowl while you prepare the marinade.

Marinade:
2 cups dry red wine
¾ cup wine vinegar
1 cup water

1 clove garlic, crushed
2 bay leaves
Dash of cayenne
1 teaspoon allspice

To make the marinade: Mix all ingredients together, pour over beef, and refrigerate overnight. The next day, drain beef (save the marinade) and pat dry with paper towels. Sprinkle with salt and pepper. Melt shortening in a large skillet and brown beef on all sides over high heat. Discard all excess fat. Add chopped onion and 1½ cups of the marinade. Bring to a boil, then cover, and simmer for 3 hours or until beef is very tender. Remove from heat and cool in marinade.

Aspic:
3½ pounds veal shank, cracked
2½ pounds pigs' feet, cracked
2 teaspoons salt
Dash of pepper
Dash of cayenne
5 cups water

1 cup dry sherry
4 carrots
4 stalks celery
1 small green pepper
4 sprigs parsley
1 small onion, chopped
2 slightly beaten egg whites plus shells

To make the aspic: Combine all ingredients *except egg whites and shells* and cook over a low heat for 3 hours or until meat is extremely tender. Remove from heat and, when cool enough to handle, strip meat from bones and cut into small pieces. Skim all excess fat from broth, then boil with egg whites and shells for 5 to 10 minutes (this clarifies the broth). Strain through a flannel-lined sieve.

To mold or glacé *the beef:* Pour 1 cup of the liquid aspic into a loaf pan large enough to hold the meat comfortably. Place in the refrigerator and chill until slightly thickened. Garnish the surface with slices of stuffed olives, pimiento cutouts, toasted almonds, or any other suitable accompaniment. Chill until firm. Combine remaining liquid aspic with chopped veal and pig's feet. Place the piece of beef in pan on top of garnish and trim off any meat that does not fit. Pour the aspic-meat mixture around sides and on top. Refrigerate overnight or until firm. To serve, cut in slices. Serves 10 to 12.

OXTAIL STEW

2 oxtails, cut in pieces
2 tablespoons shortening or salad oil
2 teaspoons chili powder
2 teaspoons dry mustard
2 teaspoons cornstarch
2 teaspoons salt
1½ cups orange juice

2 tablespoons lemon juice
Dash of Worcestershire sauce
½ cup seedless raisins
1 jar (4-ounce size) pimientos, cut in strips
1 cup ripe olives, coarsely chopped
3 stalks celery, thinly sliced

Heat shortening or oil in a Dutch oven or heavy kettle, add meat, and brown on all sides. Make a smooth paste of the chili powder, mustard, cornstarch, salt, fruit juices, and Worcestershire sauce. Add this mixture and the raisins to the meat and cook to the boiling point. Reduce heat, cover tightly, and simmer for 2½ hours. Then add pimientos, olives, and celery. Continue cooking for 30 minutes. Serve with rice to 6.

Meat-pie mold

BEEFSTEAK AND KIDNEY PIE

Pastry for a 1-crust pie (page 164)
4 small veal kidneys
1 cup dry red wine
1½ pounds round (top or bottom) of beef
Flour
4 tablespoons shortening

1 medium onion, chopped
1 bay leaf
5 sprigs parsley, chopped
5 sprigs celery tops, chopped
½ teaspoon dried marjoram
¼ pound mushrooms, sliced

Prepare the pastry and refrigerate it while you make the filling. Trim all fat and membrane from kidneys, sprinkle with a little salt, and cover with wine. Set aside. Cut beef into thin strips and sprinkle with flour, pounding it in thoroughly. Fry onion in heated shortening for several minutes, then add beef, and cook over a brisk heat, stirring frequently, until nicely browned. Lift kidneys from wine marinade (save marinade) and separate the kidney clusters. Dust with flour, add to beef, and cook, stirring carefully, until browned. Pour in ½ cup water and season with bay leaf, parsley, celery tops, and marjoram. Cover and cook over a very low heat until meat is tender when tested with a fork (takes about 1 hour). When tender, stir in mushrooms and the wine marinade. Pour into a 2-quart casserole or baking dish that can go to the table. Cover top with thinly rolled pastry, slashed in several places to allow steam to escape, and seal the edges securely. Bake in a preheated 450° oven for 25 to 30 minutes or until crust is perfectly browned. Serves 6 to 8.

TONGUE IN SPICY ASPIC

1 smoked beef tongue
Cayenne
½ teaspoon cinnamon
½ teaspoon allspice
½ teaspoon white pepper

¼ teaspoon ground cloves
¼ teaspoon mace
Several sprigs of parsley, chopped fine
3 tablespoons vinegar

Cover beef tongue with cold water and cook over a gentle heat for 2 to 3 hours or until very tender when pierced with a fork. Lift tongue from broth. Boil broth over a high heat until it is reduced to about 1 pint. Meanwhile, skin the tongue and trim the root. Cut the meat in small cubes and season with a dash of cayenne, spices, and parsley. Pack the mixture into a bowl or mold. Mix 3 tablespoons of vinegar into the hot broth, then pour over the meat. Refrigerate overnight. Unmold and cut in slices to serve. Serves 8.

FRIZZLED BEEF

One of the most formidable problems faced by American pioneers was the preservation of meat. The most widely practiced methods of preservation were salting, pickling, and drying. The Indians had a method of drying both game and beef which they taught the white man; meat dried in this manner was called jerky. These strips of salted, peppered, and dried meat were carried by trappers and cowboys, who sometimes sustained themselves for days by chewing on them. Under more civilized circumstances, jerky was usually creamed and served on biscuits or on fried corn-meal mush.

2 tablespoons butter
¼ pound dried beef, shredded
3 tablespoons flour

2 cups milk
Dash of pepper, freshly ground

Heat butter in a saucepan, add dried beef, and fry over a moderate heat until edges begin to look crisp. Sprinkle in flour and continue cooking 3 to 4 minutes, stirring constantly. Pour in milk and cook, still stirring, until mixture bubbles. Season with a dash of pepper. Serve over toast, biscuits, or Fried Corn Meal Mush (page 116). Makes 4 servings.

CORNISH PASTIES

Pastry:
2 cups sifted all-purpose flour
1 teaspoon salt
⅔ cup shortening
4 tablespoons cold water (about)
Filling:
1 pound round steak, ground

½ pound lean pork, ground
1 cup potatoes, diced fine
½ cup onion; diced fine
½ cup parsley, chopped
1 teaspoon salt
¼ teaspoon pepper

Sift flour and salt together. Cut in shortening with a pastry blender or two knives until mixture resembles corn meal. Mix in the water with a fork. Then, using your hands, gather the pastry together in a mass. Refrigerate while you make the filling. Combine both meats, the potatoes, onion, parsley, and seasonings. Divide the pastry into 8 portions. Roll one portion at a time on a lightly floured board, making a circle about the size of a saucer. Put a heaping tablespoon of filling on half the pastry, fold over the other half, and seal edges with fork tines dipped in flour. Place on a cooky sheet and bake in a preheated 450° oven for 10 minutes. Reduce heat to 350°, and continue baking 50 minutes or until pastry is a tempting brown.

RED FLANNEL HASH

There are several stories purporting to explain the origin of Red Flannel Hash. One states that it was created in the Green Mountains of Vermont, where it was popular with Ethan Allen and his Green Mountain Boys.

3 medium beets, cooked
1 large potato, cooked
1 pound chuck steak, ground
Salt

Pepper
½ cup (1 stick) butter
1 medium onion, chopped
1 tablespoon cream

Chop the beets and potato, mix with ground chuck. Add salt and pepper. Melt *4 tablespoons of the butter* in a large skillet, add the chopped onion, and cook until limp. Stir in the meat-vegetable mixture and cook over a low heat for 10 minutes, stirring occasionally. Lift mixture into a medium-sized baking dish. Melt remaining butter and combine with cream. Spoon this over the hash. Place under a preheated broiler, 3 inches from unit or tip of flame, for 5 minutes or until hash has a rich, brown crust. May be served with poached eggs on top. Serves 4.

STUFFED CABBAGE

1 head green cabbage
1 pound ground beef
½ pound pork, ground
2 eggs, beaten
1 medium onion, chopped
½ cup cooked rice
2 teaspoons salt
¼ teaspoon pepper

⅓ cup milk (about)
1 cup tomato juice
1 cup beef broth
¼ cup cider vinegar
2 tablespoons sugar
1 bay leaf
¼ teaspoon pepper

Leave cabbage head whole but ream out some of the solid core. Cover with boiling water and cook about 10 minutes. Drain cabbage carefully and pull off 16 to 18 of the largest outer leaves. Trim off some of the thick center ribs. Combine beef, pork, eggs, onion, rice, salt, pepper, and just enough milk to make a loose mixture. Put a heaping tablespoon of the filling in the center of each cabbage leaf, roll up and tuck in the ends, making a neat package. Place side by side in a shallow baking dish and pour in a mixture of tomato juice and all remaining ingredients. Cover and bake in a preheated 350° oven for about 1 hour. Serves 6.

VEAL GRILLADES

2 pounds round of veal
2 tablespoons flour
3 tablespoons butter
2 small onions, chopped
1 clove garlic, chopped
1 stalk celery, chopped
½ green pepper, chopped
1 bay leaf

½ teaspoon dried thyme
1 teaspoon salt
¼ teaspoon pepper
Dash cayenne
2 tablespoons tomato paste
2 cups beef broth
Chopped parsley

Cut veal into slices about ½ to ¾ inch thick and dust with flour. Sauté in heated butter over a high heat until nicely browned on both sides. Add onions, garlic, celery, green pepper, bay leaf, and all the seasonings. Cook until vegetables are slightly limp. Combine tomato paste with broth and add to veal mixture. Cover and cook over a low heat for 35 to 45 minutes or until grillades are tender. At serving time, transfer meat to a hot platter, pour sauce over all, and sprinkle generously with chopped parsley. Serve with steamed rice, Hominy Pudding (page 115), or new potatoes. Serves 4.

Butcher's advertisement

VEAL BIRDS

12 thin slices veal cutlet
½ cup (1 stick) butter
1 medium onion, chopped
2 cups fine bread crumbs
½ cup chopped parsley
½ teaspoon salt
¼ teaspoon pepper
½ teaspoon dried thyme

½ teaspoon dried marjoram
½ teaspoon dried basil
2 to 3 tablespoons milk
Flour
1½ cups beef broth
Bay leaf
Several celery tops
Several sprigs parsley

Veal slices should be pounded as thin as for Veal Scallopini. Melt *half the butter*, stir in onion, and cook several minutes. Combine with bread crumbs and chopped parsley, salt, pepper, and the three herbs. Add just enough milk to moisten the stuffing (it should not be wet). Spread equal amounts of the stuffing on each slice of veal, making it into a small roll and attaching the end with a toothpick. Dust the rolls lightly with flour. Heat remaining half of the butter in a skillet. Add veal birds and brown over a moderate heat. Pour in meat stock, add bay leaf, celery tops, and parsley. Cover tightly and simmer slowly for 30 to 40 minutes or until meat is tender. Serve with pan gravy. Serves 4 to 6.

VEAL CHOPS EN PAPILLOTE

This recipe is adapted from Practical Housekeeping, 1895.

6 veal chops
Salt
Pepper
Flour
4 tablespoons butter
1 tablespoon onion, minced
12 mushroom caps, thinly sliced

½ cup boiled ham, minced
½ cup cooked chicken or veal, minced
3 truffles, thinly sliced (optional)
1 tablespoon parsley, minced
½ cup dry sherry
1 can (7½-ounce size) beef gravy

Slash the fat on edges of chops to keep them from curling. Season with salt and pepper and dust lightly with flour. Melt *2 tablespoons of the butter* in a large, heavy skillet, add the chops, and sauté over medium heat for 25 minutes or until nicely browned and well done. Turn once. Remove chops from skillet and keep them hot. Add remainder of the butter to the same skillet, toss in onion, and cook a few minutes. Then add the mushrooms and cook about 5 minutes longer. Add the ham, chicken or veal, truffles, and parsley. Turn the mixture a few times. Finally, pour in the sherry and beef gravy. Bring to a boil, scraping bottom and sides of the skillet to loosen the rich brown particles. Reduce heat to simmer, and cook a few more minutes. Taste for seasoning. Meanwhile, cut 6 heart-shaped pieces of parchment paper, large enough to overlap each chop by 2 inches or slightly more all around. Butter one side of the paper with softened butter. Place a chop on buttered side of each "heart" and spoon some of the stuffing on top. Divide the mixture evenly among the six. Fold the paper over the chops and roll the edges as you would a hem, sealing the package so that steam and juices cannot escape. Place in a buttered, shallow baking dish and bake in a preheated 400° oven until the paper browns slightly and swells up like a small balloon. This takes only a short time. Serve in the paper packages.

VEAL IN SOUR CREAM

2 pounds veal steak, cut in 1½-inch cubes
3 tablespoons butter
2 tablespoons flour
1 cup commercial sour cream

1 tablespoon minced onion
½ pound mushrooms
2 tablespoons butter
1 teaspoon salt

Melt 3 tablespoons butter in heavy frying pan and sauté meat over high heat until lightly browned on all sides. Do not crowd in the pan; rather do a few pieces at a time. Place meat in baking dish or casserole that has a cover. Add flour to fat remaining in frying pan, and stir until smooth. Then stir in the sour cream thoroughly. Remove from heat. In a separate pan, melt 2 tablespoons butter and cook minced onion until slightly golden, then add mushrooms (if large, slice thin; if small, leave whole), and simmer over low heat for about 5 minutes. Combine mushrooms with sour cream mixture and salt. Pour over veal, cover, and bake in a 325° oven for 1 hour or until meat is tender when pierced with a fork. Serve with steamed rice. Serves 4.

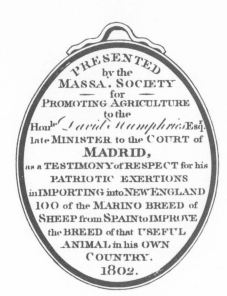

Medal presented to David Humphrey for importing Merino sheep

LAMB SHANKS

6 lamb shanks or chops
1 egg, slightly beaten
1 cup fine dry bread crumbs
Few sprigs parsley, chopped
¼ teaspoon dried thyme
¼ teaspoon dried marjoram

¼ teaspoon dried savory
½ teaspoon salt
½ teaspoon grated lemon rind
3 tablespoons butter
Sherry

Dip the shanks in egg, then coat with a mixture of crumbs, parsley, thyme, marjoram, savory, salt, and lemon rind. Heat butter in a skillet. Add shanks and sauté over a low heat until nicely browned on both sides. Add sherry to pan gravy and serve over shanks. Serves 4.

CROWN ROAST OF LAMB WITH SARATOGA CHIPS

In *The American Frugal Housewife*, published in 1836 and "Dedicated to Those Who Are Not Ashamed of Economy," Lydia Maria Child wrote: "That part of mutton called the rack...is cheap food. It is not more than four or five cents a pound; and four pounds will make a dinner for six people. . . . If your family be small, a rack of mutton will make you two dinners...."

Buy as much of the rack of lamb as you will need (they range in size from 12 to 16 chops) and have the butcher make it into a crown roast. Place it in a shallow roasting pan, stuffing the center with foil so the crown will keep its shape. Put bits of salt pork on the tips of the bones or wrap the ends in foil to prevent charring. Roast in a preheated 300° oven for 1½ hours. Season with salt and pepper and place on a hot platter. Remove foil and fill the center of roast with Saratoga Chips (page 112) which have been heated in the oven. Or, if you prefer, fill center with Puréed Chestnuts (page 100). The number it will serve depends on the size of the crown. To serve the crown in proper style, put paper frills around the tips of the bones.

MINT-STUFFED BARBECUED LAMB

A 7-pound leg of lamb, boned
2 cups fresh mint leaves
Sauce:
1½ cups cider vinegar

½ cup (1 stick) butter
1 tablespoon Worcestershire sauce
Red pepper to taste
1 or 2 garlic cloves, crushed

Stuff the boned lamb with mint leaves that have been washed and dried. Pack them into the cavity as tightly as possible, then skewer and tie the meat securely. Wrap in foil and allow to stand in the refrigerator for several hours (preferably overnight) so that the flavor of the mint can permeate the meat. Bring to room temperature before cooking. To roast over charcoal, place lamb on a rack 4 inches from bed of coals (which have been prepared ahead of time). Brush the meat frequently with the barbecue sauce and turn occasionally during the entire cooking period. It will take about 1½ to 1¾ hours for rare, and better than 2 hours for well done. To roast in the oven, place the lamb in a roasting pan on a rack, pour the barbecue sauce over the meat, and roast in a preheated 325° oven for 1¼ to 1½ hours for rare; 2 to 2½ hours for well done. Baste frequently with the sauce, using either a brush or baster. Although the mint contributes enormously to the flavor of the lamb, one does not eat it. Serve with new potatoes steamed in butter.

To make the barbecue sauce: Combine vinegar, butter, Worcestershire sauce, red pepper, and crushed garlic in a saucepan. Bring to a boil, then simmer for about 20 minutes.

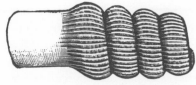
Lamb chop frill

IRISH LAMB STEW

2 pounds boned shoulder of lamb
1 cup sliced raw potatoes
¼ small head cabbage, shredded
2 leeks, sliced thin
2 medium onions, sliced
1 stalk celery, sliced
1½ teaspoons salt
¼ teaspoon freshly ground pepper

1 bay leaf
1 clove garlic, crushed
¼ teaspoon dried thyme
8 small onions
4 carrots
2 white turnips, quartered
1 pound green peas, shelled
Few sprigs parsley

Have meat cut into 2-inch cubes. Arrange alternate layers of lamb and the mixed sliced vegetables in a casserole or baking dish. Season with salt, pepper, bay leaf, garlic, and thyme. Cover with water and bring to a boil on top of the stove. Cover casserole, place in a preheated 350° oven, and bake for 1½ hours or until meat is tender. Cook onions, carrots, turnips, and peas—each separately—until tender. Drain. Lift meat out of casserole onto a plate and keep it warm. Strain liquid from stew and reserve. Work vegetables (from stew) through a sieve, ricer, or in a blender, then combine with the strained liquid, the whole cooked vegetables, and the meat. Taste and adjust seasoning. Serve hot with parsley, chopped fine, sprinkled on top. Serves 4.

HAM

Shortly after President James K. Polk left office in 1849, he visited New Orleans and, after looking over the French dishes offered in one restaurant, "asked a servant in a low tone if he could give me a piece of cornbread and boiled ham." Polk was born in North Carolina, which is considered part of Smithfield ham country. Quite a number of southern states—Tennessee, Georgia, and Kentucky among them—claim to produce the best ham; but Smithfield, Virginia, has long enjoyed the most prestigious reputation for its product. As early as 1639 (the town of Smithfield was not founded until 113 years later), settlers in Virginia were exporting pork and bacon to New England. Over a century ago, Queen Victoria placed an order for six hams a week to come from Smithfield.

In 1818, the New England poet Henry C. Knight wrote of life in Virginia in his book *Letters from the South and West:* "A meat-house is one of the first houses built; hung on all sides with chines, middlings, joles, and hams; perhaps finer flavoured for having run wild [and fed on the peanuts grown in Virginia]. One of the common petty larcenies of the slaves, is breaking into the smoke-house. It is remarked that, north of the Potomac, one may find good beef, and bad bacon; and south of the Potomac, good bacon and bad beef."

Smithfield hams have been so highly esteemed that several other parts of the country have attempted to raise imitations. In 1926, in order to protect its industry and its traditions, the General Assembly of Virginia placed a statute in its books: "Genuine Smithfield hams [are those] cut from the carcasses of peanut-fed hogs, raised in the peanut-belt of the State of Virginia or the State of North Carolina, and which are cured, treated, smoked, and processed in the town of Smithfield, in the State of Virginia."

TO COOK AGED, COUNTRY-CURED HAMS

Soak the ham overnight (at least 12 to 18 hours) in enough water to cover it entirely. Drain, cover meat again with fresh cold water, and bring to the simmering point only. Do not boil. Simmer the ham for just 2 hours, regardless of the size or weight, then remove from stove, and allow ham to cool in the liquor. When ham is cold, cut off the rind, score, stud with cloves, and glaze with one of the following:

Brown Sugar Glaze: Mix 1 cup brown sugar with 1 teaspoon dry mustard and ½ teaspoon ground cloves. Add a little of the fat from the pan (just enough to make a stiff paste) and spread this mixture over the fat.

Honey Glaze: Spoon honey over the fat.

Apricot Jam Glaze: Spoon apricot jam over the fat.

Bake in a preheated 400° oven for 30 minutes. Serve cut in paper-thin slices, hot or cold.

TO BAKE MODERN HAMS

These hams do not require boiling as country-cured hams do. Put ham, skin side up, in roasting pan. Place in a preheated 300° oven and bake approximately 20 to 22 minutes per pound for a 10- to 12-pound ham; 18 to 20 minutes per pound for a 12- to 15-pound ham; 15 to 18 minutes per pound for a ham 15 pounds or over. If you use a meat thermometer, insert it in the fleshiest part of the ham and bake until thermometer reads 165°. Remove ham from the oven, cut off the rind, and score the fat. Glaze with any of the glazes on page 88, return to a 400° oven, and bake another 15 minutes to set the glaze. Serve hot or cold.

HAM BAKED IN MAPLE SYRUP

Cut off the rind from a slice of ham about 1¼ to 1½ inches thick, and slash the fat in several places to keep it from curling. Mix 2 teaspoons dry mustard with 2 tablespoons cider vinegar until smooth, then add ¾ cup pure maple syrup. Pour over ham (some cooks stud the ham with cloves to add flavor) and place in a 350° oven for 50 to 60 minutes. Baste frequently with the sauce. When ham is cooked, remove from baking pan and place on warm serving platter. Put baking pan, with sauce, on top of stove over high heat and cook the sauce, stirring constantly, until it is a good consistency for gravy. Pour over ham slice or serve separately in a sauceboat. Ham prepared this old-fashioned way is especially good when served with new potatoes and asparagus, broccoli, or cauliflower with Hollandaise Sauce (page 126). Serves 4.

HAM WITH ORANGE

Slash the fatty rim of a nice thick slice of ham to keep it from curling. Sauté in 1 tablespoon melted butter over a low heat until lightly browned on both sides. Place on a hot platter and keep it warm. Pour 1 cup orange juice into pan drippings, stirring until you have mixed in all the rich, brown particles. Add 1 tablespoon of arrowroot or cornstarch, mixed with a little water until smooth, and cook, stirring constantly, until sauce thickens. Last of all, mix in 1 tablespoon honey and the sections from 2 small oranges (be sure to remove all membrane). Heat through, then pour sauce over ham slice, and garnish with parsley. A generous slice should serve 4.

RED-EYE GRAVY

After frying a slice of country ham about ¼ inch thick, drain off any excess fat, add a little water to the drippings and about a tablespoon of strong coffee to give it color. Bring to a boil and serve with the ham and, traditionally, grits and hot biscuits.

BAKED STUFFED HAM PONTALBA

A 14-pound ham, boned
4 cups shelled pecans, ground
3 onions, chopped fine
1 small can truffles, cut in pieces
6 bay leaves
2 sprigs (½ teaspoon dried) thyme
3 teaspoons dried sage

3 teaspoons ground cloves
¼ teaspoon cayenne
½ cup Madeira wine
1 apple
1 cup cane syrup
Brown sugar
Fine dry bread crumbs

Ask your butcher to bone the ham. If a dry smoked ham is used, the ham must be soaked in cold water for 12 hours. When a modern cured ham is used, soaking is unnecessary. To make the stuffing: cut out about ½ pound of ham to make a cavity, and work the ham through a food grinder. Blend thoroughly with the pecans, *1 chopped onion*, truffles, *2 bay leaves (crumbled)*, thyme, *1 teaspoon sage*, *1 teaspoon ground cloves*, cayenne, and Madeira to make the stuffing. Pack into ham cavity, sewing or skewering it securely. Put these seasonings on the ham: *1 chopped onion, 2 bay leaves, 1 teaspoon sage, 1 teaspoon cloves*. Sew a cloth securely around ham and place in a large kettle. Add enough water to cover, and the remaining chopped onion, bay leaves, sage, cloves, the whole unpared apple, and the syrup. Bring to a boil, cover, reduce heat, and simmer for about 6 hours or until tender. Allow ham to cool in the liquid. When cool, remove rind, pat ham with a mixture of brown sugar and crumbs, and bake in a preheated 375° oven until surface is well browned and ham is hot.

SCHNITZ-UN-GNEPP

Schnitz means "cut" and, in Pennsylvania Dutch usage, it has come to mean cut dried apples. There are both sweet and sour *Schnitz:* the sour *Schnitz* are used for pies; the sweet apples go into sweet *Schnitz*, served with dumplings *(gnepp)* as in this recipe.

2½- to 3-pound smoked ham with bone
2 cups dried apples

2 tablespoons brown sugar

Cover ham almost completely with cold water. Bring to a boil, reduce heat, cover, and simmer gently for 2 hours. Meanwhile, put dried apples in a bowl and cover with cold water to soak. When ham has been cooked 2 hours, add drained apples and brown sugar. Simmer 1 hour, then lift ham onto a large platter and spoon apples around it. Reserve ham broth.

Dumplings:
1½ cups sifted all-purpose flour
3 teaspoons baking powder
½ teaspoon salt

1 tablespoon butter
¼ cup milk (about)
1 egg, well beaten

Sift together flour, baking powder, and salt into a bowl. Pinch in the butter with your finger tips until well distributed, then stir in enough milk to make a soft dough. Add egg. Drop dumplings from a soup spoon into the boiling ham broth, cover tightly, and simmer 10 to 12 minutes. Arrange dumplings on the platter around the meat and spoon a little broth over them. The liquid may be thickened by stirring in a little flour mixed to a smooth paste with water. Serves 6 to 8.

HAM MOUSSE

In *Society As I Have Found It*, Ward McAllister wrote, "We ask [the chef] for a novelty, and his great genius suggests, under pressure, *mousse aux jambon* [Ham Mousse], which is attractive to the eye, and, if well made, at once establishes the reputation of the artist, satisfies the guests . . . and allays their fears for their dinner."

2 envelopes gelatin	2 eggs, separated
¼ cup sherry	3½ cups cooked ham, ground
1⅓ cups chicken broth	1 cup heavy cream

Sprinkle gelatin over sherry to soften. Heat chicken broth until bubbling. Beat egg yolks slightly, stir in a little heated broth, then pour back into broth. Cook over a low heat, stirring constantly, for a minute or two. Remove from heat, mix in gelatin until dissolved, then add the ham. Fold in stiffly beaten egg whites and stiffly beaten cream. Spoon into a 1-quart mold and refrigerate until firm. Unmold on a platter. Serves 6.

GLAZED HAM AND PORK LOAF

To make the loaf:

2 pounds ham, ground
1½ pounds lean pork, ground
1 teaspoon salt
¼ teaspoon pepper
2 eggs, well beaten
1 cup milk
1 cup cracker crumbs

Glaze:

1½ cups brown sugar, firmly packed
1 tablespoon prepared mustard
½ cup cider vinegar
½ cup water

Combine thoroughly ground ham and pork, salt, pepper, eggs, milk, and crumbs. Shape the mixture into a loaf, place in a shallow baking pan, and bake in a preheated 350° oven for 1½ hours. When loaf goes in the oven, mix brown sugar, mustard, vinegar, and water in a saucepan and cook for about 5 minutes. As the ham loaf browns, baste it with the glaze. Baste frequently during remaining baking time. Serve hot or cold to 6 or 8.

CHARLES COUNTY, MARYLAND, STUFFED HAM

In Charles County, Maryland (named for Charles Calvert, Third Lord Baltimore), ham has been prepared by this method for three centuries.

Cook aged, country-cured ham (page 88) to the point where ham is cooled in the liquor. When meat is cool, remove from liquor and set aside. Heat liquor to the boiling point, then toss in 8 quarts (1 peck) of well-washed, tender spring greens. A favorite combination includes: mustard and turnip greens, spinach or kale, small green onions with their tops, and land cress (not to be confused with watercress). When greens are wilted, drain thoroughly and chop fine. Season with celery seed and freshly ground pepper. With a sharp knife make deep crescent-shaped incisions in the ham, top and bottom, and stuff the openings tightly with the chopped greens. Wrap the ham in unbleached muslin and sew securely. Return ham to liquor and simmer 5 minutes per pound. Remove muslin. May be served hot or cold. If a precooked ham is used, cook greens in boiling water and proceed as above.

STUFFED SPARERIBS

"Many people buy the upper part of the spare-rib of pork," Lydia Maria Child observed in 1836 in *The American Frugal Housewife*, "thinking it the most genteel; but the lower part of the spare-rib toward the neck is much more sweet and juicy, and there is more meat in proportion to the bone."

4 to 5 cooking apples	Salt
1 box (1 pound) prunes	Pepper
2 strips lean spareribs (about	Brown sugar
10 inches long)	Cinnamon

Pare apples, core, and cut into thick slices. Cook in a small amount of water until almost tender. Drain. Cook prunes according to package directions. Drain and remove pits. Place one strip of the spareribs in a shallow roasting pan and sprinkle with salt and pepper. Spread the cooked apples over the ribs evenly. Cover with prunes, then sprinkle with a little brown sugar, cinnamon, and more salt. Place second strip of ribs on top and link edges together, here and there, with skewers. Bake in a preheated 325° oven for about 2 hours or until fork pierces the meat easily. Serves 6.

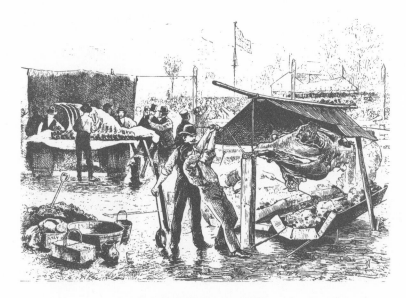

Political barbecue, 1876

BARBECUED SPARERIBS

Section the ribs from 2 racks of spareribs into easy-to-eat pieces. Sprinkle with salt and pepper and place on a rack in roasting pan. Bake in a preheated 350° oven for 35 minutes, turning them occasionally. Brush lavishly with Barbecue Sauce (page 129), increase oven heat to 400°, and continue baking for another 35 minutes or until well browned. Turn ribs frequently, brushing each time with the sauce. Serves 4 to 6.

To make Barbecued Lamb Riblets: Section 2 racks of lamb breast. Sprinkle with salt and pepper and brush with the Barbecue Sauce (page 129). Roast in a preheated 400° oven for 1 hour, turning occasionally and brushing with sauce each time. Serves 4.

PORK AND APPLE PIE

The cookbook *(La Cuisine Creole)* from which this recipe was adapted advises: "This is a plain and wholesome dish; when the family is large and apples plentiful, it will be an economical way of giving the boys 'apple pie.'"

Pastry for a 2-crust pie (page 164)
4 greening apples
2 pounds lean pork, cubed
½ teaspoon dried thyme
2 tablespoons sugar

1 teaspoon salt
¼ teaspoon pepper
1 tablespoon butter
1 egg, beaten

Line bottom and sides of a deep pie dish with pastry. Pare apples, core, and cut into slices. Arrange alternate layers of pork and apples in the pie shell, sprinkling the layers as you go along with a mixture of thyme, sugar, salt, and pepper. Dot the last layer with butter and cover with pastry. Slash pastry in several places, then brush it lavishly with egg, and bake in a preheated 350° oven for 1½ to 2 hours. Serve either lukewarm or cold—but not chilled, and never hot from the oven. If you do not mind departing from tradition, serve a mixture of freshly grated horse-radish and sour cream with it.

ROAST SUCKLING PIG

Mrs. Leslie's *American Family Cook Book,* from which this recipe is adapted, instructs: "A sucking-pig, like a young child, must not be left for an instant."

1 suckling pig (about 10 to 15 pounds)
2 loaves (1 pound each) white bread
3 cups water
1 large onion, chopped
½ cup butter

1 tablespoon dried sage
1½ teaspoons salt
¼ teaspoon freshly ground pepper
1 tart apple, peeled and grated

Ask the butcher to clean the pig thoroughly. Crumble bread into a large bowl, add water, and set aside to soak. Cook onion in melted butter until limp. Remove from heat and stir in sage, salt, pepper, and apple. Squeeze moisture from bread and combine bread with onion mixture. Fill the pig with this dressing and place in a kneeling position in a roasting pan. Put a block of wood in its mouth and tie the legs in place. Sprinkle skin with salt and cover ears and tail with foil to prevent charring. Pour 1 cup hot water into the pan and roast pig in a preheated 325° oven for 3½ to 4 hours or until tender when tested with a fork. Baste frequently with pan drippings. About 30 minutes before pig has finished cooking, remove foil. To serve, place roasted pig on a hot platter, replace wooden block in mouth with a small red apple, insert cranberries or grapes in eye sockets. Surround with water-cress. Serves 8 to 10.

To carve: Cut at right angles to the backbone, making cuts about one inch apart. Run the knife along the backbone and under meat to loosen, then lift off each piece.

GLAZED ROAST PORK

Kitchen stoves, although invented in the late eighteenth century, were not immediately taken up by American housewives. Indeed, they were resisted well into the nineteenth century. One of Eliza Leslie's books giving instructions for fireplace cookery was still being published in 1870. This pork roast, then, was cooked even until that late date in a reflecting oven, a device with its open side facing the fireplace and its curved metal back facing out. The meat was placed on a spit in the reflecting oven and turned by hand. Today the same effect can be achieved in a modern rotisserie.

A 5- to 6-pound loin of pork　　　　*Glaze:*
Flour　　　　　　　　　　　　　　1 cup sugar
Salt　　　　　　　　　　　　　　　⅓ cup cider vinegar
Pepper　　　　　　　　　　　　　1 teaspoon hickory-smoked salt

Score the fat on the roast lightly, then rub the entire surface with flour, salt, and pepper. Place on a rack in a shallow roasting pan. Roast in a preheated 450° oven for 15 minutes, then reduce heat to 350°, and continue roasting 30 to 35 minutes per pound, basting frequently with the glaze. Serves 6.

To make the glaze: Pour sugar in a heavy skillet and cook over a moderate heat until it becomes a rich, golden brown liquid. Pour in half a cup of boiling water, a little at a time (mixture sputters at this point, so stand back), and cook, stirring constantly with a wooden spoon, until all lumps have dissolved. Measure ½ cup of the caramel syrup and combine it with vinegar and hickory-smoked salt.

To roast in a rotisserie: Prepare pork as directed above, start rotisserie at 450°, and revolve slowly for 15 minutes or until meat begins to turn brown. Then reduce heat to 350° and baste, at frequent intervals, with glaze. Allow 30 to 35 minutes per pound.

SCRAPPLE

Scrapple, or *ponhaws* as the Pennsylvania Dutch called it, was originated as a thrifty way to use scraps of pork after hogs had been slaughtered.

1½ pounds pork shoulder　　　　Dash of ground cloves
¼ pound pork liver　　　　　　　¼ teaspoon dried thyme
1 cup yellow corn meal　　　　　1 teaspoon dried sage
2 teaspoons salt　　　　　　　　1 teaspoon dried marjoram
¼ cup onions, chopped fine　　　½ teaspoon freshly ground pepper

Combine pork shoulder and liver in a saucepan with 1 quart water and cook, over a moderate heat, for 1 hour. Drain, reserving the broth. Discard all bones and chop meat fine. Blend corn meal, salt, 1 cup water, and 2 cups of the broth in a saucepan. Cook, stirring constantly, until thick. Stir in meat, onions, all the spices and herbs. Cover and simmer gently for about 1 hour over a very low heat. Pour into a 9 x 5 x 3-inch loaf pan and chill until firm. Cut into slices about ½ to ¾ inch thick, dust lightly with flour, and fry in a little heated shortening over a moderate heat until crisp on both sides. Serve at once.

HOMEMADE SAUSAGE, COUNTRY STYLE

Combine 2 pounds of fresh lean pork, coarsely ground, with ½ tablespoon dried thyme or sage, dash of cayenne, ¾ teaspoon freshly ground black pepper, and 1 teaspoon salt. Mix well with your hand. Divide in half and shape into two rolls, wrapping each roll securely in foil. Sausage will keep several weeks under refrigeration.

To fry sausages: Cut off slices about ¾ inch thick. Place in a cold skillet and fry over a low heat until well browned on both sides and thoroughly cooked. Serve with applesauce.

CREOLE SAUSAGE

1 pound lean pork, ground
½ pound pork fat, ground
½ large onion, chopped fine
½ garlic, crushed
½ teaspoon salt
½ teaspoon pepper, freshly ground

¼ teaspoon ground chili pepper
¼ teaspoon cayenne
¼ teaspoon dried thyme
¼ teaspoon allspice
1 small bay leaf, crumbled
1 tablespoon chopped parsley

Combine ground pork and pork fat with onion, garlic, salt, pepper, chili pepper, cayenne, thyme, allspice, bay leaf, and parsley. Shape into a roll, wrap securely in foil, and refrigerate. Keeps well for several weeks. This is a hot, highly seasoned sausage meat. To fry, follow directions for Homemade Sausage, Country Style (above).

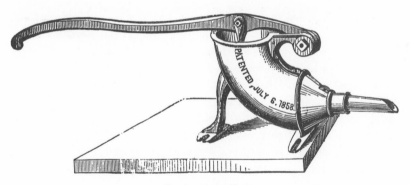

Sausage stuffer

COUNTRY SAUSAGE WITH FRIED APPLE RINGS

Core unpared apples (choose a crisp, tart variety) and cut into rings about ½ inch thick. Allow 2 to 3 rings per serving. Shape sausage meat into patties. Fry in a heavy skillet, over a low heat, until well done but not crisp. Transfer to a heated platter, set aside, and keep warm. Leave about ½ inch of fat in the skillet (pour off the excess) and add as many apple rings as will fit comfortably. Sprinkle lightly with brown sugar and cinnamon and cook, turning frequently (use care so that they do not lose their shape). Cover pan for a few minutes to soften apples, then remove cover, and cook a little longer or until rings have a rich glaze. As you finish cooking each batch, place them on the platter with the sausages.

ROAST RACK OF VENISON

William Byrd, in *Histories of the Dividing Line Betwixt Virginia and North Carolina*, stated: "Our Indian kill'd a Deer, & the other men some Turkeys, but the Indian begg'd very hard that our Cook might not boil Venison & Turkey together, because it wou'd certainly spoil his luck in Hunting, & we shou'd repent it with fasting and Prayer."

A rack of venison weighs 6 to 8 pounds. Bring the meat to room temperature before roasting. Place in a roasting pan, rub generously with butter, or cover with a piece of salt pork, secured with string. If you use butter, baste occasionally during the roasting period. Place in a preheated 325° oven and roast 18 minutes per pound. Do not overcook. Venison should be rare, not well done. Let stand on a warm platter before carving to allow the juices to settle. Salt and pepper to taste. Then serve with Cumberland Sauce (page 128). Puréed Chestnuts (page 100), potatoes, squash, or wild rice are all excellent accompaniments.

CREAMED SWEETBREADS AND OYSTERS

2 pairs sweetbreads
1 tablespoon vinegar
1 stalk celery with leaves
Few sprigs of parsley
4 tablespoons flour
½ teaspoon paprika

4 tablespoons butter
1 cup heavy cream
1 pint oysters in liquor
1 teaspoon salt
Dash of mace or nutmeg
¼ cup dry sherry

Soak sweetbreads in cold salted water for 20 minutes. Drain, add vinegar, celery, parsley, and enough cold water to cover. Cook to the boiling point, then simmer slowly for 15 to 20 minutes, depending on the size of the sweetbreads. Drain and plunge immediately in ice water to blanch. When cold, trim off any tubes and cartilage. Place in a pie dish, cover with wax paper, and put a weight on top. (Pressing the sweetbreads ensures a firm texture.) Separate into small sections with your hands, leaving the tender membrane covering the clusters intact. Coat sweetbreads with flour and paprika. Sauté in heated butter until a delicate golden color. Stir in cream and cook over a low heat, stirring constantly, until smooth and thick. Heat oysters in their liquor until the edges begin to curl. Combine with sweetbreads. Season with salt, mace or nutmeg, and sherry. Serve over crisp hot waffles. Serves 4.

To make Oyster and Sweetbread Pie: Pour into a deep pie dish or casserole (one that can go to the table) and cover with pastry (page 164). Seal edges securely and bake in a preheated 425° oven for 15 to 20 minutes or until nicely browned.

SWEETBREADS EUGÉNIE

Prepare and cook sweetbreads as directed in Creamed Oysters and Sweetbreads. Dip sweetbreads in beaten egg, then in a mixture of flour, salt, and paprika. In a skillet, heat 4 tablespoons butter until it begins to bubble. Add the sweetbreads and sauté over a low heat until golden brown on both sides. Place on a slice of toast, cover with Béchamel Sauce (page 126), and garnish with slices of truffles or lightly sautéed mushrooms. Serves 4.

RABBIT FRICASSEE

"As to their being fresh," Amelia Simmons counseled in speaking of how to buy a good rabbit, "judge by the scent." Though rabbit may seem a frontier food, in recipes like this one it was served at such civilized ménages as Monticello.

1 rabbit	Rind from ¼ lemon
Flour	Few sprigs parsley
¼ cup butter	2 stalks celery with leaves
Salt	1 bay leaf
Pepper	1 tablespoon flour
1 medium onion, chopped fine	1 tablespoon butter
1½ cups red wine	Chopped parsley

Cut rabbit into serving pieces and dust with flour. Heat butter in a skillet with a tight-fitting lid, add rabbit pieces, and sprinkle with salt and pepper. Fry until nicely browned on all sides. Now stir in onion and cook for a few minutes. Next, pour in the wine. Tie lemon rind, parsley, celery, and bay leaf in a little cheesecloth and drop into the skillet. Cover and simmer gently until meat is tender—takes about 1 hour. Lift rabbit onto a hot serving platter. Discard seasoning bag. Work flour and butter together until well blended, then add to liquid, and cook, stirring constantly, until sauce bubbles. Pour over rabbit and sprinkle top with chopped parsley. Serves 4.

The Christians stayed three months in Autiamque, enjoying the greatest plenty of maize, beans, walnuts, and dried plums (persimmons); also rabbits, which they had never had ingenuity enough to ensnare until the Indians there taught them.

—The Gentleman of Elvas, the Lord Inquisitor,
Expedition of Hernando de Soto, 1541

KIDNEY STEW

1 pound small veal kidneys	⅓ cup dry red wine
1 teaspoon salt	2 carrots, diced fine
¼ teaspoon pepper	Flour
2 bay leaves	4 tablespoons butter or bacon drippings
6 peppercorns	¼ pound mushrooms, sliced
1 large onion	

Wash kidneys, trim away any fat, membrane, or connective tissue, and put in a bowl. Add salt, pepper, bay leaves, peppercorns, *2 slices of the onion* (save the rest to use later on), and wine. Cook diced carrots in 2 cups salted water until almost tender. Lift kidneys from bowl (save marinade) and slice in small pieces. Coat generously with flour and fry in heated butter or bacon drippings until nicely browned. Stir in remaining piece of onion, chopped, and continue cooking until onion is limp. Add carrots and the water in which they cooked. Heat, stirring constantly, until sauce thickens. Add mushrooms and cook a few minutes longer. Last of all, stir in the strained marinade. Bring to a boil but do not cook further. May be served from a chafing dish over crisp toast or waffles. Makes 4 to 6 servings.

VEGETABLES

GLAZED PARSNIPS

"Parsnips," Amelia Simmons noted rather enigmatically in *American Cookery*, "are a valuable root, cultivated best in rich old grounds, and doubly deep plowed, late sown, they grow thrifty, and are not so prongy."

6 medium parsnips
3 tablespoons butter, melted
¼ cup brown sugar, firmly packed

½ cup cider
1 teaspoon salt

Peel parsnips, cut in quarters lengthwise, trim out any woody core. Cook in boiling, salted water until tender when tested with a fork. Drain thoroughly. Lay parsnips in a shallow baking dish. Mix together the butter, brown sugar, cider, and salt. Spoon this mixture over the parsnips. Bake 20 minutes in a 400° oven. Baste occasionally with the glaze. Serves 4.

BAKED STUFFED EGGPLANT

1 large or 2 small eggplants
½ cup (1 stick) butter
1 medium onion, chopped fine
1 can (1 pound, 3 ounces) solid-pack
  tomatoes or 6 ripe tomatoes, skinned
1 cup celery, diced

1 teaspoon dried basil
½ teaspoon dried thyme
¾ teaspoon salt
Pepper, freshly ground
1 cup fresh bread crumbs

Cut eggplant in half lengthwise. Remove pulp, leaving the shell about ½ inch thick, and butter inside of shell. Dice the pulp and set aside. Melt *half the butter* in a saucepan. Stir in onion and cook until straw colored. Add diced eggplant, tomatoes, celery, basil, thyme, salt, and pepper. Cook over a moderate heat until mixture is thick and celery is tender. Spoon vegetable mixture into eggplant cavities. Cover with crumbs, lightly sautéed in remaining butter, and place in a shallow baking pan. Pour ½ inch boiling water in the pan. Place in a preheated 325° oven and bake for 15 to 20 minutes. To serve as an entree, substitute 1½ cups cooked shrimp or crab meat for one cup of the eggplant. Serves 4 to 6.

GREEN PEAS WITH MINT

Of the great variety of vegetables Jefferson grew at Monticello, his favorite was the pea. In Albemarle County, Virginia, it was customary for the neighboring gentlemen-farmers to compete each spring for the distinction of serving the first green peas. Jefferson took the honors so frequently that one year he told his children not to speak of the peas in his garden so that his friend George Divers of Farmington might give the annual dinner.

Cook frozen peas according to package directions or shell fresh peas and cook in boiling, salted water. In either case, do not overcook. Dot with butter and sprinkle with fresh chopped mint. Serves 4.

AMBUSHED ASPARAGUS

This recipe is adapted from Common Sense in the Household.

Cut the tops from 6 hard dinner rolls (either square or rectangular) and hollow out most of the center. Brush centers with melted butter and place them, along with the tops, in a 300° oven to dry while you prepare the asparagus. Cook 1 pound fresh asparagus (or 1 package frozen) until tender. Drain and cut the spears into small pieces. Set aside. Make 2 cups of well-seasoned Cream Sauce (page 126). Stir in asparagus, season with a dash of nutmeg, then spoon the mixture into the hot, crisp rolls. Cover with tops and put back in the oven for 3 minutes. May be served with crisp bacon for breakfast or lunch.

TURNIP GREENS

Cook 1 pound pork or salt pork in boiling, lightly salted water until tender when tested with a fork. Add water as needed. Wash thoroughly 2 bunches turnip greens and 1 bunch mustard greens. Pare and chop coarsely 4 white turnips. Add greens and turnips to pork and cook over a low heat for 40 to 45 minutes. Drain and serve with Corn Meal Dumplings (page 116) cooked in the pot liquor, Spider Corncake (page 35), or Corn Meal Biscuits (page 26). Serves 4.

MASHED TURNIPS

This recipe is adapted from the New England Economical House-keeper, where it was called "Turnip Sauce."

Pare 2 medium-sized yellow turnips (rutabagas) and 2 large potatoes. Cut into chunks of equivalent size. Place in a saucepan, cover with boiling, salted water, and cook until tender. Drain and dry thoroughly, then put through a ricer. Beat in a generous amount of butter, salt and pepper to taste, a big pinch of sugar, and some heavy cream, heated. Continue beating until turnips are very smooth. These can be made ahead of time and kept warm in a double boiler. Serves 4 to 6.

ONIONS IN CREAM

24 small white onions	½ teaspoon salt
2 tablespoons butter	Dash of cloves
2 tablespoons flour	¼ cup chopped parsley
1 cup half-and-half (milk and cream)	

Cover peeled onions with cold, salted water and bring to a boil. Reduce heat and cook slowly until onions are tender when tested with a fork. Drain thoroughly. Melt butter in a saucepan, add flour a little at a time, stir until smooth, and cook over a low heat for several minutes. Stir in half-and-half and continue cooking, stirring constantly, until sauce is smooth and bubbly. Remove from heat, stir in salt, cloves, and parsley. Combine with onions. Serves 4.

PLANTATION STRING BEANS

1 pound green beans
4 slices bacon
4 to 6 scallions

1 teaspoon salt
¼ teaspoon pepper

Snip off ends and slice green beans into thin slivers. Dice bacon and fry until crisp. Scoop out the bits of bacon, drain on paper towels, and set aside. Chop scallions and sauté in bacon fat until limp. Add beans, stir thoroughly, and cook over a moderate heat for about 1 minute. Add 1 tablespoon water, cover tightly, and cook 4 minutes. Remove cover and continue cooking and stirring until beans are tender but still crisp. Before serving, season with salt and pepper and sprinkle the beans with the drained bacon bits. Serves 4 to 6.

GREEN BEANS WITH CHESTNUTS

Take enough cooked chestnuts, chopped coarsely, to make about ⅓ cup. Sauté lightly (only a minute or two) in 6 tablespoons of butter. Add 1 pound cooked green beans and mix well. Taste for seasoning. Serves 4.

In July, when the chestnuts and corn are green and full grown, they half boil the former, and take off the rind; and having sliced the milky, swelled, long rows of the latter, the women pound it in a large wooden mortar, which is wide at the mouth, and gradually narrows to the bottom; then they knead both together, wrap them up in green corn-blades of various sizes, about an inch-thick, and boil them well, as they do every kind of seethed food. This sort of bread is very tempting to the taste, and reckoned most delicious to their strong palates.

—James Adair,
The History of the American Indian, 1775

PURÉED CHESTNUTS

1 pound chestnuts
1 teaspoon oil
1 tablespoon vinegar
3 stalks celery, coarsely chopped
1 small onion, coarsely chopped

2 tablespoons butter
½ teaspoon pepper, freshly ground
2 to 3 tablespoons heavy cream
Salt

Make a gash in the flat side of each chestnut, place them in a pan with the oil, and shake until well coated. Heat in a preheated 350° oven until the shells and inner skins can be removed easily. Shell the chestnuts, cover with water, and add the vinegar, celery, and onion. Boil until tender. Drain, discard celery and onion, and purée or mash until free of lumps. Beat in the butter, pepper, and cream. Add salt to taste. A rich and delicious accompaniment to venison, game, or turkey.

RUTABAGA PUDDING

Rutabagas were the subject of a bitter dispute that was aired in the New York newspapers in 1818. William Cobbett, the proprietor of a seed store in New York, maintained that he sold the best dollar-a-pound seeds in the City. As a gratuitous jab at his competitor, Grant Thorburn, Cobbett made the additional claim that he had introduced the rutabaga to America. Thorburn retorted by saying that *he* sold the best seed at a dollar a pound—and then devastated his opponent with the facts: "In the year 1796 a large field of these turnips was grown by Wm. Prout on that piece of ground now occupied by the navy yard, at the city of Washington."

2 pounds rutabagas (yellow turnips)
½ cup fine dry bread crumbs
½ cup milk
2 tablespoons melted butter

1½ teaspoons salt
Big pinch of sugar
2 eggs, well beaten

Peel rutabaga and cut in cubes, then cover with boiling water. Place a lid on the pan and cook vegetable over moderate heat until tender when pierced with a fork. Drain thoroughly. Mash as smooth as possible or put through a ricer, then beat in all remaining ingredients. Spoon into a 1½-quart baking dish or casserole and bake in a preheated 350° oven for 1 hour. Serves 4 to 6.

CHARTREUSE OF VEGETABLES

According to Mary Ronald's *Century Cook Book*, "Chartreuse is a liqueur made by the monks of the French monastery of Grand Chartreuse; but a class of dishes has also been given this name, where two or more foods are used which conceals the others. The story goes that on fast days the monks were thus able to indulge in forbidden food, and savory viands were hidden under cabbage or other severely plain articles." Thomas Jefferson was partial to the chartreuse recipe below, adapted from the Monticello manuscript collection.

6 small kohlrabi
8 carrots
6 small beets or small white turnips
2 medium-sized yellow turnips

Parsley
Salt
Pepper

Each vegetable must be cooked separately. Peel and slice, rather thin, the kohlrabi, carrots, white turnips (if you use them), and the yellow turnips. The beets are cooked whole in their skins. Drop each vegetable in a pot of boiling, salted water and cook until tender. Drain. Peel and slice the beets. Layer the vegetables, alternating the color, in a 1½-quart mold or the bottom of a double boiler (any deep, straight-sided vessel will do). Sprinkle finely chopped parsley and a dash of salt and pepper between the layers. Place the vessel in a pan of hot water, cover tightly (lacking a cover, use foil), and bake 20 minutes in a 350° oven. Unmold on a warm serving platter and serve with Hollandaise Sauce (page 126). Serves 6.

SQUASH

Indians grew a wide variety of squash long before the first white men reached America. Crooknecks and bush-scallops grew in the Northeast, cushaws and sweet potato squashes in the South, the Boston marrow and autumn turban in New England. Captain John Smith described the squash ("macocks") he found in the early days of Virginia, saying that the Indians "plant amongst their corn pumpions, and a fruit like unto our muskmelon, but less and worse, which they call macocks." Surely the best-known and most popular American squash is the Hubbard, whose history was revealed in a letter by James J. H. Gregory, written in December, 1857, for *The Magazine of Horticulture*. "Of the origin of the Hubbard squash we have no certain knowledge," Mr. Gregory said. "The facts relative to its cultivation in Marblehead are simply these. Upwards of twenty years ago, a single specimen was brought into town, the seed from which was planted in the garden of a lady, now deceased; a specimen from this yield was given to Captain Knott Martin, of this town, who raised it for family use for a few years, when it was brought to our notice in the year 1842 or '43. We were first informed of its good qualities by Mrs. Elizabeth Hubbard, a very worthy lady, through whom we obtained seed from Capt. Martin. As the squash up to this time had no specific name to designate it from other varieties, my father termed it the 'Hubbard Squash.'"

BAKED SQUASH

Wash 2 squash (acorn, Hubbard, etc.) and cut them in half. Spoon out seeds and fibers from the cavity. Put 4 slices of bacon in a shallow baking pan and bake in a preheated 350° oven until crisp. Remove from oven, drain on paper towels, and set aside. Sprinkle squash with salt and pepper and place, cut side down, in the bacon fat. Bake at 350° about 1 hour or until tender when tested with a fork. Just before serving, sprinkle lightly with brown sugar, brush with some of the bacon fat, and drop the bacon, crumbled, into squash cavities. Serves 4.

COLACHE

(Summer Squash, Mexican Style)

4 summer squash	1 small onion, chopped
4 ears of corn	Salt
3 ripe tomatoes	Pepper
¼ cup butter	

Wash squash and cut in small pieces; cut corn kernels from the cob; skin tomatoes and cut in cubes. Heat butter in a saucepan, stir in onion, and cook until limp but not brown. Add squash, corn, tomatoes, salt, and pepper. Cover and cook over a low heat for 30 to 40 minutes, stirring occasionally. Makes 6 servings.

PENNSYLVANIA RED CABBAGE

2 tablespoons shortening or bacon
  drippings
1 large onion, chopped fine
2 apples, pared, cored, and thinly sliced
1 cup water
½ cup red wine vinegar

2 tablespoons sugar
1 teaspoon salt
Dash pepper
1 bay leaf
1 medium-sized head red cabbage
1 tablespoon flour

Heat shortening or bacon drippings in a large, heavy saucepan. Add the onion and sauté 3 to 4 minutes. Toss in apple slices and cook several minutes longer. Stir in water, vinegar, sugar, salt, pepper, and bay leaf and bring to the boiling point. Remove from heat while you shred the cabbage, and stir it into the vinegar mixture. Cover tightly, and cook over a low heat for 40 to 45 minutes, stirring occasionally. Just before serving, add the flour, stirring constantly until mixture thickens slightly. Excellent with pork, goose, duck, suckling pig, or game. Serves 4.

JERUSALEM ARTICHOKES

The roots of Jerusalem artichokes were eaten in this country by the Indians before the arrival of Columbus. They were cultivated in Italy as *girasole* (meaning "a flower that turns toward the sun"), which became "Jerusalem" in English. They are entirely different from the globe, or French, artichoke, which is an edible thistle.

1½ pounds Jerusalem artichokes
⅓ cup melted butter
3 tablespoons fresh lemon juice

½ teaspoon salt
Few sprigs parsley, chopped

Peel artichokes and cook in boiling, salted water until tender. Test with a toothpick after 15 minutes—artichokes should not be overcooked. Drain thoroughly. Dress with a mixture of butter, lemon juice, salt, and chopped parsley. Serves 4 to 6.

GLAZED BABY CARROTS

2 bunches baby carrots
6 tablespoons butter

6 tablespoons sugar
½ teaspoon cinnamon or ginger

Wash carrots, scrape if necessary, and leave whole. Cook in a small amount of boiling, salted water about 12 to 15 minutes or until tender when tested with a fork. The time depends on size and degree of freshness. Drain thoroughly. Combine butter, sugar, and cinnamon or ginger in a large skillet. Cook, stirring constantly, until well blended. Add carrots and cook over a low heat, shaking the pan frequently to glaze carrots on all sides. When shiny and well glazed, serve to 6.

HARVARD BEETS

1 can (1 pound) baby beets
¼ cup sugar
½ teaspoon salt
½ tablespoon cornstarch

¼ cup cider vinegar
1½ tablespoons ginger marmalade
2 tablespoons butter

Drain beets thoroughly and set aside. Combine sugar, salt, and cornstarch in top of a double boiler. Pour in vinegar and cook over direct heat, stirring constantly, until smooth and bubbly. Add beets, ginger marmalade, and butter. Place over simmering water for about 30 minutes. Serves 4.

BAKED CELERY WITH SLIVERED ALMONDS

1 large bunch Pascal celery
4 tablespoons butter
2 tablespoons flour
1 cup milk

½ cup celery water
½ cup blanched, slivered almonds
2 tablespoons dry bread crumbs

Wash celery and cut into slices about ½ inch thick (save a generous handful of the celery tops). Place the celery in a saucepan, cover halfway with boiling, salted water, and lay the celery leaves on top. Cook for 10 to 15 minutes after water has reached the boiling point or until tender. Discard leaves and drain celery thoroughly, saving ½ cup of the celery water. While celery cooks, melt *2 tablespoons of the butter* in a saucepan, stir in flour until smooth, add milk. Cook over a low heat, stirring constantly, until smooth and bubbly. Stir in ½ cup celery water and taste to see if more salt is needed. Place a layer of the cooked celery in a shallow baking dish, spoon half the sauce over it, and sprinkle with half the almonds. Add the remaining celery, then the sauce. Sprinkle the top with bread crumbs, dot with the remaining butter, and sprinkle remaining almonds over all. Bake in a preheated 350° oven for 30 minutes. Serves 4.

MUSHROOMS IN CREAM

½ cup (1 stick) butter
¼ cup olive oil
1½ pounds fresh mushrooms
Salt

Pepper, freshly ground
1 teaspoon dried tarragon
¾ cup heavy cream
1 teaspoon fresh lemon juice

Heat butter and oil in a large heavy skillet over a low heat. Meanwhile, wash mushrooms, remove stems, and slice fairly thin. Add to butter-oil mixture and cook about 5 minutes, stirring frequently. Add butter if needed. Sprinkle in salt and a large amount of pepper (more than seems reasonable). The freshly ground pepper adds wonderful flavor. Stir in tarragon, crumbled fine. Continue cooking 5 minutes longer, giving mixture an occasional stir. Add the cream and simmer until sauce has thickened slightly—it should have body but should not be really thick. If sauce seems too thin, stir in a little cornstarch or arrowroot and cook until it reaches a good consistency. Just before serving, add the fresh lemon juice. Serve with steak or over crisp toast as a luncheon dish. Serves 4.

FRIED MUSHROOMS

1 pound fresh small button mushrooms	Cracker crumbs
1 beaten egg	Salt

Wash and dry fresh, firm mushrooms. Dip in beaten egg and cracker crumbs. Preheat fat to 375° on deep-fat thermometer or until a 1-inch cube of bread browns in 60 seconds. Fry mushrooms until brown, then drain on paper towels. Salt to taste. Serves 4 to 6.

SPINACH TIMBALES

4 eggs	Dash of nutmeg
1½ cups warm milk or ½ cup heavy cream and 1 cup chicken stock	1 teaspoon lemon juice
1 teaspoon salt	1 cup cooked spinach, well drained and chopped fine
Dash of pepper	

Beat together eggs, warm milk, salt, pepper, nutmeg, and lemon juice until frothy. Stir in spinach. Pour mixture into 6 to 8 buttered custard cups, depending on size of the cups. Set in a pan of hot water and bake in a preheated 325° oven for 20 to 30 minutes or until a knife tested in the center comes out dry. Unmold onto hot plates and serve plain or with Hollandaise Sauce (page 126).

SHAKER SPINACH WITH ROSEMARY

2 pounds spinach	1 green onion, chopped
¼ teaspoon fresh rosemary or large pinch of dried rosemary	2 tablespoons butter
3 sprigs parsley, chopped	Salt
	Pepper

Trim thick stems from spinach, wash the leaves several times in cold water. Chop coarsely and pile in a large saucepan with all remaining ingredients. Cook, covered, in its own juices about 5 minutes or until spinach is limp but still bright green. Serves 4.

SAUTÉED OR FRIED CUCUMBERS

Pare 2 medium-sized cucumbers, then cut in slices about ¼ inch thick. Pat with paper towels to remove all moisture.

To sauté: Sprinkle with salt and pepper and coat lightly with flour. Cook in ¼ cup melted butter until golden brown on both sides.

To fry: Dip each slice in fine dry bread crumbs, then in slightly beaten egg, then again in the crumbs. Fry several at a time in deep fat heated to 385° on deep-fat thermometer or until a 1-inch cube of bread browns in 60 seconds. When slices are golden brown, drain on paper towels and season with salt and pepper. Serve at once to 4.

CREOLE TOMATOES

3 large tomatoes
1 green pepper, chopped
1 small onion, chopped
4 tablespoons butter
Salt

Pepper
6 rounds of toast
1 tablespoon butter
1 tablespoon flour
½ cup light cream

Pour boiling water over tomatoes, let stand several minutes, then slip off the skins. Cut tomatoes in half crosswise and place in a flame-proof baking dish. Cover the tops generously with a mixture of green pepper and onion. Dot each tomato with butter and sprinkle with a little salt and pepper. Bake in a preheated 350° oven for 15 to 20 minutes or until tomatoes are very tender. Place each tomato on a round of buttered toast and keep warm. To make the sauce, add the tablespoon of butter to the pan drippings. When it has melted, add the flour and stir until smooth. Then add the cream. Cook, stirring constantly, until sauce thickens. Season to taste. Pour sauce over tomatoes and serve to 6.

A De Bry engraving of Indians transporting vegetables

SCALLOPED TOMATOES

6 ripe tomatoes or 1 can (1 pound,
  3 ounce size) solid-pack tomatoes
1 cup coarse dry bread crumbs
1 teaspoon sugar

Salt
Pepper
3 tablespoons butter

Skin the ripe tomatoes and cut in slices. Combine crumbs, sugar, salt, pepper, and butter. Place a layer of tomatoes in the bottom of a buttered casserole and sprinkle with some of the crumb mixture. Repeat with tomato layers and crumb mixture until dish is filled, then top with remaining crumb mixture. Bake in a preheated 350° oven for 30 minutes. Serves 4 to 6.

VARIATION: To make Scalloped Tomatoes, Southern Style, use the above ingredients, but increase the sugar to ¾ cup. Melt butter in a heavy skillet, add all remaining ingredients, and heat to a boil. Reduce heat and cook very, very slowly about 1 hour. Stir occasionally. When done, the tomatoes should be lightly glazed and most of the liquid absorbed. If they look too dry before they start to glaze, stir in a little more butter.

FRIED TOMATO SLICES

Choose firm, almost ripe tomatoes and cut in slices about ½ inch thick. Plan on 2 to 3 slices per person. Dip each slice of tomato into corn meal seasoned with salt and pepper, coating both sides. Fry some bacon until crisp (allow at least 2 slices per person). Drain on paper towels. Add tomato slices to bacon fat (a thin film of fat is sufficient) and fry several minutes on each side or until coating is crisp. To fry more than one panful of tomato slices, wipe out pan and add more fat before proceeding with second batch.

DELAWARE SUCCOTASH

Originally, succotash—or *misickquatash,* as the Narragansett Indians called it—was made of corn and kidney beans, and cooked in bear grease. One of the early settlers wrote of *misickquatash,* "In Winter [the Indians] esteeme their Corne being boyled with Beanes for a rare dish." Indeed, the Pilgrims probably thought it a rare dish themselves; it may have been one of the first recipes taught by friendly Indians to the settlers at Plymouth Rock, to be made from the sparse materials at hand.

2 thin slices salt pork
1 pint shelled (2 pounds unshelled)
   Lima beans or 1 package (2 cups)
   frozen, thawed Lima beans
8 ears corn or 1 package (2 cups)
   frozen, thawed corn

1 large ripe tomato, skinned and cubed
1 teaspoon salt
¼ teaspoon pepper
Dash of nutmeg

Lay slices of salt pork in bottom of a saucepan and cover with Lima beans. Add enough water to cover, and cook over a low heat until the beans are tender. Cut the kernels from fresh corn and combine with beans, cubed tomato, and seasonings. Cover and continue cooking over a low heat for 10 to 15 minutes. Stir frequently to prevent scorching. Serves 6.

SUCCOTASH

2 cups fresh Lima beans or
   2 packages frozen Lima beans
2 cups whole kernel corn (fresh, frozen,
   or canned)
2 tablespoons butter

1 teaspoon salt
Dash of pepper
1 teaspoon sugar
½ cup water
¼ cup heavy cream

Cook Lima beans in boiling, salted water until tender (if frozen Lima beans are used, cook according to package directions). Mix cooked beans with corn (if fresh, cut from the cob; if canned, drain; if frozen, use straight from the package), butter, salt, pepper, sugar, and water. Cook over a low heat for 10 to 15 minutes. Drain, then add cream. Heat through but do not boil. Serves 4 to 6.

CORN ON THE COB

"Some people take the whole stem," Fredrika Bremer wrote on her visit to America in 1850, "and gnaw [the kernels] out with their teeth: two gentlemen do so who sit opposite . . . myself at table, and whom we call 'the sharks,' because of their remarkable ability in gobbling up large and often double portions of everything which comes to table, and it really troubles me to see how their wide mouths . . . ravenously grind up the beautiful white, pearly maize ears."

Ideally, corn should be husked and cooked within a few minutes from the time it leaves the garden. Since this is not always possible, corn should be refrigerated until ready to use—but never longer than absolutely necessary. To test corn for ripeness, open the husks and pierce a kernel with your fingernail. If it is as young as it should be, it will be milky inside. Fill a large kettle with enough water to cover the corn and bring water to a rolling boil. *Do not add salt* (it tends to toughen the corn). Add instead 1 or 2 teaspoons of sugar. Husk the ears, remove the silk, and plunge into the boiling water. When water comes to a boil again, cook 3 to 5 minutes. Very young tender corn needs only about 3 minutes of boiling. The shorter the cooking time, the better the corn will be. Place corn in a dish lined with a linen napkin and fold it over the corn to hold in the heat. Serve with salt, pepper, and butter.

It is not elegant to gnaw *Indian corn. The kernels should be scored with a knife, scraped off into the plate, and then eaten with a fork. Ladies should be particularly careful how* they *manage so ticklish a dainty, lest the exhibition rub off a little desirable romance.*
—Charles Day, *Hints on Etiquette,* 1844

SHAKER DRIED CORN

Until well into the nineteenth century, drying was the principal means of preserving fruits and vegetables—and the Shakers made a specialty of dried corn. At one time the chief occupation of the Sisters of North Union, Ohio—a Shaker settlement that flourished between 1822 and 1889—was the drying of sweet corn.

1 cup dried corn	½ teaspoon salt
2 cups boiling water	2 tablespoons butter
2 teaspoons sugar	½ cup light or heavy cream

Place corn in a saucepan, pour in boiling water, and let stand at least 1 hour. At the end of this soaking period, stir in sugar, salt, and butter. Cook, uncovered, over a low heat for about 30 minutes. (To prevent scorching, make certain heat is low because the corn will absorb most of the liquid.) Stir in cream and cook 5 minutes longer. Serves 4.

CORN PUDDING

This recipe has been handed down in the family of General Daniel Morgan, a Revolutionary War hero.

2 cups fresh corn or
  1 package frozen corn
3 eggs
¼ cup flour

1 teaspoon salt
½ teaspoon white pepper
2 tablespoons butter, melted
2 cups light cream

Cut corn from the cob or thaw the frozen corn. Beat eggs vigorously, then stir in corn and a mixture of flour, salt, and white pepper. Add butter and cream. Pour into a buttered 1½-quart baking dish or casserole, place in a pan of hot water, and bake in a preheated 325° oven for 1 hour or until a knife tested in center comes out dry. Serves 6 to 8.

CORN CUSTARD WITH TOMATOES

1 cup grated fresh corn
4 eggs
1 small onion, grated
½ teaspoon salt
Dash cayenne
1½ cups milk

4 medium tomatoes
Flour
Salt
4 tablespoons butter
1 cup light cream

Grate corn from cobs into a bowl and measure correct amount. Beat eggs vigorously and stir in onion, salt, and cayenne. Heat milk until a film forms, skim, and stir into corn mixture. Pour into 6 buttered custard cups and place in a shallow pan containing about 1 inch of boiling water. Bake in a preheated 325° oven for 50 to 60 minutes or until a knife inserted in center of custard comes out clean. Shortly before custards are done, cut tomatoes in slices, dust both sides with flour, sprinkle with salt, and sauté in heated butter over a brisk heat. Fry several minutes on each side. Remove from skillet, stir in 1 or 2 teaspoons of flour, and pour in cream. Cook, stirring constantly, until sauce thickens just enough to make a smooth gravy. Taste and add salt if necessary. Remove custards from cups, place on a hot platter, surround with tomatoes, and spoon sauce over tomatoes. Serves 6.

CORN OYSTERS

2 cups grated fresh corn
2 eggs, separated
½ teaspoon salt

Dash pepper
¼ cup flour
¼ cup shortening

Grate corn from cobs into a bowl and measure correct amount. Stir in well-beaten egg yolks, salt, pepper, and flour. Beat egg whites until stiff but not dry. Fold them into corn mixture gently. Heat shortening in a skillet. Drop corn batter from a teaspoon into hot fat and brown quickly on both sides. Serve very hot with chops, a roast, or a cold fowl. Makes 12 to 14.

BRUNA BÖNER
(Swedish Beans)

1¼ cups dry brown beans or kidney beans
1½ quarts cold water
1 tablespoon salt
2 tablespoons cider vinegar

2 tablespoons molasses
1 tablespoon brown sugar
1 tablespoon butter
1 tablespoon cornstarch

Soak the beans overnight in cold water. The following day, cook in the same water, with salt added, for about two hours or until the beans are tender but still hold their shape. (During the cooking period there should always be enough water on the beans so that the water can be seen.) Stir in vinegar, molasses, brown sugar, and butter and continue cooking 10 minutes longer. Make a smooth paste of cornstarch and a little water and stir into the beans. Cook a few minutes longer until the liquid thickens slightly. Serves 6 to 8.

Advertisement for equipment for sorting beans

COWPOKE BEANS

1 pound dried pinto or red beans
Ham bone
1 red chili pepper (optional)
1 teaspoon salt
¼ pound suet, chopped
1 large onion, chopped
1 clove garlic, chopped

4 ripe tomatoes, chopped
½ cup chopped parsley
½ teaspoon ground cumin
½ teaspoon dried marjoram
1½ tablespoons chili powder
1 teaspoon salt

Cover beans with cold water and soak overnight. Next day add the ham bone, red chili pepper, and salt to the undrained beans. Bring to a boil, reduce heat, cover, and simmer gently for several hours or until beans are tender. Drain and save liquid. Toward the end of the cooking period, heat suet in a large skillet, stir in onion and garlic, and cook 5 minutes or until onions take on a little color. Add tomatoes, parsley, 1 cup of the bean liquid, and all remaining ingredients. Cook over a low heat, stirring frequently, for 45 minutes. Combine with beans and continue simmering gently for 20 minutes. Serves 6 to 8.

BOSTON BAKED BEANS

It is for baked beans that Boston is known as Bean Town. The Puritan Sabbath lasted from sundown on Saturday until sundown on Sunday, and baked beans provided the Puritans with a dish that was easy to prepare. The bean pot could be kept in the slow heat of a fireplace to serve at Saturday supper and Sunday breakfast. Housewives too busy with other chores were able to turn the baking of the beans over to a local baker. The baker called each Saturday morning to pick up the family's bean pot and take it to a community oven, usually in the cellar of a nearby tavern. The free-lance baker then returned the baked beans, with a bit of brown bread, on Saturday evening or Sunday morning.

6 cups pea or navy beans
1 pound salt pork
1 tablespoon dry mustard
1 tablespoon salt

1 teaspoon black pepper
1 cup molasses
1 small onion (optional)

Pick over beans, cover with cold water, and soak overnight. In the morning, drain, cover with fresh water, bring to a boil very slowly, then simmer until the skins burst, "which is best determined," wrote Fannie Farmer, "by taking a few beans on the tip of a spoon and blowing on them, when skins will burst if sufficiently cooked." Miss Farmer adds that beans tested this way "must, of course, be thrown away." Drain beans. Scald the salt pork, which should be well streaked with lean, by letting it stand in boiling water for 5 to 10 minutes. Cut off two thin slices, one to place in bottom of pot, the other to be cut into bits. Score rind of the remaining piece with a sharp knife. Mix dry mustard, salt, black pepper, and molasses. Alternate the layers of beans in the pot with the molasses mixture and the bits of pork. If you use an onion, bury it in the middle. When the bean pot is full, push the large piece of pork down into the beans with the rind sticking up. Add boiling water to cover, put the lid on, and bake all day (a minimum of 6 to 8 hours) in a 250° oven. Check from time to time and add boiling water if needed. Uncover pot during last hour of baking so the rind can brown and crisp. To this day many old-timers believe the rich brown goodness of Boston Baked Beans is largely due to the earthenware bean pot, with its narrow throat and big bulging sides. Lacking one of these pots, you can successfully use any deep earthenware casserole that has a cover. Serves 10 to 12.

FRIJOLES REFRITOS
(Refried Beans)

1 can (20 ounces) kidney or Mexican beans
3 tablespoons olive oil or bacon drippings
1 small onion, chopped fine
1 clove garlic, chopped fine

½ green pepper, chopped fine
1 teaspoon chili powder
3 tablespoons hot beef broth

Drain beans (reserve the liquid) and mash thoroughly. Heat oil or drippings in a skillet, add onion, garlic, green pepper, and cook over a low heat until tender. Stir in chili powder mixed with hot beef broth, then add the beans. Cook slowly, stirring continuously. Add bean liquid as needed. Beans are cooked properly when they are completely dry. Serves 6.

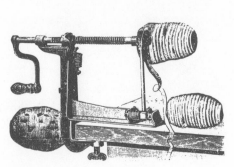

Above: a potato parer. Right: an implement used to make Saratoga Chips.

SARATOGA CHIPS

The invention of Saratoga Chips is usually attributed to George Crum, the chef of Moon's Lake House at New York's fashionable nineteenth-century spa, Saratoga Springs. One of the fussier patrons persisted in returning orders of French fried potatoes to the chef, insisting that they were not thin enough. In a rage, Crum disdainfully sliced some potatoes paper-thin, dropped them into boiling fat, and had his triumphant gibe served to the guest (who loved them).

To make Saratoga, or Potato, Chips: Pare potatoes and slice paper-thin with a vegetable slicer. Soak in cold water for 2 hours. Dry thoroughly and fry in deep fat until crisp and golden. Drain on paper towels and sprinkle with salt.

POTATO OLIVES

Pare 6 large potatoes and cut into balls with a melon-ball cutter. Drop the potatoes into boiling, salted water and cook until almost tender. Drain and cool. Melt ½ cup butter in a saucepan, add potato balls, and cook over a low heat until potatoes are golden on all sides. Shake the pan frequently to brown potatoes on all sides. Serve immediately with a sprinkling of chopped parsley on top. Serves 6.

POTATO PANCAKES

Combine in the blender 2 eggs, 1 slice onion, 1 teaspoon salt, a few sprigs of parsley, 1 cup diced raw potatoes. Turn blender on high, remove cover, and add ¼ cup flour and a second cup of diced potatoes. Do not overblend. Pour onto a hot greased griddle and cook until brown on both sides. This makes a soft pancake, more like a griddlecake. Makes 12.

POTATOES DUCHESSE

2 cups hot mashed potatoes
2 eggs, beaten
1 teaspoon baking powder

½ teaspoon salt
½ teaspoon nutmeg (optional)
Beaten egg or melted butter

Combine potatoes, eggs, baking powder, salt, and nutmeg, beating hard. Form into cakes or shape with a pastry tube and place on a buttered baking sheet. Brush with slightly beaten egg or melted butter. Brown under broiler flame or bake in a preheated 400° oven until golden. The potato mixture may also be dropped by spoonfuls into deep fat preheated to 385° to 395° on deep-fat thermometer or until a 1-inch cube of bread browns in 60 seconds. When well browned, drain on paper towels. May be prepared ahead and reheated in a preheated 425° oven for 8 to 10 minutes.

SCALLOPED POTATOES

Slice pared potatoes as thin as possible. Place a layer of potatoes in a casserole, dust with a little flour, season with salt, pepper, chopped onion (about 1 slice) and dot with butter. Repeat the layers of potatoes, with seasonings between, until the casserole is full. Then add enough milk to reach the top layer. Bake in a preheated 325° oven for 1½ hours. The number it will serve depends, of course, on the size of your casserole.

JANSON'S TEMPTATION

Eric Janson, the Swedish religious reformer who founded Bishop Hill, Illinois, in 1846, preached rigorous asceticism to his followers—no liquor and a diet that barely sustained life. One day, according to legend, a zealous Jansonist discovered the prophet feasting, secretively, on a casserole of anchovies and potatoes, bound together with golden butter and rich milk. The dish became known as Janson's Temptation.

Fine dry bread crumbs
6 medium potatoes
1 medium onion, chopped fine
2 small cans flat anchovy fillets, drained

¼ teaspoon pepper
5 tablespoons butter
2 cups milk

Butter a 2-quart casserole or baking dish and coat bottom and sides with crumbs. Pare potatoes and cut into paper-thin slices. Combine onion, anchovies (cut into pieces), pepper, and butter. Place a layer of potatoes in bottom of dish and sprinkle half the onion mixture over it. Add another layer of potatoes and the rest of the seasonings. Top with remaining potatoes and pour in the milk. Sprinkle top with ⅓ cup of crumbs and dot with butter. Bake in a preheated 350° oven for about 1 hour. Potatoes should be tender when tested with a fork and milk should be largely absorbed. Do not add salt because anchovies contribute all the salt necessary. Makes 6 servings.

CANDIED SWEET POTATOES

Sweet potatoes (the dark orange variety are often called yams) have been grown in this country since at least the early seventeenth century and are associated with southern cooking. Robert Beverley described the sweet potatoes of Virginia in 1705 as "about as long as a Boy's leg, and sometimes as long and big as both the Leg and Thigh of a young Child, and very much resembling it in Shape."

6 sweet potatoes
½ teaspoon salt
1 cup dark brown sugar

½ cup water
4 tablespoons butter
1 tablespoon lemon juice

Cook the sweet potatoes in their jackets in boiling, salted water until nearly tender. Drain, peel, and cut in slices about ½ inch thick. Place in a greased, shallow baking dish and sprinkle with salt. Cook together brown sugar, water, and butter in a separate pan for several minutes. Then stir in lemon juice and pour over potatoes. Bake in a preheated 375° oven for 20 to 25 minutes, basting occasionally with the syrup. Serves 4 to 6.

YAMS WITH APPLES

Bake 4 large yams until tender. Meanwhile, pare 4 tart cooking apples, core, and cut into thin slices. Peel yams, cut into slices about ½ inch thick, and arrange alternate layers of yams and apples in a buttered baking dish. Sprinkle each layer with sugar and a dash of nutmeg. Dot with butter. Cover and bake in a preheated 350° oven for 30 to 35 minutes. The tartness of the apples cuts the sweet flavor of the yams. Serve as an accompaniment for roast duck, game, or ham. Makes 4 to 6 servings.

MACARONI AND CHEESE PUDDING

On February 6, 1802, after dinner with President Jefferson at the White House, Mr. Manasseh Cutler wrote that there was "a pie called macaroni, which appeared to be a rich crust filled with the strillions of onions, or shallots, which I took them to be, tasted very strong, and not agreeable. Mr. Lewis told me there were none in it; it was made of flour and butter, with a particularly strong liquor mixed with them."

2½ cups elbow macaroni
¼ cup butter
¼ cup flour
2¼ cups milk

1 teaspoon salt
Dash pepper
2 cups grated Cheddar cheese

Cook macaroni according to package directions until tender, then drain thoroughly. While macaroni cooks, melt butter in a saucepan, stir in flour until smooth, and cook a minute or two. Add the milk a little at a time, and cook, stirring constantly, until sauce bubbles. Add salt and pepper. Arrange alternate layers of macaroni and cheese in a medium-sized baking dish or casserole, reserving some of the cheese (about ¼ cup) to sprinkle over top. Pour hot sauce over all, sprinkle with the cheese, and dot with bits of butter. Bake 35 minutes in a preheated 400° oven. Serves 4 to 6.

NOODLES JEFFERSON

Cook 2 cups (1 package) noodles according to package directions. Drain well. Add 1 cup (2 sticks) soft or melted sweet butter and 2 cups freshly grated Parmesan cheese. Toss gently until well mixed. Season with freshly ground pepper to taste. Serves 4.

Advertisement, Collection of F. Hal Higgins

HOMINY PUDDING

Hominy was adopted from the Indians and became an important basic food for American pioneers. It is, simply, hulled corn—the pioneers removed the hulls by soaking the grains of corn in a weak wood lye. Washed and boiled until it was tender, hominy was often served in place of potatoes. It was ground, too, into grits—fragments slightly coarser than corn meal—which have become closely identified with the South. Grits are traditionally eaten for breakfast with butter and milk, or made into breads and puddings. G. W. Featherstonhaugh, an Englishman traveling in the South in 1837, wrote: "Our breakfast was admirable, excellent coffee with delicious cream, and that capital, national dish of South Carolina, snow-white homminy brought hot to table like maccaroni, which ought always to be eaten, with lumps of sweet fresh butter buried in it! this is certainly one of the best things imaginable to begin the day liberally with."

1 cup hominy grits
5 cups boiling water
2 eggs, separated

½ cup light cream
1 teaspoon salt
¼ teaspoon white pepper

Stir grits into boiling water. Cover and cook over a low heat for 25 to 30 minutes. Set aside to cool. Then measure exactly 2 cups of the cooled grits into a bowl and beat until smooth. Beat yolks soundly and stir into grits. Add cream, salt, and pepper. Beat egg whites until they stand in peaks and fold into grit mixture, lightly but thoroughly. Spoon into a well-buttered 1-quart casserole and bake in a preheated 350° oven for 40 minutes or until surface is golden. Serve immediately to 4.

CORN MEAL

FRIED CORN MEAL MUSH

"...how I blush/To hear the Pennsylvanians call thee *Mush*," Joel Barlow wrote in his poem "The Hasty Pudding." The Fried Corn Meal Mush recipe here is, indeed, simply a fried Hasty Pudding. "Nasaump," as Roger Williams described it in 1643 in *A Key into the Language of America...*, is "a kind of meale pottage, unpartch'd. From this," Williams said, "the *English* call their *Samp*, which is the *Indian* corne, beaten and boil'd, and eaten hot or cold with milke or butter ... and which is a dish exceeding wholesome for the *English* bodies."

5 cups boiling water
1½ cups yellow corn meal
1 teaspoon salt
1 egg yolk

2 tablespoons milk
Bread or cracker crumbs
Butter or bacon fat

Boil water in the top of a double boiler. Then combine corn meal with salt and 1½ cups cold water. Stir into boiling water a little at a time, stirring constantly. Cook over high heat about 3 minutes. Cover and cook over boiling water for 15 minutes. Pour into a greased loaf pan and cool. Cut the firm mush into slices about ¾ inch thick. Beat egg yolk with milk, dip slices in mixture, then coat with fine dry bread or cracker crumbs. Fry in heated butter or bacon fat until crisp and golden. Serve hot with warm maple syrup.

Fath'r and I went down to camp
Along with Captain Goodin,
And there we saw the men and boys
As thick as hasty puddin'.

—Verse from *Yankee Doodle*

CORN MEAL DUMPLINGS

1 cup corn meal
¼ cup all-purpose flour
1 teaspoon baking powder
½ teaspoon salt

2 eggs
½ cup milk
1 tablespoon melted butter

Sift together corn meal, flour, baking powder, and salt. Beat eggs and milk together, then stir into dry ingredients. Add the melted butter. Drop batter from a spoon into a pot of boiled greens or heated stock. Cover tightly and cook over a low heat for 15 minutes.

CHEESE AND CORN MEAL LOAF

1 cup corn meal
1 cup milk
2 cups boiling water
1 teaspoon salt

½ pound Cheddar cheese, cubed
Flour
½ cup shortening

Combine corn meal and milk in a saucepan. Add boiling water and cook over a moderate heat, stirring constantly, until thick. Reduce heat, cover, and cook over a low heat for 10 minutes. Stir occasionally. Remove from heat. Add salt and cheese, stirring until cheese melts. Spoon into a loaf pan and cool. When cold and solid, turn out of pan and cut into slices about ¾ inch thick. Dust slices lightly with flour and fry in heated shortening until crisp and golden on both sides. Serve for breakfast or lunch with fried ham, sausages, or crisp bacon. Serves 4 to 6.

HUSH PUPPIES

According to one old southern legend, the hounds that went along on hunting expeditions were a hungry lot and would start yelping as soon as they caught the smell of fish frying for their masters' dinner. To quiet the hounds, the hunters dropped bits of corn-meal batter into the fish pan and then tossed the tidbits to the dogs with the gentle rebuke, "Hush, puppy!"

1½ cups corn meal
½ cup all-purpose flour
2 teaspoons baking powder
½ teaspoon salt

1 egg, well beaten
¾ cup milk
1 small onion, grated
Fat for deep-fat frying

Sift together corn meal, flour, baking powder, and salt. Mix egg, milk, and onion in a bowl. Combine with dry ingredients and drop from a spoon into hot fat. When Hush Puppies are crisp and golden (about 1 minute), lift from fat with slotted spoon and drain on paper towels. Serve hot. In the South, Hush Puppies are usually served with fried fish. Made bite-sized, they are delicious served with drinks. Makes about 20.

POLENTA

This recipe is adapted from Mary Randolph's *Virginia Housewife.*

1 cup corn meal
1 teaspoon salt
½ cup grated Parmesan cheese

3 tablespoons butter
Paprika

Bring 3 cups of water to a rolling boil. Combine corn meal with 1 cup cold water and salt. Stir into boiling water and cook, stirring frequently, for about 10 minutes. Pour into a loaf pan and refrigerate until firm. Shortly before serving, cut the Polenta into slices about ½ inch thick and place in a shallow baking dish. Sprinkle with Parmesan cheese, dot with butter, and shake paprika over all. Broil about 4 inches from tip of preheated broiling unit until brown—about 4 to 5 minutes. Serves 6.

RICE DISHES

CREOLE JAMBALAYA

Jambalaya (derived from the Spanish word *jamon*, meaning ham) was introduced to New Orleans by the Spanish in the late 1700's. It was made, at first, only with ham; when the Creole cooks took the recipe into their repertoire, they added shrimp from the Gulf waters. Creole Jambalaya, considered one of the classic Creole dishes, can be made with crab, shrimp, chicken, ham, and a variety of other ingredients—one at a time, or all together.

1 tablespoon shortening
1 pound smoked pork sausage or ham,
    cut into ½-inch cubes
½ cup chopped green pepper
1 tablespoon flour
3 cups cooked shrimp, cleaned
3 cups skinned tomatoes, diced
2½ cups water

1 large onion, sliced
1 clove garlic, minced
2 tablespoons parsley, chopped
2 cups uncooked long-grain rice
2 tablespoons Worcestershire sauce
1¼ teaspoons salt
½ teaspoon dried thyme
¼ teaspoon red pepper

Melt shortening in a large skillet, add sausage or ham and green pepper. Cook, stirring frequently, for 5 minutes. Stir in flour until smooth and cook a minute or two longer. Add shrimp, tomatoes, water, onion, garlic, and parsley. Cook to the boiling point, then stir in rice and all remaining ingredients. Cover and cook over a low heat for 30 minutes or until rice is tender and all the liquid is absorbed. Sprinkle with chopped parsley. Serves 8.

WILD RICE AND CHICKEN LIVER PILAU

Technically, wild rice is not a true rice but the seed of a tall aquatic grass native to both North America and eastern Asia. It was such an important food for the Indians that the Sioux and Chippewa fought many battles for better stands.

1 cup uncooked wild rice
½ cup (1 stick) butter
1 medium onion, chopped fine
1 green pepper, chopped fine

16 chicken livers, cut in half
1 teaspoon salt
¼ teaspoon pepper
3 tablespoons brandy

Cook rice in boiling, salted water until tender but still firm. Do not overcook. Drain. Heat *half the butter* in a skillet, add onions and green pepper, and sauté for 5 minutes or until limp. Push vegetables aside and sauté *half the chicken livers* until nicely browned on all sides. Combine vegetable-liver mixture with rice and season with salt and pepper. Set aside, keeping it warm. Heat remaining butter in a saucepan and add remaining chicken livers. Sauté until cooked through. Heat brandy and ignite with a match. Pour over chicken livers, spooning the brandy over them until flame dies. Serve separately with the wild rice mixture. Serves 4.

SOUTH CAROLINA DRY RICE

"The finest rice in the world," Dr. Sturtevant said in his *Notes on Edible Plants*, "is that raised in North and South Carolina." Carolina rice is said to have been first introduced to Charleston in 1694, brought there by a Dutch brig out of Madagascar.

1 cup long-grain rice
1½ cups water
Salt

Juice of ¼ lemon
2 tablespoons butter

Combine all ingredients in a heavy saucepan and heat to a boil. Stir once (no more) with a long-pronged fork. Turn heat down low and cook until all the water has disappeared and rice is dry and flaky—takes about 20 minutes. Serves 4.

HOPPING JOHN

It is said in the South that without a dish of Hopping John on New Year's Day, a year of bad luck will follow. The name may have derived from a custom that children must hop once around the table before the dish is served or may have been the sobriquet of a lively waiter.

½ pound bacon, in one piece
2 cups black-eyed peas, fresh, frozen,
   or dried

1 teaspoon salt
1 cup long-grain rice

If you use dried peas, soak them overnight in cold water. Cook the bacon in 2 quarts water about 1 hour. Then add black-eyed peas and salt. Continue cooking for 30 minutes or until peas are almost tender. Add rice and boil about 15 to 18 minutes longer. Lift out bacon, slice, and set aside, keeping it warm. Drain peas and rice thoroughly, then place in a warm oven for a few minutes or until rice is fluffy. Serve with sliced bacon on top. Serves 6.

RED RICE

4 slices bacon
2 onions, chopped fine
1 can (6-ounce size) tomato paste
1½ cups water
1 tablespoon salt

¼ teaspoon pepper
1 tablespoon sugar
2 cups uncooked rice
½ cup bacon drippings

Fry the bacon in a saucepan until almost crisp. Lift from pan and set aside. Drain off all but 2 tablespoons of the drippings and reserve. Stir onions into the saucepan and cook until wilted, then add tomato paste, water, salt, pepper, and sugar. Cook over a low heat about 10 minutes. There should be 2 cups of sauce. Put rice in a large saucepan or the top of a steamer. Add sauce and ½ cup bacon drippings (if you do not have enough drippings, make up the necessary amount with butter). Cover and steam or cook over a very low heat for 30 minutes. Fork in the crumbled bacon and continue cooking 30 to 45 minutes or until rice is tender and all liquid absorbed. Serves 6 to 8.

GUMBO Z'HERBES

Gumbo z'herbes can be made with almost any greens, seasonings, and herbs. It originated in the Congo and was introduced to New Orleans by Negroes; it was then modified with herbs sold there in the French market by Cherokee and Choctaw Indians.

1 pound salt pork
4 to 5 bunches fresh young greens selected
  from the following: mustard, radish
  tops, spinach, lettuce, beet tops,
  collards, watercress, carrot tops,
  turnip tops, broccoli, endive
1 head cabbage, kale, or kohlrabi, or 1 box
  Brussels sprouts
Selection of herbs to taste: dill, tarragon,
  chives, thyme, parsley, sorrel, dandelion,
  fennel, leeks, celeriac, sage

1 heaping tablespoon lard
2 tablespoons flour
2 large onions, chopped
4 cloves garlic, chopped fine
2 tablespoons vinegar
1 pod red pepper
Salt
Pepper

Cover salt pork with water and cook until tender. Drain, then chop into small cubes. While meat cooks, trim and wash greens and break cabbage into pieces. Place all greens in a large kettle, add enough water to cover, and cook until very tender. Drain thoroughly, saving water in which greens cooked. Add herbs to greens and chop very fine or blend in an electric blender. Set aside. Heat lard in a deep kettle, stir in flour until smooth, and cook, stirring constantly, until *roux* begins to take on color. Add onions and garlic and cook several minutes. Stir in cubed salt pork and the chopped greens. Cook 5 minutes, stirring constantly. Pour in 1½ quarts of liquid in which greens cooked and simmer until mixture becomes a thick purée. Stir in vinegar and red pepper pod, broken into pieces. Add salt and pepper to taste. Serve hot with rice. Serves 6.

PILAU WITH PIGNON NUTS

Pilau (rice blended with shrimp, chicken, or other ingredients) is of Oriental origin. The dish seems to have been brought to America by early traders. Charleston, a great seaport before the Revolutionary War, may have been the first landing spot for pilau brought from India. Pilau is still associated with the Carolinas.

1 cup long-grain rice
¼ cup pistachio nuts
½ cup pignon nuts or toasted slivered
  almonds

3 tablespoons butter
2 teaspoons powdered mace

Cook rice. Meanwhile, remove shells and inner skin from pistachios. Leave the nuts whole. Melt butter in a heavy saucepan, toss in both kinds of nuts, and cook several minutes, stirring frequently. Add rice and mace and stir with a fork until heated through. Makes about 6 servings.

CHICKEN GUMBO FILÉ

Filé—dried and powdered sassafras leaves—seems to have been made first by Louisiana's Choctaw Indians. It was included in a great number of Creole recipes for thickening stews and soups. As used in these dishes, filé imparted a distinct flavor which, as Dr. Sturtevant stated in *Notes on Edible Plants*, is "much relished by those accustomed to it."

A 3- to 4-pound chicken
1 tablespoon lard
½ pound lean ham, diced
2 tablespoons chopped parsley
1 bay leaf, crumbled
1 sprig (½ teaspoon dried) thyme

1½ dozen oysters in liquor
Salt
¼ pod red pepper
2 tablespoons filé powder
Boiled rice

Cook chicken in boiling water until tender. Remove from saucepan (save the broth), cool, strip meat from bones, and cut into serving pieces. Set aside. Heat lard in a soup kettle, add ham, and cook for 5 minutes, stirring frequently. Stir in parsley, bay leaf, and thyme and cook several minutes longer or until browned. Measure liquor from oysters, add enough chicken broth and boiling water to make 1½ quarts of liquid, and pour into soup kettle. Season with salt and red pepper pod. Simmer for 30 minutes, then add the oysters, and simmer a few minutes until edges begin to curl. Add the chicken. Remove from heat and stir in filé, a little at a time (if filé is cooked, even simmered, it makes the gumbo stringy). Serve immediately in soup plates over boiled rice. Serves 4.

SEAFOOD-OKRA GUMBO

"Shrimps are much eaten here," a visitor to New Orleans in 1805 said, "also a dish called *gumbo*. This last is made of every eatable substance, and especially of those shrimps which can be caught at any time."

1 pound uncooked shrimp in shell
¼ cup butter
1 pound okra, sliced
2 onions, chopped fine
1½ tablespoons flour
1 cup tomatoes
12 oysters in liquor

2 teaspoons salt
1 clove garlic, crushed
Pinch of cayenne or ¼ pod red pepper
Tabasco
Worcestershire sauce
½ pound crab meat
Boiled rice

Shell shrimp and sauté in *2 tablespoons of the butter* for several minutes or until they turn a bright coral color. Set aside. Heat remaining 2 tablespoons butter in a soup kettle, add okra, and cook, stirring frequently, until tender. Stir in onion and cook several minutes, then stir in flour until smooth. Add tomatoes and cook the mixture several minutes longer. Add enough water to the oyster liquor to make 2 quarts of liquid. Stir into okra mixture and add salt, garlic, and cayenne or red pepper pod. Simmer for 1 hour, then add shrimp, and simmer another half hour. Fifteen minutes before serving, add the oysters and cook over a low heat until edges begin to curl. Then add Tabasco, Worcestershire sauce, and crab meat and heat through. Serve gumbo in soup plates over boiled rice. Serves 6 to 8.

Egg carrier

OMELETTE

2 eggs
1 tablespoon water
½ teaspoon salt

Dash of pepper
2 tablespoons butter

Beat together eggs, water, salt, and pepper. Melt butter in an omelette pan or skillet until very hot but not brown or smoking. Pour in egg mixture and cook over a medium heat, lifting the edges with a spatula to allow the liquid to run underneath. When omelette is golden brown on the bottom but still creamy on top, fold one half over the other and slide onto a warm platter. May be served with Mushrooms in Cream (page 104) or Creole Sauce (page 129). Spoon sauce around the omelette and garnish with watercress.

HANGTOWN FRY

According to some Californians, Hangtown Fry was created in 1849. A miner from Shirttail Bend hailed into Hangtown with a poke full of nuggets, plunked his fortune down on the counter of Cary House, and said he wanted the finest, most expensive meal they had. When he was told that oysters and eggs were the most expensive items on the menu (in those days whiskey was $1,500 a barrel, turnips a dollar each), he told the cook to put them together and serve up the food. The dish was made, originally, with the small Pacific Coast Olympia oysters.

1 dozen oysters
Flour
9 eggs

Fine cracker crumbs
3 tablespoons butter

Drain oysters on paper towels. Dip each one in flour seasoned with salt and pepper, then in *1 well-beaten egg*, last of all in cracker crumbs. Fry in heated butter for a few minutes or until nicely browned on both sides. Beat remaining 8 eggs with salt and pepper. Pour over oysters and cook until firm on the bottom. Turn with a large spatula and cook the second side a minute or two longer. Serves 4.

WILD ONIONS AND EGGS

4 bunches wild onions or green onions
2 to 3 tablespoons bacon fat

6 eggs
1 teaspoon salt

Wash the onions and chop fine (chop both the bulb and green tops). Cook in heated bacon fat, with 1 tablespoon of water added, until onions are tender. Season eggs with salt and beat until yolks and whites are well blended. Pour over onions and scramble. Serves 4.

122

SISTER ABIGAIL'S BLUE FLOWER OMELETTE

It is not unusual to use flowers—nasturtiums, squash and pumpkin blossoms, rose petals—in cooking. The use of chive blossoms, however, seems peculiarly a Shaker innovation, or perhaps Sister Abigail's.

Break 4 eggs into a bowl. Add 4 tablespoons of water or milk, ½ teaspoon salt, dash of pepper, 1 tablespoon finely chopped parsley, 1 tablespoon chopped chives, and 12 chive blossoms (these can be eliminated if chives are not in blossom). Beat until well blended. Heat 2 tablespoons butter in an omelette pan or skillet. When butter is bubbly but not brown, pour in omelette mixture. Stir with a fork until eggs begin to set, then cook a little longer, without stirring. Loosen sides of omelette with a fork and roll out onto a heated platter. Serve at once to 2.

KENTUCKY SCRAMBLE

1 cup cooked whole-kernel corn (fresh, canned, or frozen)
3 tablespoons butter or bacon drippings
1 green pepper, chopped
Few sprigs of parsley, chopped
2 slices pimiento, chopped
6 eggs
1 teaspoon salt
¼ teaspoon pepper

Drain corn and sauté in heated butter or bacon drippings for several minutes. Stir in green pepper, parsley, and pimiento and continue cooking about 5 minutes longer. Just before serving, beat together the eggs, salt, and pepper, then pour into corn mixture, and scramble until eggs are set but still moist. Serves 4.

WESTERN SANDWICH

The sandwich is generally thought to be an American food, but its inventor was John Montagu, Fourth Earl of Sandwich. Montagu was a renowned British politician, and an even more renowned gambler. His fondness for gambling was so extreme that he neglected lunch, and usually bolted a piece of meat between slices of bread to sustain himself at the poker table. The Western Sandwich was invented by pioneers. It was common for eggs to get "high" after a long haul over hot trails. In order to salvage the eggs, and kill the bad flavor of them, pioneer women mixed eggs with onions and any other seasonings on hand.

¼ pound ham or 4 slices bacon, diced
1 green pepper, chopped
1 medium onion, chopped
4 eggs
Salt
Pepper
Bread or round buns

Fry ham or bacon in a skillet for several minutes. Toss in green pepper and onion and cook until vegetables are almost tender. Beat eggs in a bowl with salt and pepper. Pour over mixture in skillet and cook until eggs are set. Turn with a broad spatula and brown second side lightly. Place between slices of buttered bread or buns. Makes 4 sandwiches.

DEVILED EGGS WITH ANCHOVIES

6 hard-cooked eggs
1 teaspoon prepared mustard
Few sprigs parsley, chopped
½ teaspoon salt
1 tablespoon lemon juice

1 tablespoon salad oil
1 tablespoon capers, drained well
6 rolled anchovy fillets
Watercress

Cut eggs in half lengthwise. Remove yolks and mash until smooth. Stir in mustard, parsley, salt, lemon juice, oil, and capers thoroughly. Pile mixture back into egg whites. Garnish with anchovies and serve on a bed of watercress.

Cheese press

CHEESE BLINTZES

½ cup all-purpose flour
¼ teaspoon salt
2 eggs

½ cup milk
1 cup water
Butter

Sift flour and salt together. Beat eggs in a bowl until frothy, then blend in flour mixture. Add milk, a little at a time, stirring until smooth. Mix in water last of all. Batter should be very thin. Heat a small skillet (6 to 7 inches in diameter), adding just enough butter to coat the bottom. When butter starts to sizzle, pour in a little of the batter (enough to coat bottom of the pan when you tilt it back and forth). Cook blintzes until edges look slightly dry and lacy (these little crêpes are cooked only on one side). Invert skillet over a tea towel and hit side of pan to loosen the crêpe. Do not stack them on top of each other while they are warm.

Cheese Filling:
½ pound farmer cheese
¼ pound small-curd cottage cheese
¼ pound cream cheese
2 egg yolks, slightly beaten

¼ cup sugar
¼ teaspoon salt
½ teaspoon cinnamon
1 tablespoon grated lemon rind

Blend the cheeses together until smooth. Beat in egg yolks and all remaining ingredients. Divide filling evenly among the crêpes, placing it in the center on the cooked side. Fold edges over the filling to make a neat, square package. Melt 2 tablespoons butter in a large skillet. Arrange blintzes in the pan and fry over a moderate heat until golden brown on both sides. Serve very hot with cold sour cream.

WELSH RABBIT

Welsh Rabbit was reputedly improvised when a Welsh chieftain ran out of game for his banquet table and asked his cook to devise something from whatever stores were on hand. The cook produced this cheese dish, which he named—presumably not to call the guests' attention to the fact that the meat supply had vanished—"rabbit." It persisted as Welsh Rabbit in most American kitchens (though some befuddled cookbook writers have "corrected" matters by referring to the dish as "rarebit"). This recipe is adapted from one given in Sarah Josepha Hale's *New Cook Book*.

1 pound sharp natural Cheddar cheese
2 teaspoons Worcestershire sauce
½ teaspoon dry mustard

Dash of cayenne
Dash of paprika
½ cup ale or beer

Shred the cheese and set aside. Mix all remaining ingredients in a saucepan and place over a very low heat until ale or beer is hot. Add the cheese and stir until it has melted. Pour over hot toast triangles. Serves 4 to 6.

CAILLETTE

Large head green cabbage
1 cup milk
3 cups dry bread crumbs
2 eggs, lightly beaten
1 cup grated Cheddar or Swiss cheese

Salt
Pepper
Dash of nutmeg
Chicken or beef broth

Remove 12 to 14 large outer leaves from cabbage and cut off some of the thick rib. Cover with boiling water to soften. Heat milk and pour over crumbs. Mix in eggs, cheese, salt, pepper, and nutmeg thoroughly. Put a heaping tablespoon of the mixture on each drained cabbage leaf, folding in sides and ends to make a neat package. Fasten with toothpicks or tie with string and drop into gently boiling broth. Cook for 30 minutes or until cabbage is tender. Lift from broth and serve immediately. Serves 4 to 6.

LIEDERKRANZ CANAPÉS

Liederkranz, one of the few native American cheeses, was discovered by accident in 1892 by Emil Frey, a young Swiss who was working as an apprentice cheese maker in a factory in Monroe, New York. Frey's boss took a sample of the new cheese to some of his friends at the Liederkranz Club in New York. Their response was enthusiastic, and the cheese was immediately named Liederkranz.

Combine 1 cake of Liederkranz cheese with 2 tablespoons softened butter and several drops of Tabasco and mash until very smooth. Mix in a sprinkling of chopped chives, about 2 green onions (chopped very fine), and freshly ground pepper. Spread on thin slices of rye or pumpernickel bread and cut into small squares or triangles.

SAUCES

CREAM SAUCE

1 cup milk
1 slice onion
1 sprig parsley
2 tablespoons butter
2 tablespoons flour

2 tablespoons heavy cream
Salt
White pepper
Nutmeg

Scald a mixture of the milk, onion, and parsley. Melt butter in a saucepan, stir in flour until smooth, and cook over a low heat for several minutes. Do not brown. Strain hot milk into butter-flour combination and continue cooking over a low heat, stirring constantly, until sauce bubbles. Then simmer gently for several minutes. Stir in cream and season to taste with salt, pepper, and nutmeg. Makes 1 generous cup.

BÉCHAMEL SAUCE
(White Sauce)

2 tablespoons butter
2 tablespoons flour
1 cup milk

Salt
White pepper
Nutmeg (optional)

Melt butter in a saucepan. Stir in flour until smooth and cook over a low heat for several minutes. Do not brown. Stir milk into mixture and continue cooking over a low heat, stirring constantly, until sauce bubbles. Cook very gently for several minutes until sauce has thickened. Season with salt, pepper, and, if you wish, a pinch of nutmeg. Makes 1 cup.

HOLLANDAISE SAUCE

½ cup (1 stick) butter
1 tablespoon lemon juice
2 egg yolks

½ teaspoon salt
Dash of cayenne

Divide the butter into three equal parts. Place one portion in top of double boiler, add lemon juice and egg yolks. Cook over hot water, stirring constantly with a wire whisk. When butter has melted, add second portion, and, as mixture begins to thicken, add the third. Remove from heat and stir in salt and cayenne. *Do not let the water under the saucepan boil at any time.* Serve at once or keep sauce warm over hot water. Makes about ¾ cup.

VIRGINIA BOILED DRESSING

4 egg yolks
2 tablespoons cold water
2 tablespoons cider vinegar
1 teaspoon dry mustard

1 teaspoon sugar
1 teaspoon salt
1 cup commercial sour cream

Mix together egg yolks, cold water, vinegar, mustard, sugar, and salt in the top of a double boiler. Cook over boiling water, stirring constantly, until thick. Cool, then fold in sour cream. Makes about 1½ cups.

DILL AND MUSTARD SAUCE

2½ tablespoons dry mustard
5 tablespoons sugar
½ teaspoon salt
2 tablespoons olive oil

1 tablespoon vinegar
½ cup commercial sour cream
2 tablespoons chopped fresh dill or
   1 tablespoon dill weed

Blend together mustard, sugar, and salt. Add the oil and vinegar alternately. Stir slowly until blended, then beat hard. Fold in sour cream and dill. Serve with cold fish and shellfish. Makes about 1 cup.

LEMON BUTTER

To make Lemon Butter, melt butter (about 2 to 3 tablespoons per person) and add fresh lemon juice to taste. Especially good with fish.

TARTARE SAUCE

1 cup mayonnaise
1 teaspoon fresh tarragon, chopped fine, or
   ⅓ teaspoon dried tarragon
1 tablespoon onion, chopped fine

1 tablespoon parsley, chopped fine
1 tablespoon capers, drained
1½ tablespoons sour pickle, chopped fine

Combine all the ingredients thoroughly and let stand an hour or two to develop flavor. Makes about 1¼ cups.

OYSTER SAUCE

Season 1 cup of Cream Sauce (page 126) with 1 teaspoon Worcestershire sauce. Before serving, heat to a boil, then stir in 3 tablespoons chopped parsley and 1 cup finely chopped or ground oysters with their liquor. Serve with roast turkey or chicken or as a sauce for poached fish.

MUSHROOM SAUCE

¼ pound mushrooms
2 tablespoons butter
½ teaspoon salt
¼ teaspoon white pepper

2 tablespoons flour
2 cups cream
1 tablespoon dry sherry

Cut mushrooms in half or slice (depending on the size) and sauté in heated butter for about 5 minutes. Sprinkle in salt, pepper, and flour, then stir until smooth. Add cream and cook, stirring constantly, until sauce bubbles and thickens. Continue simmering for another 5 to 8 minutes. Just before serving, stir in sherry. Add salt to taste.

CUMBERLAND SAUCE

2 oranges
2 lemons
½ cup red currant jelly

1 cup port wine
1 tablespoon arrowroot
1 tablespoon Grand Marnier (optional)

Peel the rind of *1 orange and 1 lemon* with a vegetable peeler, then shred, and set aside. Squeeze the juice from both oranges and lemons and strain. Combine with the jelly in a saucepan, bring slowly to a boil, and simmer about 3 minutes. Add the port. Mix arrowroot with 1 tablespoon water until smooth and stir into the boiling liquid. Cook for a few minutes until sauce has thickened slightly. Add the rind and, if you like, the Grand Marnier. This sauce improves if made a day ahead and then reheated. Serve with ham, duck, or game.

MINT SAUCE

Strip leaves from enough fresh mint to make about ½ cup when packed tightly. Chop fine and place in a small, sturdy jar or in a mortar and pestle if you have one. Add 2 tablespoons sugar and ¼ teaspoon salt. Pound with the handle of a wooden spoon until leaves are bruised thoroughly. Stir in ⅓ cup cider vinegar and the same amount of water. Prepared in this way, Mint Sauce keeps its fresh flavor for a long time when refrigerated in a sealed jar. Good with any cold meat except beef but especially good with lamb, hot or cold.

CURRANT SAUCE

Combine 1 cup currant jelly or whole currant preserves with 1 cup port wine in the top of a double boiler. Heat over boiling water until ingredients are thoroughly blended. Serve hot.

SAUCE PIQUANTE

Heat 1 can (7½-ounce size) brown gravy and blend with 1 tablespoon each of lemon juice, finely chopped onion, chopped green pepper, drained capers or chopped sour pickles, and a dash of cayenne.

PLUM SAUCE

Wash 1 pound Damson plums, cut in half, and remove pits. Combine fruit with ½ cup sugar in a saucepan. Add 1 stick cinnamon, 1 teaspoon whole mace, and 1 teaspoon whole cloves tied together with cheesecloth. Bring to a boil, reduce heat, and simmer gently until sauce has the consistency of jam. Remove spices and chill sauce. Makes 1 cup.

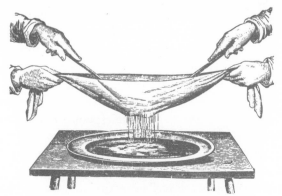

Straining sauce

CREOLE SAUCE

4 cups canned or fresh tomatoes, skinned
2 tablespoons butter
1 clove garlic, chopped fine
¼ teaspoon dried thyme
1 bay leaf, crumbled

1 teaspoon salt
Dash pepper
Dash cayenne
1 tablespoon flour

Combine tomatoes, *1 tablespoon of the butter*, garlic, thyme, bay leaf, salt, pepper, and cayenne in a saucepan. Cook over a moderate heat, stirring occasionally, until quantity has been reduced to about half. Melt remaining 1 tablespoon butter in a small saucepan. Stir in flour and cook until lightly browned. Add to tomatoes and cook a few minutes longer. Remove from heat and strain through a fine sieve or blend in an electric blender. Sautéed onions, green and red peppers, and mushrooms may be added. If this is done, do not strain or blend.

BARBECUE SAUCE

1 can (1 pound, 3 ounce size) tomatoes
1 medium onion, chopped
1 clove garlic, chopped
1 tablespoon brown sugar
1 tablespoon butter
½ cup ketchup

½ cup Worcestershire sauce
½ cup vinegar
1 teaspoon salt
¼ teaspoon pepper
Dash cayenne
¼ teaspoon dry mustard

Pour tomatoes into a saucepan, breaking up the large chunks with a fork. Add all remaining ingredients, cook to boil, then reduce heat, and simmer slowly for about 45 minutes.

SAUCE FOR COLD MEAT

Combine a few sprigs of parsley (minced fine) with a pinch of dried thyme (or, if available, a sprig or two of fresh thyme), 3 or 4 stems of fresh chives (chopped fine), 6 tablespoons dry bread crumbs, ½ teaspoon salt, and a big pinch of freshly ground pepper. Place this mixture over thinly sliced cold lamb, cold veal, or cold chicken, and sprinkle with a bit of tart French Dressing (page 137).

SAUCE REMOULADE

1¼ cups mayonnaise
¼ cup chopped sour pickles
¼ cup chopped capers, drained

2 tablespoons chopped parsley, chives, or
   fresh tarragon
½ teaspoon anchovy paste

Combine all ingredients and serve cold. Excellent with cold fish or shellfish.

CREOLE SAUCE REMOULADE

3 hard-cooked eggs
½ teaspoon dry mustard
2 teaspoons cold water
½ clove garlic, minced fine
Salt

Cayenne
1 tablespoon tarragon or wine vinegar
3 tablespoons olive oil
1 raw egg yolk
Juice of ½ lemon

Separate whites from yolks of hard-cooked eggs. Work whites through a coarse sieve and set aside. Put yolks in a bowl and mash thoroughly. Add mustard (blended to a paste with water), minced garlic, salt, cayenne, and vinegar. Mix until smooth. Beat in oil, drop by drop, then add raw egg yolk and lemon juice. Taste and beat in more oil or vinegar, if needed. Use the shredded egg whites as a garnish. Serve with shrimp, lobster, or other cold, cooked fish.

HORSE-RADISH SAUCE

½ teaspoon dry mustard
6 tablespoons freshly ground horse-radish
1 teaspoon salt

½ teaspoon white pepper
½ cup heavy cream, whipped

Mix mustard with 1 tablespoon cold water, stir until smooth, then combine with horse-radish, salt, and pepper. Allow to stand for 10 minutes. Fold thoroughly into the whipped cream. Excellent with hot or cold meats, especially beef or tongue. Makes 1 cup.

SALADS

OKRA SALAD

Cook a box of frozen whole okra according to package directions. Drain and chill. Shortly before serving, garnish with sliced fresh tomatoes and season with a tart French Dressing (page 137). Serves 3 to 4.

GREEN BEAN SALAD

1 pound green beans
2 cups shredded lettuce
2 scallions, chopped

2 sprigs summer savory
  or ¼ teaspoon dried savory
French Dressing (page 137)

Trim ends from whole green beans. Cook in a little boiling, salted water until tender but still crisp. Drain thoroughly and cool. Shortly before serving, toss beans with all remaining ingredients. Use only enough French Dressing to coat the various ingredients lightly. The Shakers, who conceived this excellent summer salad, tossed in "6 nasturtium leaves" and "12 nasturtium pods." Serves 4.

BOHEMIAN SALAD

8 medium potatoes
1 onion, chopped fine
2 tart apples (pared, cored, and
  coarsely diced)
½ cup thin strips boiled ham
½ cup thin strips roast veal or chicken
½ cup thin strips of smoked tongue

1 herring (cleaned, boned, and chopped
  coarsely)
2 tablespoons capers, drained
½ to ¾ cup French Dressing (page 137)
1 can flat anchovy fillets
4 hard-cooked eggs
1 cup baby beets
Lettuce and watercress

Cook potatoes in their jackets in boiling, salted water until tender. When cool, peel and cut into thin slices. Place in a large salad bowl. Add onion, diced apples, ham, veal or chicken, tongue, herring, and capers. Pour French Dressing over all (start with a small amount, then add more if potatoes absorb it quickly) and toss gently. Add salt and pepper, if needed. Let stand at room temperature about 30 minutes before serving. Garnish the salad as follows: arrange drained anchovy fillets, spoke-fashion, on top. Separate yolks from whites of eggs and work separately through a coarse sieve. Spoon alternate mounds of these between anchovies. Marinate beets in a little vinegar to which several cloves have been added; when they are tart, arrange beets in a garland around the salad bowl. Garnish with tufts of lettuce and watercress. Serves 6.

RED-BEET EGGS

1 teaspoon dried mustard
2 tablespoons sugar
1 teaspoon salt

½ cup cider vinegar
1 can (1 pound) baby beets
4 eggs, hard cooked

Mix together mustard, sugar, salt, and vinegar and cook to the boiling point. Pour over well-drained beets and set aside to cool. When cool, add the shelled hard-cooked eggs and refrigerate overnight. Shake container occasionally so eggs will pick up the beet color all over. Serve beets as a salad on watercress. The pickled eggs may be used as a garnish for the salad or served separately. Makes 4 servings.

COLESLAW

The Dutch word for salad, *sla*, was quickly absorbed into the American language. Concerning cabbage, Amelia Simmons noted: "The . . . small tight heads, are best for slaw."

1 small head green cabbage
½ cup heavy cream or commercial
　　sour cream
2 tablespoons sugar

1 teaspoon salt
¼ teaspoon pepper
2 tablespoons cider vinegar

Shred cabbage very fine (1 head should make about 1 quart when shredded). Mix cream with all remaining ingredients, add the cabbage, and toss gently until coated. Serve immediately, otherwise salad will become limp and soggy. Serves 4.

FOUR-BEAN SALAD

2 cups canned kidney beans, heated
2 cups whole cooked green beans (fresh, canned, or frozen)
2 cups cut cooked Italian green beans (fresh or frozen)
2 cups cooked baby Lima beans (fresh or frozen)

1 cup French Dressing (page 137)
1 cup celery hearts and leaves, chopped
Crisp lettuce
2 cups Sour Cream Salad Dressing (page 136)
1 large Bermuda onion
1 large green pepper
12 large stuffed olives

Rinse and drain kidney beans, then mix with whole green beans, cut Italian green beans, and baby Lima beans. While still warm, toss with French Dressing. Allow to marinate an hour or two, then add celery. Arrange lettuce in a large salad bowl. Combine beans with *1 cup Sour Cream Salad Dressing* and pile on top of lettuce. Garnish with rings of Bermuda onion, rings of green pepper (remove the seeds), and sliced stuffed olives. Serve with remaining Sour Cream Salad Dressing in a separate bowl. Serves 8 to 10.

BETABEL RELLENO
(Stuffed Beets)

6 medium-sized cooked beets
2 celery stalks, with leaves, chopped fine
1 green onion (scallion) with top

½ cup cooked peas or other leftover vegetable
Mayonnaise

Scoop out centers of beets. Chop the centers quite fine and mix with the celery, onion, and vegetable. Season with salt and pepper. Add just enough mayonnaise to bind the vegetables together. Fill the cavities of the beets. Serve on a bed of shredded lettuce. Serves 6.

WALDORF SALAD

Although Oscar Tschirky, known as Oscar of the Waldorf, was the maître d' rather than the chef at the Waldorf-Astoria (and once said, "my job is the serving of food, never the cooking"), he did create the Waldorf Salad. The original recipe called only for equal parts of raw apples, cut in small pieces, and celery, moistened with mayonnaise and served on lettuce leaves. Later someone added coarsely chopped walnuts, and it is this version that has become famous.

GAZPACHO SALAD

In *The Virginia Housewife,* Mary Randolph identifies *gazpacho* as Spanish in origin. Although one of Mrs. Randolph's competitors suggests that it "is a kind of raw soup, eaten with a spoon," Mrs. Randolph's recipe is more like a salad.

Arrange in a glass or crystal bowl alternate layers of unpeeled and very thinly sliced cucumbers, skinned and thinly sliced tomatoes, very thinly sliced Bermuda onions, coarse crumbs of dry French bread. Pour a tart French Dressing (page 137) over all and refrigerate until icy cold.

RUSSIAN SALAD

Naming the proper dishes for a dinner party in *Society As I Have Found It,* Ward McAllister punctiliously noted that a Russian Salad "is a pleasing novelty at times."

Cook equal amounts of the following vegetables separately: finely diced carrots, finely diced potatoes, green beans cut into ½-inch pieces, and shelled peas. When tender but still firm, drain and place in a bowl. Drain and dice an equal amount of canned beets and combine with all the other vegetables. Add 1 or 2 chopped scallions, then enough French Dressing (page 137) to moisten the salad. Marinate for 1 hour. Just before serving, drain off excess dressing and add enough mayonnaise to hold the vegetables together. Season to taste. Arrange in a salad bowl with a garnish of greens.

SAUERKRAUT SALAD

Sauerkraut, a Pennsylvania Dutch staple, has been celebrated in sermons, songs, poetry, and quite a few tired old jokes. It has been so famous that, according to a note by the editor of *The Guardian* in 1869, "when General Lee took possession of Chambersburg on his way to Gettysburg, we happened to be a member of the Committee representing the town. Among the first things he demanded for his army was twenty-five barrels of Saur-Kraut."

1 can (1-pound size) sauerkraut
1 green pepper, chopped fine
1 small onion, chopped fine
3 stalks celery, chopped fine

1 cup chili sauce
⅓ cup brown sugar
1 teaspoon paprika
3 tablespoons fresh lemon juice

Drain sauerkraut and place in a salad bowl. Toss in green pepper, onion, and celery. Set aside. Blend together chili sauce, brown sugar, paprika, and lemon juice. Pour over salad mixture and toss well. Serves 4 to 6.

SOUTHERN SALAD

1 package frozen black-eyed peas
1 cup celery, chopped fine
1 cup diced tomatoes, drained

French Dressing (page 137)
Watercress
Sweet onion

Cook peas according to directions on the package. Drain and cool. Add celery, tomatoes, and enough French Dressing to flavor the salad (about 4 to 5 tablespoons). Toss lightly and serve on a bed of watercress with a garnish of onion rings. Serves 4.

PERSIMMON AND GRAPEFRUIT SALAD

Native American persimmons drew comments from early explorers—many of them, since the discoverers had not taken the time to ripen the fruit, were negative. But the plumlike fruit gradually became popular for a variety of recipes. Francis Peyre Porcher wrote in 1869 that it made a good drink when fermented; it was used for beer, bread, puddings, and salads. The Japanese persimmon is possibly more popular in America than the country's own variety. Commodore Perry brought it to America in 1855, when he returned from his expedition to Japan.

Cut ripe, peeled persimmons in long slices and arrange on a salad plate alternating with sections of fresh grapefruit. Garnish with watercress and dress lightly with a tart French Dressing (page 137), preferably made with lemon juice rather than vinegar.

CUCUMBER SALAD

"We recommend," Mrs. Leslie said in *The American Family Cook Book*, "the eaters to be mindful of the duty of mastication, without the due performance of which, all undressed vegetables are troublesome company for the principal viscera, and some are even dangerously indigestible." Mrs. Leslie notwithstanding, General Ulysses S. Grant was inordinately fond of cucumbers. As General Horace Porter remarked in an article, "Campaigning with Grant," the General "often made his entire meal upon a sliced cucumber and a cup of coffee."

2 cucumbers	¾ teaspoon salt
1 small onion	¼ teaspoon pepper
½ cup commercial sour cream	3 tablespoons sugar
⅓ cup vinegar	¼ teaspoon dry mustard

Slice unpared cucumbers very thin, then combine with the onion, sliced equally thin. Mix all remaining ingredients in a bowl and stir until smooth. Just before serving, pour the dressing over the cucumbers and onion and toss gently. If dressing is added too far in advance, the salad will become too soggy. Serves 6.

BIRDS-NEST SALAD

Rub a little green coloring paste into cream cheese, giving it a delicate color like birds' eggs. Roll it into balls the size of birds' eggs, using the back or smooth side of butter-pats. Arrange on a flat dish some small well-crimped lettuce leaves; group them to look like nests, moisten them with French dressing, and place five of the cheese balls in each nest of leaves. The cheese balls may be varied by flecking them with black, white, or red pepper.

—From *The Century Cook Book*, 1895

SALAD OF MIXED GARDEN STUFF

Salads were usually served at the principal meals at Monticello; Jefferson's fondness for them is reflected in an inventory of his garden, which included nineteen varieties of lettuce alone.

1 head Bibb lettuce	1 small head chicory
1 bunch watercress	Few sprigs tender spinach leaves
1 small head endive	1 tablespoon chopped chives or scallions
1 small head iceberg lettuce	

Wash the salad greens in ice water, drain, and pat completely dry. Tear apart (do not cut) and place in the refrigerator to crisp. To serve, toss with Monticello Dressing (page 137).

SHAKER POTATO SALAD

Cook 6 medium potatoes in their jackets in boiling, salted water until tender when pierced with a fork. When cool enough to handle, peel and cut into thin slices. Dice 3 slices of bacon and fry until crisp. Stir in 1 medium-sized onion, chopped, and cook a few minutes longer. Take care not to brown the onion. Stir in 1 teaspoon salt, dash of pepper, 1 tablespoon of sugar, and ½ cup vinegar mixed with the same amount of water. Heat to a boil, pour over potatoes, and toss gently. Serve with finely chopped parsley on top. Serves 6.

Nor do I say, that it is filthy to eat potatoes. I do not ridicule the using of them as sauce. What I laugh at is, the idea of the use of them being a saving; of their going further than bread; of the cultivation of them in lieu of wheat adding to the human sustenance of a country. . . . As food for cattle, sheep or hogs, this is the worst of all the green and root crops; but of this I have said enough before; and therefore, I now dismiss the Potatoe with the hope, that I shall never again have to write the word, or see the thing.

—William Cobbett, *A Year's Residence in the United States of America*, 1819

CREAM POTATO SALAD

6 large potatoes
¾ cup heavy cream (about)
4 tablespoons cider vinegar
1 tablespoon salad oil
1½ teaspoons salt

¼ teaspoon pepper
1 medium onion, sliced thin
8 red radishes, sliced thin
Salad greens

Cook potatoes in their jackets in boiling, salted water until tender when pierced with a fork. Peel and dice. Combine the cream, vinegar, oil, salt, and pepper. Pour over warm potatoes and toss gently. Potatoes should absorb almost all the cream. Add onion slices, separated into rings, and the radishes. Mellow at least 30 minutes, then garnish with greens, and serve at room temperature. Serves 6.

SOUR CREAM SALAD DRESSING

1 cup mayonnaise
1 cup commercial sour cream

1 tablespoon chives or green
onion tops, chopped
1 teaspoon dill weed (optional)

Combine mayonnaise with sour cream. Stir in chives or onion and dill. Makes 2 cups.

FRENCH DRESSING

Basic French Dressing is a mixture of good wine vinegar, good oil, salt, pepper, and, if you wish, fresh green herbs and mustard. Lemon juice may be used in place of vinegar. The correct proportions are 1 of vinegar to 3 of oil, with salt and freshly ground pepper to taste. As is true of so many things, French Dressing is always best when freshly made.

HOT CREAM DRESSING

4 slices bacon	1 tablespoon water
3 tablespoons vinegar	1 teaspoon flour
2 tablespoons commercial sour cream	1 tablespoon sugar
1 egg yolk	½ teaspoon salt

Fry bacon until crisp. Remove from pan, drain, and set aside. Pour off all but 2 tablespoons of bacon fat and stir in vinegar and sour cream. Mix together egg yolk, water, and flour until smooth. Stir into pan mixture and cook over a very low heat, stirring constantly, until dressing thickens. Remove from heat and stir in sugar and salt. Pour the hot dressing over fresh, washed greens (either dandelion, endive, lettuce, or spinach or a combination of them) and scatter the crumbled bacon over the top.

RUSSIAN DRESSING

Blend ½ cup mayonnaise with ¼ cup chili sauce, 1 tablespoon finely chopped green pepper, 1 tablespoon finely chopped pimiento, and 1 teaspoon finely chopped chives. Makes ¾ cup.

MONTICELLO DRESSING

Jefferson took a great interest in developing benne (sesame) oil for salad dressings as a substitute for the olive oil imported from Europe. On January 6, 1808, he wrote from Monticello to John Taylor of South Carolina: "The African negroes brought over to Georgia a seed which they called Beni, & the botanists Sesamum. I lately received a bottle of the oil, which was eaten with sallad by various companies. all agree it is equal to the olive oil. a bushel of seed yields 3. gallons of oil. I propose to cultivate it for my own use at least."

Combine 1 small clove of garlic (crushed), 1 teaspoon salt, ½ teaspoon white pepper, ⅓ cup olive oil, ⅓ cup sesame oil, ⅓ cup tarragon or wine vinegar. Place in a covered jar and shake well before pouring over salad.

SUN-COOKED STRAWBERRY JAM

Choose brightly colored berries that are not too ripe. It is difficult to prepare more than 4 to 5 quarts at a time. Wash, then drain very thoroughly. Remove hulls and slice small berries in half, large ones in quarters. Weigh the fruit, place in a large kettle, and add sugar. For each pound of fruit allow ¾ pound sugar. Stir until all berries are coated with sugar. Bring to a rolling boil and boil *exactly 3 minutes*. Pour immediately into flat glass, enamel, or china dishes to a depth of ½ inch—the fruit should lie flat in the syrup. Cover completely with panes of glass and place outside in unobstructed sunlight. Turn glass covers each time enough moisture accumulates on top to pour off (this may be every few minutes for an hour or two, with intervals longer after that). Stir occasionally with a spoon to expose all surfaces of berries and syrup to the action of the sun. Strawberries are "cooked" when syrup forms jellied ridges or waves when container is tilted at one end. This usually takes about 1½ days of full sunshine. Bottle immediately. A paraffin cover is not necessary. (If rainy or cloudy weather should interfere, bring dishes, still covered tightly, inside. Strawberries will keep safely for several days if fruit has cooked 4 or 5 hours.)

GRAPE CONSERVE

4 pounds Concord grapes
Grated rind and juice of 2 oranges
5 cups sugar

Dash of salt
1 cup seedless raisins
1 cup walnuts, finely chopped

Wash grapes, pluck from stems, and pinch skins from pulp, putting skins into a bowl and pulp into a saucepan. Cook pulp over a low heat for about 5 to 8 minutes to loosen the seeds, then work through a sieve. Return purée to saucepan, stir in grated orange rind and juice, the sugar, salt, and raisins. Cook over a low heat, stirring constantly, until the sugar has dissolved. Increase heat and boil until mixture thickens, stirring constantly. Add skins and continue boiling 5 minutes longer or until conserve is quite thick. Stir in walnuts, pour into sterilized 6-ounce jelly glasses, and seal securely. Makes 8 glasses.

PEAR MARMALADE

4 pounds ripe pears
1 lemon

1 large orange
3 pounds sugar

Wash pears, cut in half, and remove cores. Wash lemon and orange, cut off ends, and quarter. Work all the fruit through a food grinder. Put into a kettle and stir in sugar thoroughly. Cook to boil, then reduce heat, and continue cooking over a low heat for 35 to 40 minutes or until shiny and almost transparent. Stir frequently. Spoon into sterilized jars and seal. Makes about 3 pints.

CANDIED CRANBERRIES

Cranberries may have been known at first as "crane berries," since cranes living in the New England bogs ate the berries. They were early recognized as a good preventive of scurvy, and ships putting out to sea from Down East ports always carried casks of this "bogland medicine" in their stores. Though they are now commercially grown in Wisconsin, Washington, Oregon, and New Jersey, cranberries were associated first with Massachusetts. John Josselyn, visiting New England in 1663, wrote: "The *Indians* and *English* use them much, boyling them with Sugar for Sauce to eat with their Meat, and it is a delicate Sauce." In Josselyn's day they were known, too, as "bounce berries," since they were, and still are, tested for ripeness by their ability to bounce.

Wash 2 cups of fresh cranberries and spread an even layer on the bottom of a shallow baking dish. Sprinkle with 1 cup of sugar, cover tightly, and bake in a preheated 350° oven for 1 hour. Give them an occasional stir during baking period. Chill before serving. Serve with meat or fowl.

"The Jelly wont Jell."– illustration from *Success with Small Fruits* (1881)

CRANBERRY SAUCE

Pick over and wash 4 cups of cranberries. Combine 2 cups sugar with 1½ cups water, bring to a boil, and cook for 10 minutes. Add the cranberries, cover, and cook until they stop popping. Skim off froth. Cool before serving. Add a dash of cognac if you wish.

SPICED CRAB APPLES

4 pounds crab apples
4½ cups sugar
1 quart vinegar

2 sticks cinnamon
½ tablespoon whole cloves

Choose firm, ripe crab apples, free from blemishes. Do not pare; leave the stems attached. In a kettle large enough to contain the fruit, combine sugar, vinegar, and spices. Bring slowly to a boil and cook for 5 minutes. Add fruit, again bring to a boil, then turn down heat, and cook slowly until apples are tender. Allow fruit to stand in syrup overnight. The next day, drain off the syrup and cook it until it is the consistency of honey. Pack fruit into 1-pint sterilized jars and fill with syrup. Seal. Makes 6 jars.

Advertisement, *Harper's Weekly*

APPLE BUTTER

Apple Butter has always been associated with the Pennsylvania Dutch, and it has a special meaning for the Schwenkfelders. Every September for the last 226 years, the Schwenkfelders have held *Gedaechtnisz Tag*—a thanksgiving service. The Schwenkfelders began their arduous voyage to America in July, 1734. Christopher Schultz, a sixteen-year-old orphan, kept a diary during the trip and, on September 21, 1734, he recorded "it was again calm, and the anchor was dropped near New Castle, and we obtained our first *fresh water* out of the river today. The captain rowed over and brought back a bag of *apples*." With rolls that were provided, the Schwenkfelders had a meal of fresh food, the first after their long voyage. Their traditional thanksgiving— water, bread, butter, Apple Butter—commemorates that fact each year.

3 quarts sweet cider
8 pounds ripe, well-flavored apples
2½ cups brown sugar, firmly packed
2 teaspoons cloves

2 teaspoons cinnamon
1 teaspoon allspice
½ teaspoon salt

Cook cider over a high heat, uncovered, about 30 minutes or until it is reduced to half. Wash, quarter, and core unpeeled apples, add to cider, and cook over a low heat until very tender. Stir frequently. Work apple mixture through a sieve, returning the purée to the kettle. Stir in sugar, all the spices, and salt. Cook over a very low heat, stirring almost continuously, until Apple Butter thickens. Pour into sterilized pint jars and seal securely. Makes 4 jars.

APPLESAUCE

In *American Cookery*, Amelia Simmons strongly urged Americans to plant their own apple trees, "excepting in the compactest cities." She argued that many otherwise useless spots might be turned into orchards, and cautioned families to "preserve the orchard from the intrusions of boys, &c. which is too common in America." Miss Simmons concluded that the "net saving would in time extinguish the public debt."

Pare, core, and slice thin 10 greening apples. Add 1 cup water and cook over a low heat, covered, for 15 minutes, stirring occasionally. Remove from heat and rub apples through a sieve or, preferably, blend in an electric blender to make a smooth sauce. Add 1 cup granulated sugar, return to a brisk heat, and cook about 5 minutes longer. Cool, but do not chill, and serve with cold heavy cream. Makes 5 to 6 cups, depending on the size of the apples.

ALBEMARLE PEACH CHUTNEY

Chutney (from the Hindu *catni*) was probably introduced to America by schooner captains plying the Indian spice trade.

7 pounds firm fresh peaches
1 pint cider vinegar
2 pounds dark brown sugar
½ cup grated onion
2 boxes (1-pound size) seedless raisins
5 apples, pared and diced
2 tablespoons white mustard seed

¼ cup scraped ginger root or
   3 tablespoons ground ginger
1½ tablespoons salt
2 tablespoons paprika
1 tablespoon cumin powder
Grated rind and juice of 2 lemons

Peel and cut peaches (enough to make about 4 quarts) in slices about ¾ inch thick. Cover with vinegar and brown sugar. Set aside. Combine all remaining ingredients and cook over a low heat, stirring constantly, until the mixture is thoroughly blended. In a separate saucepan, cook the peach mixture for several minutes or until peaches are tender but still hold their shape. Combine both mixtures and cook together for a few minutes. Pour into sterilized jars and seal securely. Makes about 5 quarts.

SWEET PICKLED PEACHES

6 pounds firm fresh peaches
3 cups cider vinegar
3 cups sugar

½ teaspoon whole cloves
½ teaspoon whole allspice
½ teaspoon mace

Pour boiling water over peaches and let stand several minutes, then drain and skin. (Some varieties resist this method and must be pared with a knife.) Cut each peach in half, remove the pit, and pack into 2 or 3 sterilized quart jars (the size of the peaches and the way in which they are packed is the determining factor). Bring vinegar and sugar to the boiling point. Add all the spices and continue boiling for 5 minutes. Pour over the peaches immediately and seal securely. Makes 2 to 3 jars.

CANTALOUPE PICKLE

Peel a large unripe cantaloupe, remove seeds and membrane, cut into small pieces. Cover with white vinegar, then pour off all the vinegar and measure it. To every pint of vinegar add 1¾ cups of brown sugar (firmly packed), 8 whole cloves, ½ teaspoon cinnamon, and ¼ teaspoon mace. Bring the mixture to a boil. Add melon and cook over a low heat until tender and almost transparent. With a slotted spoon, transfer cantaloupe to a bowl. Continue to boil pickling liquid for about 12 minutes. Pour over melon. Cool completely before using. Makes about 1 quart.

CORN RELISH

2 packages frozen corn or
  4 cups fresh corn
¼ head cabbage, shredded
1 sweet red pepper, chopped fine
5 stalks celery, thinly sliced

¼ cup sugar
1 tablespoon salt
1 tablespoon dry mustard
½ cup white vinegar
½ cup water

Cook corn until tender. Drain and set aside. Combine cabbage, red pepper, and celery in a saucepan. Add about 1 cup of water, cover, and cook 5 minutes. Drain and combine with corn. Mix together sugar, salt, and dry mustard. Then stir in vinegar and water. Pour over vegetables, heat to a boil, then continue cooking 15 minutes longer. Stir occasionally. Pour into sterilized pint jars and seal, or refrigerate and use immediately. Makes 2 jars.

GINGER PEARS

2 pounds hard late pears
Juice and rind of 1 lemon
½ cup water

2 pounds sugar
2 ounces ginger root or crystallized ginger

Pare, quarter, core, and cut pears into thin slices. Squeeze lemon juice, then cut rind into thin slices. Combine both rind and juice with water, sugar, and small chunks of ginger. Cook over a low heat for 45 minutes or until mixture is clear and syrupy. Add pears and continue simmering for 45 minutes (the pears should be transparent and the syrup quite thick). Pour into sterilized jars and seal. Makes 3 to 4 half-pint jars.

CARROT PICKLES

4 cups sliced, uncooked carrots
2 medium onions, sliced
¾ cup sugar
¾ teaspoon salt
½ teaspoon cinnamon

¼ teaspoon ginger
¼ teaspoon cloves
¼ teaspoon celery seed
1 tablespoon salad oil
2 cups vinegar

Cook carrot and onion slices in 1 cup of water over a low heat for 10 minutes. Drain, add all remaining ingredients, and simmer gently for 15 minutes. Ladle into 4 sterilized pint jars and seal securely.

YANKEE TOMATO RELISH

2 cups skinned and chopped tomatoes
½ cup onion, chopped fine
1 cup chopped celery
¼ cup green pepper, chopped fine

6 tablespoons sugar
1 tablespoon mustard seed
½ cup cider vinegar

Before measuring tomatoes, squeeze out most of the juice, then combine tomatoes with all remaining ingredients. Pour into a sterilized jar, cover, and let stand for at least 24 hours before using. Makes about 1 quart.

TOMATO KETCHUP

Get them quite ripe on a dry day, squeeze them with your hands till reduced to a pulp, then put half a pound of fine salt to one hundred tomatoes, and boil them for two hours. Stir them to prevent burning. While hot press them through a fine sieve, with a silver spoon till nought but the skin remains, then add a little mace, 3 nutmegs, allspice, cloves, cinnamon, ginger and pepper to taste. Boil over a slow fire till quite thick, stir all the time. Bottle when cold. One hundred tomatoes will make four or five bottles and keep good for two or three years.
—Mrs. Samuel Whitehorne, *Sugar House Book*, 1801,
Collection of Newport Historical Society

TOMATO PRESERVES

5 large ripe tomatoes
3½ cups sugar

Juice and rind of 1½ lemons
½ cup crystallized ginger, chopped

Pour boiling water over tomatoes, let stand for several minutes, then slip off the skins. Chop tomatoes in small cubes. Cover with sugar and allow to stand for 1 hour. Squeeze juice from lemons and cut rind in fine slivers. Combine with tomato mixture and crystallized ginger. Cook over a low heat, stirring frequently, until preserves thicken. A good test is to spoon some into a saucer; if the liquid turns syrupy thick on cooling, preserves are done. Makes about 1½ pints.

PICKLED JERUSALEM ARTICHOKES

2 pounds Jerusalem artichokes
1 cup white vinegar
1 cup water

1 cup sugar
5 whole cloves
½ teaspoon salt

Peel artichokes and cook whole in boiling, salted water until tender. Start testing with a toothpick after about 15 minutes. Do not overcook. Drain thoroughly. Combine all remaining ingredients and cook to a boil. Pour over artichokes and let stand at least 8 hours before using. Makes about 1 quart.

DESSERTS

NEW ORLEANS CALAS
(*Rice Cakes*)

Vendors used to sell *calas* on the streets in the French Quarter of New Orleans with the cry, *"Belles calas! Calas tout chaud!"*

½ cup uncooked rice
3 cups boiling water
1 package active dry yeast or
  1 cake compressed
3 eggs, well beaten
¼ cup flour (about)

½ cup sugar
½ teaspoon salt
Dash of nutmeg
Fat for deep-fat frying
Confectioners' sugar

Cook rice in boiling water until very tender. Drain and set aside to cool. Dissolve yeast in 2 tablespoons warm water. Mix with cold rice and let stand in a warm spot overnight. The following day, beat in eggs, flour, sugar, salt, and nutmeg, adding more flour, if necessary, to make a thick batter. Heat fat to 370° on deep-fat thermometer or until a 1-inch cube of bread browns in 60 seconds. Drop batter from tablespoons into hot fat and fry until golden brown. Drain on paper towels and sprinkle with confectioners' sugar. Serve hot.

A NUN'S SIGH

These *Beignet Soufflés*—as light as a nun's sigh—are made of chou paste, the base for cream puffs and éclairs. The recipe was adapted from *French Dishes for American Tables* by Pierre Caron, *chef d'entremets* at the old Delmonico's.

1 cup sifted all-purpose flour
Pinch of salt
1 tablespoon sugar
1 cup water
⅓ cup butter

4 eggs
1 teaspoon vanilla
Fat for deep-fat frying
Confectioners' sugar

Sift together flour, salt, sugar, and set aside. Heat water and butter together until butter melts. Add flour combination all at once, and stir rapidly with a wooden spoon until dough leaves sides of pan and forms a lump. Remove from heat and beat in eggs, one at a time, beating hard after each addition. When dough is no longer slippery-looking, stir in vanilla. Scoop up a heaping teaspoon of the dough and, with a second teaspoon, push it off into pre-heated fat (350° on deep-fat thermometer or until a 1-inch cube of bread browns in 60 seconds). When puffed and golden brown, drain on paper towels. Sprinkle with confectioners' sugar and serve hot. Makes several dozen.

FRUIT FRITTERS

1 cup sifted all-purpose flour
¼ teaspoon salt
2 tablespoons sugar
2 eggs, separated
⅔ cup milk

1 tablespoon melted butter
1 teaspoon fresh lemon juice
2 cups cubed fruit
Fat for deep-fat frying
Cinnamon

Sift together the flour, salt, and sugar. Set aside. Combine egg yolks and milk, then beat in butter and lemon juice. Stir in flour mixture with as few strokes as possible and gently fold in stiffly beaten egg whites. If you use canned fruit, drain on paper towels. Heat deep fat to 350° or until a 1-inch cube of bread browns in 60 seconds. Drop a piece of fruit into batter, drain slightly, and fry in hot fat until golden brown on each side. Drain on paper towels and sprinkle with a mixture of granulated sugar and a little cinnamon. Serves 8.

Deep-fat fryers

DOUGHNUTS

1 cup sugar
3½ teaspoons baking powder
½ teaspoon cinnamon
½ teaspoon nutmeg
½ teaspoon salt

4 cups all-purpose flour (about)
2 eggs
1 cup milk
3 tablespoons melted butter
Fat for deep-fat frying

Sift together sugar, baking powder, cinnamon, nutmeg, salt, and flour. Beat eggs thoroughly, then stir into dry ingredients. Add the milk and melted butter. Roll about ⅓ inch thick on a floured board and cut with a doughnut cutter (lacking this, use a biscuit cutter and make a hole in the center with a large thimble). Fry several at a time in hot fat (375° on deep-fat thermometer or until a 1-inch cube of bread browns in 60 seconds) until nicely browned. Drain on paper towels. Dust with granulated or confectioners' sugar. Makes 2 dozen.

TRIFLE

The Trifle was brought to America by the British colonists. In this country, the wine-soaked cake was also known as Tipsy Squire and Tipsy Parson.

Place a layer of spongecake in a crystal bowl. Saturate it with sherry, rum, or brandy. Stud with ½ cup toasted almonds, then refrigerate until serving time. Make custard according to directions given in Snow Eggs (page 155). Combine 1 cup heavy cream with 1 tablespoon confectioners' sugar and 1 teaspoon vanilla, then beat until stiff. Before serving, pour custard over spongecake, then pile whipped cream on top. Jam may be spread over the cake before the custard and cream are added. Serves 6 to 8.

EMPAÑADAS DE CAMOTE CON PIÑA
(Pineapple-Yam Turnovers)

Filling:
1 cup cooked yam, mashed
½ cup crushed pineapple, drained
1 tablespoon lime or lemon juice
¼ teaspoon salt
1 egg, beaten
½ cup light brown sugar
½ cup blanched almonds, chopped
½ teaspoon cinnamon

Pastry:
2 cups sifted all-purpose flour
2 tablespoons sugar
2 teaspoons baking powder
½ teaspoon salt
⅔ cup shortening
5 or 6 tablespoons ice water

To make the filling: Combine mashed yam with pineapple and all remaining ingredients for the filling. Set aside.

To make pastry: Sift together flour, sugar, baking powder, and salt. Cut in shortening with a pastry blender or two knives until mixture looks mealy. Add water, just enough to hold pastry together when kneaded lightly. Roll as thin as pie pastry on a lightly floured board and cut into circles, 3 to 4 inches in diameter. Spoon filling on one half of the circle, wet edge of pastry with a little water, then fold other half of pastry over, and press edges together with fork tines. Prick pastry tops. Bake in a preheated 375° oven for 15 to 20 minutes or until delicately browned. Serve at room temperature. Makes 15.

OLYKOEKS
(Raised Doughnuts)

In his *History of New York...by Diedrich Knickerbocker,* Washington Irving wrote of a large "dish of balls of sweetened dough fried in hog's fat, and called dough nuts or oly koeks." The Dutch introduced doughnuts—they called them oily cakes—to the New World.

1 cup milk
1 package active dry yeast or
 1 cake compressed
¼ cup lukewarm water
1 cup brown sugar, firmly packed
6 cups sifted all-purpose flour

1 teaspoon salt
1 teaspoon cinnamon or nutmeg
2 eggs, well beaten
1 cup softened butter
Fat for deep-fat frying

Scald milk, then cool to lukewarm. Sprinkle yeast over lukewarm water to dissolve. Sift together sugar, flour, salt, and cinnamon or nutmeg. Combine milk and yeast in a large bowl. Stir in the flour with your hands (the dough will be very heavy), then stir in beaten eggs. Cover and let rise in a warm place until double in size. Punch down the dough, then work in the butter with your hands until dough is smooth and well blended. Roll about ½ inch thick on a lightly floured board and cut with a doughnut cutter. Place doughnuts on a tray lined with wax paper, cover again, and let rise in a warm place until light and puffy. Drop several at a time into deep fat preheated to 375° on deep-fat thermometer or until a 1-inch cube of bread browns in 60 seconds. Fry until nicely browned on both sides. Lift from fat, drain on paper towels, and sprinkle with confectioners' sugar, granulated sugar, or a mixture of granulated sugar and a little cinnamon. Makes about 40.

FASTNACHTS

These Pennsylvania Dutch doughnuts were served traditionally on Fastnacht Day (Shrove Tuesday)—a last sweet treat before the Lenten season began.

1 package active dry yeast or
  1 cake compressed
¼ cup warm water
2 cups milk
1 teaspoon sugar
6 to 7 cups sifted all-purpose flour

2 eggs
4 tablespoons butter, melted
¾ cup sugar, plus 2 tablespoons
1¼ teaspoons salt
Fat for deep-fat frying
Confectioners' sugar

Sprinkle yeast over warm water to dissolve. Scald milk, remove from heat, and cool. Add *1 teaspoon of the sugar, 3 cups of the flour,* and the yeast, and stir thoroughly. Cover and let stand in a warm place until double in size. Beat eggs vigorously and combine with butter, sugar, salt, and remaining flour. When the dough rises, stir in the egg mixture. At this point, mixture should be stiff enough to roll. Add more flour, if needed. Cover and let rise in a warm place a second time until double in size. Punch down with your fist, then roll about ½ inch thick on a lightly floured board. Cut into 2-inch squares, making a slit in the middle. Cover and let rise a third time. Fry several at a time in deep fat preheated to 350° on deep-fat thermometer or until hot enough to brown a 1-inch cube of bread in 60 seconds. Drain on paper towels and sprinkle with confectioners' sugar.

PANNEQUAIQUES

Jefferson seems to have delighted as much in the spelling as in the recipes of his steward in Washington, Étienne Lemaire. The President once wrote his daughter: "I enclose you Lemaire's receipts. The orthography will be puzzling and amusing but the receipts are valuable." Among Jefferson's favorites was this recipe for *Pannequaiques*—now called crêpes.

1 cup sifted all-purpose flour
1 tablespoon sugar
¼ teaspoon salt
2 eggs

2 additional egg yolks
1¾ cups milk
2 tablespoons melted butter
1 teaspoon rum or cognac

Combine all ingredients in a mixing bowl and beat with a rotary or electric beater until smooth. If you prefer to use a blender, put all ingredients in the container and blend until as thick as heavy cream. Heat a 6-inch skillet until a drop of water tested on the bottom sizzles. Grease the skillet, then add a generous tablespoonful of the batter. Tip the pan back and forth so there will be a thin coating of batter over the bottom of the pan. When crêpe is brown on the bottom, turn and brown the other side. Lift out of skillet and place on wax paper. Sprinkle each pancake as it comes from the pan with confectioners' sugar, then stack on top of each other, keeping them warm. Place on dessert platter and cut in wedges, or spread currant jelly between each layer and sprinkle confectioners' sugar on top.

STRAWBERRY SHORTCAKE

Roger Williams, founder of Providence in 1636, wrote in his *Key into the Language of America*...that the strawberry "is the wonder of all the Fruits growing naturally in those parts.... In some parts where the *Natives* have planted, I have many times seen as many as would fill a good ship, within few miles compasse." Williams went on to say: "The *Indians* bruise them in a Morter, and mixe them with meale and make Strawberry bread." From the time the colonists first discovered strawberries, a proliferation of Strawberry Shortcake recipes has sprung up.

2 cups sifted all-purpose flour
1 tablespoon baking powder
¼ teaspoon salt
½ cup softened butter

½ cup milk (about)
1 quart strawberries
Sugar
3 tablespoons butter

Sift together flour, baking powder, and salt. Add butter, working it thoroughly into the flour mixture. Using a fork, lightly mix in the milk—just enough to make a soft dough. Divide in half and pat each portion on the bottom of an inverted 8-inch cake pan. Prick surface with fork tines. Bake in a preheated 400° oven for about 15 minutes or until golden. While shortcakes bake, wash and hull berries. Crush half the berries and sprinkle generously with sugar. Sugar remaining whole berries. Take shortcakes from oven and, while still hot, dot surfaces with butter. Drain crushed berries (save the juice) and spoon on one layer, cover with second shortcake, and place drained whole berries on top. Return to oven for about 5 minutes, then pour fresh strawberry juice over the top and serve warm with plain or whipped cream.

Strawberry vendor

BLUEBERRY SHORTCAKE

3½ cups sifted all-purpose flour
1 tablespoon baking powder
½ teaspoon salt
½ cup (1 stick) butter

1 egg
¾ cup milk (about)
1 pint blueberries
½ cup sugar

Sift together flour, baking powder, and salt. Cut in butter with a pastry blender or two knives until mixture resembles corn meal. In a separate bowl, beat egg thoroughly, then stir in milk. Stir this lightly into the flour combination with a fork. Divide dough in half and roll one portion to fit in the bottom of a 9-inch pie pan. Cover with blueberries, then sprinkle with sugar. Cover with remaining dough rolled into a circle. Bake in a preheated 400° oven for 30 minutes or until dough takes on a golden tone. Serve warm with butter and sugar or cream. Serves 6.

PLUMS IN WINE JELLY

1 can (1 pound, 13 ounce size) plums
Red or white wine

2 envelopes unflavored gelatin

Drain plums, measure the syrup, and pour it into a saucepan. Pit the plums and place in a bowl. If you choose greengage plums, use a light white wine such as Chablis; if you use red or purple plums, then select a not-too-dry red wine. Measure wine (the wine plus the syrup should equal 1 pint). Pour the wine over the plums. Sprinkle gelatin over ½ cup cold water to soften. Heat plum syrup and stir in gelatin until dissolved. Combine with plums and wine and pour into a mold. Refrigerate until firm. Turn out of mold onto serving plate. Serves 4 to 6.

AMBROSIA

Ambrosia, the food eaten by Greek gods to preserve their immortality, is familiarly known to Americans as a combination of oranges and coconut—a very popular dessert in the South. In some sections, it is traditionally served for Christmas dinner.

Cut rind and white membrane from juicy oranges, then cut crosswise into thin slices, discarding the seeds. Put a generous layer of orange slices in a crystal bowl, sprinkle with sugar, and cover with a layer of shredded coconut. Continue layering with oranges, sugar, and coconut, ending with the coconut. Chill several hours before serving. Today other fruits are frequently added, such as pineapple, bananas, grapes, even berries—but the orange and coconut remain as the base.

FROZEN PLUM PUDDING

½ cup chopped candied cherries
½ cup chopped citron
¼ cup sherry
1 cup sugar
Dash salt
¾ teaspoon ground cardamom seed
2 eggs, beaten

2 cups milk
2 cups heavy cream
¼ cup macaroon crumbs
¼ cup chopped blanched almonds
¾ cup heavy cream, whipped
1 tablespoon sugar

Soak cherries and citron in sherry for an hour or two. Combine sugar, salt, and cardamom in a saucepan. Stir in eggs and milk. Cook over a low heat, stirring constantly, until mixture coats a wooden spoon. Cool, then stir in 2 cups heavy cream. Pour into ice cream freezer and freeze until mushy. Then add the sherry-flavored cherries and citron, the macaroon crumbs, and almonds. Continue cranking the freezer until mixture is firm. Pack into a 6-cup plum-pudding or gelatin mold and cover securely. Place in freezer compartment of refrigerator overnight to mellow. Unmold on a serving platter and return to freezer an hour or two or until firm. Frost the pudding with whipped cream sweetened with sugar. Return to freezer until whipped cream is firm. Serves 12 to 15.

SALPICON OF FRUITS

Combine 1 cup rum and 1 cup sugar in a saucepan. Bring to a boil, then pour over 4 cups cut fruit (oranges, bananas, grapes, pineapple, etc.). Let stand until cold. Chill in refrigerator or freeze in ice cube tray for several hours, stirring occasionally.

POACHED SECKEL PEARS

The Seckel pear, the finest and best known of all American pears, is named for the farmer who first grew this variety on his farm outside Philadelphia, shortly after the Revolution.

1½ cups water
1½ cups sugar
2 pounds Seckel pears

2 tablespoons chopped crystallized ginger
Heavy cream

Combine water and sugar in a saucepan and cook over a moderate heat until syrup begins to thicken. Wash pears (do not peel) and drop them into the hot syrup. Cook over a low heat, basting occasionally, for about 30 minutes or until tender when pierced with a fork. Remove from stove and stir in crystallized ginger. Serve slightly warm or cool, not chilled, with a pitcher of cream or unsweetened whipped cream. Serves 6.

BANANAS FLAMBÉ

Remove skins from 4 green-tipped bananas and cut in half lengthwise. Heat ½ cup (1 stick) butter in a chafing dish, add bananas, and sprinkle with ¾ cup sugar and 4 tablespoons lemon or lime juice. Cook until lightly browned, turning occasionally. To *flambé*, warm ⅓ cup cognac, pour over bananas, and ignite. Spoon sauce over fruit until flame dies out.

SPICED PEACHES IN BRANDY

12 large whole spiced peaches, canned
12 cloves
1 blade mace

1 stick cinnamon
1 cup brandy

Stick one clove in each peach and place in saucepan with the juice. Add cinnamon and mace and simmer gently until heated through. With a skimmer, remove the peaches to a large stone crock or wide-mouthed glass jar which has been scalded with boiling water. Add one cup of brandy and cover. Simmer remaining peach juice until it is reduced to half its original volume, then pour it into the crock. Cover tightly and store in a cool place for at least 3 days before serving. If stored for a longer time, add brandy as needed to keep the fruit covered with liquid. Apricots may be substituted for peaches.

HAZELNUT BAVARIAN CREAM

1 envelope unflavored gelatin
¼ cup cold water
½ cup milk
4 egg yolks
¼ cup sugar

Pinch of salt
¾ cup hazelnuts or walnuts, ground
2 tablespoons dark rum
2 cups heavy cream

Sprinkle gelatin over cold water to soften. Combine milk, egg yolks, sugar, and salt in the top of a double boiler. Cook over boiling water, stirring constantly, until mixture will coat a wooden spoon. Stir in gelatin until dissolved, then add ground nuts and rum. Refrigerate until the consistency is that of raw egg whites. Fold in stiffly beaten cream and pour into a 1½-quart mold or bowl. Chill until firm. Serves 6 to 8.

BLANCMANGE

½ pound blanched almonds
¼ cup water
¼ cup milk
1 tablespoon unflavored gelatin

1 cup heavy cream
½ cup sugar
1 tablespoon flavoring (kirsch, orgeat, rum, or maraschino)

Pound almonds in a mortar until very fine or blend in an electric blender. Stir in water and milk, allow to stand for 10 to 15 minutes, then strain through cheesecloth. The mixture will be very heavy and will take time to drip through; make certain every last bit of liquid is extracted. Sprinkle gelatin over ¼ cup water to soften. Scald cream, then stir in gelatin and sugar until both are dissolved. Add almond liquid and flavoring. Pour into a small mold or bowl and refrigerate for several hours until firm. Serve with whipped cream to 4.

CAPE COD BERRY GRUNT

1 pint berries
1 cup water
½ cup sugar
1½ cups sifted all-purpose flour

1 tablespoon baking powder
¼ teaspoon salt
1 tablespoon butter
¼ cup milk (about)

Cook the washed berries in water and sugar until soft (about 5 to 10 minutes, depending on the kind of berries and degree of ripeness). If you use frozen berries, mix the thawed fruit with ½ cup sugar (do not cook). Sift together flour, baking powder, and salt. Pinch in the butter with your finger tips until well dispersed, then stir in enough milk to make a soft dough. Place berries in bottom of a 1½-quart mold or ovenproof bowl, spoon dough on top, and cover tightly with a lid or a piece of foil. Place in a deep kettle and pour in enough boiling water to reach the halfway mark. Cover the kettle and simmer slowly for 1½ hours. Turn out of mold and serve hot with cream or New England Nutmeg Sauce (page 163). Serves 6.

PEACH COBBLER

⅔ cup sugar
1 tablespoon flour
3 cups fresh peach slices
4 tablespoons butter
¾ teaspoon cinnamon

1½ cups all-purpose flour
1 tablespoon baking powder
¼ teaspoon salt
3 tablespoons butter
½ cup milk (about)

Combine sugar and flour in a saucepan. Add peaches and cook over a low heat, stirring constantly, until fruit is tender (takes about 5 minutes, depending on the variety and quality of the fruit). Pour into an 8-inch square pan, dot with butter, and sprinkle with cinnamon. Set aside. Sift together flour, baking powder, and salt. Pinch in butter with your finger tips until well distributed. With a fork, stir in milk (just enough to make a soft dough), transfer to a lightly floured board, and knead a second or two. Roll into a 9-inch square about ½ inch thick. Place on top of the peaches, pinching dough to rim of pan. Bake in a preheated 425° oven for 25 to 30 minutes or until nicely browned. Serve warm, with or without cream.

LOUISA MAY ALCOTT'S APPLE SLUMP

The author of *Little Women* was so fond of this New England dessert that she named her house in Concord, Massachusetts, Apple Slump.

6 cups apples, pared, cored, and sliced
1 cup sugar
1 teaspoon cinnamon
½ cup water

1½ cups sifted all-purpose flour
¼ teaspoon salt
1½ teaspoons baking powder
½ cup milk (about)

Combine apple slices, sugar, cinnamon, and water in a saucepan with a tight-fitting lid. Heat to the boiling point. Sift together flour, salt, baking powder. Stir in enough milk to make a soft dough. Drop dough from a tablespoon onto apple mixture. Cover tightly and cook over a low heat for 30 minutes. Serve warm with New England Nutmeg Sauce (page 163) or rich cream. This dessert can be made with various fresh or frozen berries. Serves 6.

DOWN EAST APPLE BROWN BETTY

1½ cups dry bread crumbs
¼ cup melted butter
4 medium apples, peeled and sliced
¾ cup brown sugar, firmly packed
Pinch of salt

1 teaspoon cinnamon
¼ teaspoon nutmeg
¼ teaspoon ground cloves
1 teaspoon grated lemon rind
Juice of 1 lemon

Work bread crumbs and butter together and pat a third of the mixture on the bottom of a buttered baking dish. Cover with *half the apples*. Mix together sugar, salt, cinnamon, nutmeg, cloves, and lemon rind. Sprinkle half the mixture over the apple. Add *half the lemon juice* and 1 tablespoon of water. Add another layer of crumbs. Repeat with apples, sugar mixture, lemon juice, and water. Sprinkle remaining crumbs on top, cover, and bake in a preheated 350° oven for 40 minutes. Remove cover and continue baking at 400° for 10 minutes. Serve warm with cream, vanilla ice cream, or Lemon Sauce (page 163). Serves 6.

APPLE PANDOWDY

Pastry:
1½ cups flour
Dash of salt
½ cup shortening
Ice water
¼ cup melted butter (about)
Filling:
½ cup sugar

½ teaspoon cinnamon
¼ teaspoon salt
¼ teaspoon nutmeg
10 large apples
½ cup light molasses or maple syrup
3 tablespoons melted butter
¼ cup water

Sift flour and salt together into a bowl, then blend in the shortening with a pastry blender or two knives until mixture is mealy. Sprinkle a little ice water over the mixture, just enough to hold the dough together. Roll the pastry out, brush with butter, and cut it in half. Place the halves on top of each other and cut in half again. Repeat last step two more times, each time brushing the pastry with butter. Pile the pieces (there will be 16) on top of each other and chill at least 1 hour. Then roll the pastry and divide in half, using one portion to line a deep medium-sized baking dish. Reserve the other portion for the top. Refrigerate both while you make the filling.

To make the filling: Mix together sugar, cinnamon, salt, and nutmeg. Peel and core apples, then cut in thin slices. Mix thoroughly with sugar-spice combination and pile into pastry-lined baking dish. Combine molasses or maple syrup with melted butter and water. Pour over the apples. Cover with pastry and seal. Place in a preheated 400° oven for 10 minutes, then reduce heat to 325°. At this point, "dowdy" the dessert by cutting the crust into the apples with a sharp, sturdy knife. Return to oven and bake for 1 hour. Serve hot with thick cream or ice cream. Serves 6.

PERSIMMON PUDDING

Early settlers found that the native American persimmon could "drawe a man's mouth awrie with much torment" if not properly ripe. Some dismissed the "pessemmins" as "a good kind of horse plomb," but they gradually became welcome ingredients for puddings, especially in the Middle West and the Carolinas.

2 to 3 very ripe persimmons
¾ cup brown sugar, firmly packed
1 cup milk
¼ cup butter, melted
1 cup sifted all-purpose flour

2 teaspoons baking powder
¼ teaspoon salt
¼ teaspoon cinnamon
Heavy cream

Peel persimmons and work through a sieve or blend in an electric blender. Measure one cup persimmon pulp and combine with brown sugar, milk, and butter. Sift together flour, baking powder, salt, and cinnamon and stir into persimmon pulp until smooth. Pour into a buttered 1½-quart baking dish and bake in a preheated 325° oven for about 1 hour or until pudding pulls away from sides of dish (surface should be soft). Serve warm or cold with whipped cream. Serves 4 to 6.

INDIAN PUDDING

In February, 1809, Mrs. Samuel Harrison Smith, a prominent figure in Washington society, recorded in a letter to her sister-in-law that one of her guests, a Mr. Hauto, "to our great entertainment, had some difficulty in making way with his indian pudding and molasses, but when I assured him that this dish was immortalized by the greatest poet of our country [Joel Barlow], he made out to mortalize it."

¼ cup corn meal
2 cups hot milk
¼ cup sugar
⅛ teaspoon baking soda
½ teaspoon salt
½ teaspoon ground ginger

½ teaspoon ground cinnamon
¼ cup molasses
1 cup cold milk
Whipped cream
Nutmeg

Stir corn meal, a little at a time, into the hot milk and cook over low heat or in the top of a double boiler, stirring constantly, for 15 minutes or until thick. Remove from heat. Mix together sugar, baking soda, salt, ginger, and cinnamon, then stir into the corn-meal mixture. Add molasses and cold milk, mixing thoroughly. Pour into a 1-quart casserole and bake in a preheated 275° oven for 2 hours. Serve warm with whipped cream and a light sprinkling of freshly grated nutmeg. Serves 6 to 8.

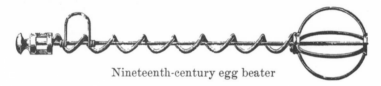

Nineteenth-century egg beater

CHARLOTTE RUSSE

The origin of the Charlotte Russe is fairly obscure, but it is generally thought to have been the creation of the famous French chef Carême. It was served at a banquet given at the White House during Van Buren's Presidency and was a popular dessert in the 1800's.

1 cup milk
1 envelope unflavored gelatin
2 tablespoons cold water
4 egg yolks
½ cup sugar

¼ teaspoon salt
Grated rind of 1 lemon
¼ cup lemon juice
6 ladyfingers, split
1 cup heavy cream

Scald milk. Sprinkle gelatin over cold water to soften. Mix together egg yolks, sugar, and salt. Pour hot milk, a little at a time, over the yolk mixture, beating hard all the time. Cook over a low heat, stirring constantly, until mixture is smooth and slightly thickened. Remove from heat, add gelatin, and stir until dissolved. Stir in lemon rind and juice, then refrigerate until cold but not set. Line a 1-quart mold or bowl with ladyfingers, placing some on the bottom and the remainder upright around the sides. Some of the ladyfingers may have to be cut to make them fit. Beat heavy cream until it holds a shape, fold into gelatin mixture gently, and pour into mold. Chill 2 to 3 hours or until firm. To serve, unmold on a crystal or silver platter or cake stand. Serves 6.

PLUM PUDDING

3 cups fine bread crumbs, one day old
½ teaspoon salt
¾ teaspoon ground cinnamon
½ teaspoon ground nutmeg
¼ teaspoon ground cloves
⅔ cup brown sugar, firmly packed
¾ cup milk, scalded
6 eggs, well beaten
⅓ pound suet, ground

1½ cups raisins
½ cup currants
¼ cup candied orange peel, chopped
¼ cup candied lemon peel, chopped
¼ cup candied citron, chopped
¼ cup dates, chopped
½ cup tart apples, chopped
¼ cup rum, brandy, or cider

Combine crumbs with salt, spices, and brown sugar. Stir in the scalded milk and cool. Mix in eggs and suet, then add all the fruits and rum, brandy, or cider. Work mixture with your hands to distribute fruit evenly. Place in a greased 2-quart mold. Seal securely with lid or foil and stand on a rack in the bottom of a kettle. Add enough boiling water to cover the mold halfway. Cover kettle tightly and steam over a low heat for 5 to 6 hours. Add more boiling water when necessary. Serve warm with Hard Sauce (page 163). Makes 12 servings.

SNOW EGGS

Oeufs à la neige, or Snow Eggs, as they were referred to at Monticello, are best known in this country as Floating Island. Jefferson's cook James used rose or orange-flower water in this recipe rather than the almond extract indicated here.

1 cup milk
1 cup light cream
3 egg whites
Dash of salt
½ cup sugar

1 teaspoon almond extract
4 egg yolks
½ cup sugar
½ teaspoon vanilla

Heat milk and cream in a shallow pan. Meanwhile, beat the egg whites with a dash of salt until they stand in peaks. Beat in the sugar a little at a time, then add the almond extract. With a dessert spoon, scoop out egg-shaped portions of the meringue. Remove milk from heat and drop the meringue "eggs" into the hot milk. (Cook only a few at a time.) Return pan to very low heat. Poach meringues for 2 to 4 minutes, turning them once with great care. With a slotted spoon lift the firm snow eggs out of the milk and onto a tea towel.

To make the custard: Beat the egg yolks with sugar until well mixed. Flavor with vanilla. Then add the cream-hot-milk mixture in a thin, steady stream, stirring constantly. Place over boiling water and cook, stirring constantly, until custard is thick enough to coat a wooden spoon. Takes about 15 minutes. Chill.

To serve, pour custard into a crystal bowl and arrange the snow eggs on top. Serves 4.

VARIATION: To make Snow Eggs in the Victorian manner, make the custard in the recipe above but do not poach the meringue eggs. Instead, after beating the egg whites until they stand in stiff peaks, beat in, a little at a time, about ⅓ cup of raspberry or strawberry preserves. Spoon little mounds of the mixture onto the chilled custard.

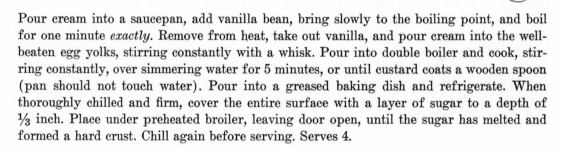

CRÈME BRÛLÉE

This recipe is adapted from one used by Julien, Thomas Jefferson's French cook in Washington. At that time, before broilers came into general use, the crust was glazed by passing a hot shovel or a salamander (shown at right) over it.

2 cups heavy cream
1 inch of vanilla bean

4 egg yolks, well beaten
Maple or brown sugar

Pour cream into a saucepan, add vanilla bean, bring slowly to the boiling point, and boil for one minute *exactly*. Remove from heat, take out vanilla, and pour cream into the well-beaten egg yolks, stirring constantly with a whisk. Pour into double boiler and cook, stirring constantly, over simmering water for 5 minutes, or until custard coats a wooden spoon (pan should not touch water). Pour into a greased baking dish and refrigerate. When thoroughly chilled and firm, cover the entire surface with a layer of sugar to a depth of ⅓ inch. Place under preheated broiler, leaving door open, until the sugar has melted and formed a hard crust. Chill again before serving. Serves 4.

POTS DE CRÈME

2 cups light cream
½ pound sweet chocolate, grated
Dash of salt

6 egg yolks, slightly beaten
1 tablespoon cognac or rum

Combine cream, chocolate, and salt in a saucepan. Cook over a low heat, stirring constantly, until mixture is thoroughly blended and cream is scalded. Pour this hot mixture, a little at a time, into the egg yolks, beating hard. Pour into mousse pots or into a large crystal or silver dessert bowl and place in the refrigerator for several hours or until firm. Serves 6 to 8.

SISTER ABIGAIL'S STRAWBERRY FLUMMERY

The Shakers were unusually attentive to the needs of their elders, and they developed a special diet, and special dishes, for the aged. This recipe is among the more popular of those dishes.

3 cups milk
⅓ cup cornstarch
5 tablespoons sugar
¼ teaspoon salt

1 egg, well beaten
½ teaspoon rose water or vanilla
1 quart fresh strawberries, raspberries,
    loganberries, or blueberries

Scald *2¼ cups of the milk*. Mix cornstarch, sugar, and salt in a bowl, then add remaining milk, a little at a time. When smooth, combine with scalded milk and cook over a moderate heat, stirring constantly, until thick and bubbly. Remove from heat and gradually beat a small amount into the egg. Blend with remaining mixture, add rose water or vanilla, and cook over a low heat for 2 minutes, stirring constantly. Pour into a 1-quart mold and chill until firm. Unmold on serving platter and surround with sweetened berries. Serves 4 to 6.

PEACH CHARLOTTE

2 envelopes unflavored gelatin
2 cups milk
4 eggs, separated
½ cup sugar
¼ teaspoon salt

1 cup heavy cream
Ladyfingers
Fresh or brandied peach halves
Brandy Sauce (page 163)

Sprinkle gelatin over ¼ cup cold water to soften. Scald milk in the top of a double boiler. Beat egg yolks vigorously, adding sugar and salt a little at a time. Pour in a little of the hot milk, beating constantly. Pour back into milk and cook over boiling water until thick enough to coat a wooden spoon. Remove from heat and stir in gelatin until dissolved. Cool, then fold in stiffly beaten egg whites and whipped cream. Line a greased 1½-quart mold with ladyfingers, pour in the charlotte mixture, and chill until firm. Turn out onto serving platter and garnish with fresh or brandied peach halves. Serve with Brandy Sauce to 6.

BAKED HONEY CUSTARD

Refined, white sugar was a scarce and high-priced commodity on the American frontier, and many families substituted tree-sweetenin', bee-sweetenin', and molasses. Sugar and syrup were made from maple trees, and honey came from beehives, which were common around frontier households. Honeybees were unknown in the New World until the early 1600's, but they soon became indispensable and gave rise to dessert recipes like this one.

2 cups milk
4 tablespoons honey
3 eggs

¼ teaspoon salt
Sprinkle of mace or nutmeg

Scald milk, then stir in the honey. Beat eggs and salt together, then slowly beat in a little of the hot milk mixture. Combine the two and pour into 6 custard cups, scattering a little mace or nutmeg on top of each. Set cups in a pan of hot water and bake in a preheated 375° oven for 30 to 40 minutes. When a knife inserted in center comes out dry, the custard is cooked. Remove cups from water immediately and serve cold. Serves 6.

GOOSEBERRY FOOL

1 quart ripe gooseberries, strawberries,
  blackberries, or raspberries
1 cup sugar

1½ teaspoons grated lemon rind
1½ cups heavy cream
½ cup crumbled macaroons

Combine the berries with ¼ cup of water in a saucepan. Cook over a low heat until fruit is extremely tender. Remove from heat and work through a sieve to make a smooth purée. While hot, stir in sugar and lemon rind. Set aside to cool. Whip cream until it holds a shape, then fold into the cool fruit purée. Spoon into a serving bowl, sprinkle surface with macaroon crumbs, and chill thoroughly. Serves 6.

157

SNOWBALLS

Pastry for a 2-crust pie (page 164)
6 large apples
Orange marmalade
¼ cup soft butter
½ cup brown sugar

4 teaspoons cinnamon
1 teaspoon allspice
1 teaspoon nutmeg
Hard Sauce (page 163)

Prepare pastry and roll out thin on a floured board. Cut into 6 squares large enough to cover the apples. Pare apples, leave whole, but remove the core. Fill each cavity with orange marmalade. Make a smooth paste of butter, brown sugar, and the three spices. Spread this paste over each apple. Wrap apples in pastry squares, pricking surface here and there with a fork. Bake in a preheated 425° oven for 15 minutes, then reduce heat to 350°, and continue baking 40 to 45 minutes. Serve warm with Hard Sauce.

ICE CREAM

What is perhaps the first written comment on ice cream in America comes from a letter written in 1744 by William Black, a guest of Thomas Bladen, proprietary governor of Maryland. Black wrote, "You saw a plain proof of the Great Plenty of the Country, a Table in the most Splendent manner set out with Great Variety of Dishes, all serv'd up in the most Elegant way, after which came a Dessert no less Curious; Among the Rarities . . . was some fine Ice Cream which, with the Strawberries and Milk, eat most Deliciously."

Ice cream is believed to be a Chinese invention. Originating as "water ices" some 3,000 years ago, it was brought to the West by Marco Polo. Its lineage and literature are imposing. In America, George Washington made it; Mrs. Alexander Hamilton served it; Dolley Madison popularized it. Ice cream was often served at elaborate dinners as the *pièce de résistance;* at Madison's second inaugural ball, in 1812, the climactic moment was marked by the serving of ice cream. The cream came from the President's dairy at Montpelier, and strawberries from Mrs. Madison's garden topped the dish.

By the early 1900's, millions of Americans ate ice cream in cones, sodas, sundaes, and out of bucket freezers. The old pot freezer (in which the ingredients were beaten by hand and then shaken up and down in a pan of ice and salt until frozen) disappeared in 1846 when Nancy Johnson invented the hand-cranked portable ice cream freezer. In 1851, Jacob Fussell, a milk dealer in Baltimore, set up the first large wholesale ice cream business. In 1874, according to legend, the ice cream soda was introduced at the semicentennial of the Franklin Institute in Philadelphia; the ice cream cone reputedly was originated at the St. Louis fair in 1904. The sundae (originally an ice cream soda without soda) came into being to skirt a law prohibiting the sale of "stimulating beverages" on Sunday.

VANILLA ICE CREAM

¾ cup light cream
¼ cup sugar
Dash of salt

2 egg yolks
1 tablespoon vanilla
1 cup heavy cream

Refrigerator method: Scald the light cream, remove from heat, stir in sugar and salt. Beat egg yolks lightly, then beat in a little of the hot cream. Pour back into cream and cook over a low heat, stirring constantly, until the custard will coat a wooden spoon (cooking the custard in the top of a double boiler is less tricky). Remove from heat, stir in vanilla, and cool. When cool, fold in stiffly beaten heavy cream and pour into an ice cube tray. Set temperature control at coldest point and freeze until firm. Serves 4.

Freezer method: Double, triple, or even quadruple the ingredients (depending on the size of your freezer). Prepare custard as above, then cool. Stir in vanilla and *unbeaten* heavy cream. Follow usual freezing technique.

VARIATION I: To make strawberry ice cream, omit vanilla. Instead add 1 cup crushed fresh strawberries or 1 package frozen strawberries, thawed, drained, and crushed. Fold into cream before mixing with custard. Any fresh fruit may be substituted for the strawberries.

VARIATION II: To make chocolate ice cream, melt 1 square (1 ounce) unsweetened chocolate in the light cream when you make the custard.

GREENGAGE ICE CREAM

1 can (1 pound, 3 ounce size) greengage plums
Juice of 1 lemon
1 cup sugar

¼ teaspoon salt
1 cup milk
1 cup heavy cream

Drain plums, remove pits, and work the fruit through a sieve or blend in an electric blender. Combine the plum purée with lemon juice, sugar, salt, and milk. Stir until sugar is dissolved. Beat cream until stiff, then fold into the plum mixture gently but thoroughly. Pour into an ice cube tray and freeze until firm but not solid. Serves 4 to 6.

CRANBERRY ICE

Outlining his prescription for a successful dinner party in *Society As I Have Found It,* Ward McAllister recommended serving a sorbet, or ice, as a refreshing diversion between courses. This ice can also be served as a dessert after smaller dinners.

Cook 2 cups fresh cranberries in 1 quart water until the berries pop. Then work through a sieve. Measure out 1½ quarts of liquid, add 2 cups of sugar, and cook until sugar has dissolved. Remove from heat and stir in 1 teaspoon unflavored gelatin which has been soaked in ¼ cup cold water. Pour into two ice cube trays and freeze until sherbet is mushy. Spoon into a bowl and beat with a rotary or electric beater until smooth. Pour back into ice trays and freeze until firm. Serves 8.

NESSELRODE PUDDING

This dessert was, according to legend, created by the chef to the Comte de Nesselrode. A number of different versions of it have been popular in this country; this one is similar to Ward McAllister's.

1 pint light cream
4 egg yolks
½ cup sugar
Chestnut purée (below) or
    1 can (8¾-ounce size) chestnut purée
¼ cup Malaga or sherry

½ cup currants
¼ cup seedless raisins
½ cup sugar
½ cup water
¾ cup heavy cream

Scald light cream. Beat egg yolks in a bowl, then beat in ½ cup sugar, a little at a time. Add scalded cream gradually and pour back into saucepan. Cook over a very low heat, stirring constantly, until custard will coat a wooden spoon. Remove from heat, then stir in chestnut purée and Malaga or sherry. Freeze the mixture (preferably in an ice cream freezer—if the mixture is not firmly frozen, the fruit, when added, will sink to the bottom). Cook currants, raisins, sugar, and water together over a moderate heat until the fruit becomes plump and the syrup thickens. Beat heavy cream until stiff. Stir the fruit and whipped cream into the frozen custard. Pack mixture into a melon or charlotte mold, cover, seal securely, and freeze until firm. This can be done in a freezer or the mold can be placed in a container of ice and salt (4 to 6 parts ice to 1 part rock salt). Unmold on a platter and serve well chilled. The pudding may be garnished with *marrons glacés* and whipped cream. Serves 6 to 8. Chopped candied fruit may be substituted for raisins and currants.

To make chestnut purée: Remove shell and inner brown skin from 20 plump chestnuts. Cook in a mixture of 1½ cups water, ½ cup sugar, and about 1 inch of vanilla bean. When tender, drain off most of the syrup and purée in a blender or work through a sieve.

Nineteenth-century mousse and pudding molds

MAPLE MOUSSE

½ cup pure maple syrup
2 eggs, separated

Pinch of salt
1 cup heavy cream

Heat maple syrup over a low heat until beads appear around the edge of the syrup. Separate eggs and place yolks in the top of a double boiler. Beat yolks vigorously, then add the heated syrup, a little at a time, beating hard all the while. Place over simmering water and cook, beating constantly with a rotary or electric beater, until the mixture will coat a wooden spoon, about 8 to 10 minutes. Cool completely. While maple combination cools, beat egg whites, with a pinch of salt added, until they stand in peaks. Beat heavy cream until stiff. Combine maple mixture, egg whites, and cream, folding gently until well blended. Pour into an ice cube tray and freeze about 1½ hours or until firm but not solid. Serves 6.

BAKED ALASKA

The idea of encasing ice cream in hot pastry was current long before the "Alaska"—as it was called on the menu at Delmonico's—was known. In 1802, a guest of President Jefferson's wrote that dessert at a White House dinner consisted of "Ice-cream very good, crust wholly dried, crumbled into thin flakes." And Benjamin Thompson, the American-born scientist who later became Count Rumford in England, laid claim to the creation of a meringue-topped ice cream, stating that his "omelette surprise" was the by-product of investigations in 1804 into the resistance of stiffly beaten egg whites to the induction of heat. As the idea of combining ice cream with warm pastry or meringue spread, and variations on the dessert were developed, it became known at first as Alaska-Florida, and later as Baked Alaska. George Augustus Sala, an Englishman who visited Delmonico's in the 1880's, reported: "The 'Alaska' is *a baked ice*. . . . The nucleus or core of the *entremet* is an ice cream. This is surrounded by an envelope of carefully whipped cream, which, just before the dainty dish is served, is popped into the oven, or is brought under the scorching influence of a red hot salamander. . . . So you go on discussing the warm cream *soufflé* till you come, with somewhat painful suddenness, on the row of ice. E'en so did the Shepherd in Virgil grow acquainted with love, and find him a native of the rocks."

Cover a thick plank, such as a bread board or chopping board, with a piece of heavy paper. Place a layer of spongecake or poundcake, cut at least 1 inch thick, on the paper. Then place a solid 1-quart brick of ice cream in the center of the cake. The cake should be large enough to extend at least ½ inch beyond the ice cream all around. Cover completely with a thick coating of meringue. Place in a preheated 500° oven for 3 to 5 minutes or until meringue is touched with gold. Serve at once to 6 or 8.

To make the meringue: Beat 4 egg whites with a dash of salt until they hold a soft shape. Add 1 cup sugar, a little at a time, and continue beating until meringue stands in peaks.

─────

A DISH OF SNOW

3 egg whites
3 tablespoons confectioners' sugar, sifted
1 cup heavy cream
1 tablespoon rose water
1 fresh coconut, grated, or
  2 cans (4-ounce size) coconut

Beat the egg whites until they stand in peaks, then beat in the sugar, a tablespoon at a time (if not sweet enough, sift in a little more sugar). Beat cream in a separate bowl until very stiff, then mix in the rose water. Gently combine egg whites and whipped cream, making certain they are well mixed. This must be done at the very last minute—the mixture won't stand up for any length of time. Heap the coconut in the center of a silver or crystal bowl and "ornament," as they used to do, "with fine leaves such as peach or honeysuckle." Spoon the sauce over the coconut and serve at once.

MINNEHAHA SAUCE

4 tablespoons butter
⅔ cup brown sugar

¼ cup heavy cream
Grated rind and juice of 1 lemon

Blend together, in the top of a double boiler, the butter, brown sugar, heavy cream, and lemon rind and juice. Cook over boiling water, beating constantly, until sauce is a creamy froth. Serve with a simple dessert. Makes about 1½ cups.

STRAWBERRY SAUCE

Beat 1 egg white until it stands in peaks. Add 1 cup mashed strawberries (fresh or frozen), and continue beating until mixture looks fluffy. Gradually beat in 1 cup confectioners' sugar and 2 tablespoons butter, beating until sauce is light and airy. Serve over a simple, not-too-sweet dessert or use as a topping for shortcake. Makes about 2 cups.

MAPLE PECAN SAUCE

Cook ¾ cup maple syrup over a moderate heat for 6 to 8 minutes or until syrup thickens slightly. Remove from heat and stir in ½ cup coarsely chopped pecans or walnuts. Serve warm over ice cream. Makes about 1 cup.

BUTTERSCOTCH SAUCE

Melt ⅓ cup butter over low heat. Stir in 1 cup brown sugar (firmly packed), 2 tablespoons light corn syrup, and ½ cup heavy cream. Cook to the boiling point. Remove from heat and cool slightly before serving. Serve over ice cream or with unfrosted cakes or plain custards.

CARAMEL SAUCE

Combine ½ pound caramel candies with 1 cup heavy cream in top of double boiler. Cook over hot water, stirring frequently, until well blended. Makes 1½ cups.

CHOCOLATE NUT SAUCE

Heat ¼ cup butter in a heavy skillet, add 1 cup coarsely chopped nuts (walnuts, pecans, cashews, peanuts, slivered Brazil nuts, or filberts), and sauté until well browned. Remove from heat and stir in 1 package (6-ounce size) semi-sweet chocolate pieces until melted. Serve warm over vanilla or coffee ice cream. Makes 1¼ cups.

LEMON SAUCE

Mix ⅓ cup sugar and 1 tablespoon cornstarch together in a saucepan. Add 1 cup water and cook, stirring constantly, until mixture bubbles. Simmer gently for a few minutes, then remove from heat. Stir in 3 tablespoons butter, ½ teaspoon grated lemon rind, 1½ tablespoons fresh lemon juice, and a pinch of salt. Serve hot with pudding.

NEW ENGLAND NUTMEG SAUCE

Mix together 1 cup sugar and 1 tablespoon flour. Stir in 1 cup boiling water and cook, stirring constantly, until sauce bubbles and thickens slightly. Add 1 tablespoon butter and simmer gently for 5 minutes. Remove from heat and stir in 1 teaspoon nutmeg. Serve hot.

HARD SAUCE

Cream ⅓ cup of butter until soft. Add, a little at a time, 1 cup confectioners' sugar and either 1 teaspoon of vanilla or 2 tablespoons cognac or rum, stirring until smooth. Serve cold with steamed puddings or on apple pie.

BRANDY SAUCE

½ cup milk	2 tablespoons sugar
½ cup heavy cream	Dash of salt
2 eggs, separated	3 tablespoons brandy

Scald milk and cream together in the top of a double boiler. Beat egg yolks until light in color, then beat in sugar, a little at a time, and salt. Add milk-cream mixture gradually, beating constantly. Pour back into double boiler and cook over boiling water until sauce thickens enough to coat a wooden spoon. Remove from heat, stir in brandy, then pour over stiffly beaten egg whites, beating vigorously. Cool before serving.

SAUCE MELBA

1 cup raspberries (fresh or frozen)	1 tablespoon cornstarch
½ cup sugar	1 tablespoon water
½ cup currant jelly	Slivered almonds

If fresh berries are used, wash and drain; if frozen, thaw. Place berries and sugar in a saucepan, mash with a fork, add the currant jelly, and cook over a low heat until mixture begins to bubble. Combine cornstarch with water to make a smooth paste. Stir into berries and cook until clear and slightly thickened. Strain and cool. Spoon over ice cream and strew with toasted slivered almonds.

To make Peach Melba: Cut peaches in half, and fill each half with vanilla ice cream. Spoon some of the sauce over them.

PIES

PASTRY FOR PIE CRUST

2 cups all-purpose flour
1 teaspoon salt

⅔ cup shortening
5 to 6 tablespoons ice water

Sift flour and salt together in a bowl. Cut in shortening with a pastry blender or two knives until mixture looks mealy. Sprinkle water over mixture (the less water you use, the better your pastry). Mix lightly with a fork, then work the pastry with your hands until it can be formed into a ball. Chill thoroughly. Divide in half and roll one portion at a time on a lightly floured board. Using light strokes, start in the center and roll toward the edge. When dough is about ⅛ inch thick, line a 9-inch pie pan, pressing pastry to bottom and sides. Refrigerate both parts while you prepare the filling.

To make pastry for a 1-crust pie: Follow directions given above, cutting the ingredients in half. To prepare a baked pastry shell, line a 9-inch pie pan with the pastry and bake in a preheated 450° oven for 12 to 15 minutes.

LEMON MERINGUE PIE

Pastry for a 1-crust pie (above)
1 cup sugar
Dash of salt
¼ cup flour
3 tablespoons cornstarch
2 cups water
3 egg yolks, beaten

1 tablespoon butter
Grated rind of 1 lemon
¼ cup lemon juice
Meringue:
3 egg whites
¼ teaspoon cream of tartar
6 tablespoons sugar

Prepare pastry, line a 9-inch pie pan, and bake in a preheated 450° oven for 12 to 15 minutes. Cool. Mix sugar, salt, flour, and cornstarch in a saucepan, stir in water, a little at a time, and cook over a low heat, stirring constantly, until mixture is thick and bubbly. Stir a little into egg yolks, very gradually, continuing to beat hard. Combine with the hot mixture and cook over a very low heat for about 2 minutes. Remove from heat and stir in butter, lemon rind, and juice. Cool for about 10 minutes, then pour into baked pastry shell, and cool completely. Pile the meringue on the cool lemon filling, spreading it until it touches rim of pastry all around the edge. Bake in a preheated 425° oven for 5 to 7 minutes or until top is lightly browned.

To make meringue: Beat egg whites until frothy, then add cream of tartar, and continue beating until whites hold a soft shape. Beat in the sugar, a little at a time, beating vigorously until meringue is satiny and stiff enough to stand in peaks.

KEY LIME PIE

Condensed milk was first manufactured in 1858, and after the Civil War it was a godsend to the devastated South. In Key West, Florida, it was not only a sorely needed food but the inspiration for this famous pie recipe.

Pastry for a 1-crust pie (page 164)
3 eggs, separated
1 can condensed milk

¾ cup fresh lime juice
6 tablespoons sugar

Line a 9-inch pie pan with pastry. Bake in a preheated 450° oven for 12 to 15 minutes, then cool. Beat egg yolks and condensed milk together, then beat in lime juice until smooth. Pour this uncooked filling into baked pie shell. Beat egg whites until they hold a shape, then beat in sugar, a little at a time, until meringue stands in peaks. Spoon meringue over top of filling, spreading it to the edge of the pastry all around. Bake in a preheated 425° oven for 5 to 7 minutes or until meringue is touched with gold. Cool before serving. Do not refrigerate. Some people prefer whipped cream to the meringue, in which case the pie should not be baked.

PEACH CRAB LANTERN

A writer in 1801 stated: "Had some peaches stewed in order to make Crab Lanterns for dinner." Crab Lanterns was the common name for fried peach pies, shaped like half-moons.

3 fresh peaches
½ cup sugar
½ cup water
½ teaspoon ground cinnamon
1 cup sifted all-purpose flour
2 tablespoons sugar
2 teaspoons baking powder

¼ teaspoon salt
¼ cup butter
1 egg yolk
3 tablespoons milk (about)
Fat for deep-fat frying
Confectioners' sugar

Skin peaches (skin will slip off easily if you let peaches stand in boiling water a few minutes), remove pits, and cut in slices about ½ inch thick. Cook sugar and water together for several minutes, then add peach slices and cinnamon. Continue cooking about 2 minutes, shaking the pan back and forth almost constantly. Remove from heat and cool. Sift together flour, sugar, baking powder, and salt into a bowl. Cut in butter with a pastry blender or two knives. Mix egg yolk and milk together, then stir into flour combination with a fork, adding only enough liquid to hold the dough together. Turn out on a floured board, divide in half, and roll, one portion at a time, about as thick as pie pastry. Cut into circles the size of a large coffee cup. Drain peach slices and place several slices on half the circle. Fold over the other half; then, with fork tines, seal edges and prick tops. Refrigerate. Heat fat to 350° on deep-fat thermometer or until a 1-inch cube of bread browns in 60 seconds. Fry the pies until they are a light, tempting brown. Drain on paper towels and sprinkle with confectioners' sugar. Applesauce (page 141), Mincemeat (page 169), Prune Filling (*see* Kolaches, page 23), stewed fruits, or preserves may be substituted for the peach filling. Makes 12.

APPLE PIE

An immigrant living in Beloit, Wisconsin, wrote on November 29, 1851, to friends back in Norway: "Strawberries, raspberries, and blackberries thrive here. From these they make a wonderful dish combined with syrup and sugar, which is called *pai*. I can tell you that is something that glides easily down your throat; they also make the same sort of *pai* out of apples or finely ground meat, with syrup added, and that is really the most superb." A hundred years earlier, in 1758, a Swedish parson named Dr. Acrelius had written home: "Apple-pie is used through the whole year, and when fresh apples are no longer to be had, dried ones are used. It is the evening meal of children. House-pie, in country places, is made of apples neither peeled nor freed from their cores, and its crust is not broken if a wagon wheel goes over it."

Apple Pie is what some things are as American as, and it has, in various forms, been eaten for breakfast, for an entree, and for dessert. Some of the first orchards in New England were planted by William Blaxton, a clergyman who owned, for a time, a farm on Beacon Hill. He moved to Rhode Island in 1635 and raised what is now called the Sweet Rhode Island greening—the first apple, as a distinct type, to be grown in the United States.

Pastry for a 2-crust pie (page 164)
4 large greenings (peeled, cored, and sliced very thin)
1 cup sugar
¼ teaspoon salt

½ teaspoon cinnamon (optional)
Grated rind of ½ lemon
1 tablespoon lemon juice
Butter
Cream

Prepare the pastry. Divide in half, line a 9-inch pie pan with one portion, and save the remainder for the top. Refrigerate both while you make the filling. Measure the sliced apples. You should have about 4 cups. Mix apple slices with sugar, salt, cinnamon (if you use it), lemon rind, and lemon juice. Arrange a row inside chilled pastry shell, about one-half inch from edge, and work toward center until shell is covered. Pile remaining slices on top. Dot with butter and cover with top crust, slashed in several places. Seal edges securely and crimp. Bake in a preheated 450° oven for 10 minutes. Reduce heat to 350° and bake 30 to 35 minutes. Five minutes before pie has finished baking, brush top with cream and sprinkle generously with sugar. Serve warm or at room temperature with Cheddar cheese or ice cream.

MARLBOROUGH TART

Pastry for a 1-crust pie (page 164)
½ cup Applesauce (page 141)
½ cup sugar
⅔ cup light cream

Grated rind and juice of 1 lemon
¼ cup sherry
3 eggs, well beaten

Line a 9-inch pie pan with pastry. Refrigerate while you make the filling. Combine applesauce with sugar, cream, lemon rind, lemon juice, and sherry. Stir in the well-beaten eggs and pour into chilled pastry shell. Bake in a preheated 400° oven for 10 minutes. Reduce oven heat to 325° and bake 45 minutes. The filling will not become firm until the pie cools.

APPLE PIE WITH CHEDDAR PASTRY

But I, when I undress me
Each night, upon my knees
Will ask the Lord to bless me
With apple-pie and cheese.
—Eugene Field, "Apple-Pie and Cheese"

1⅔ cups sifted all-purpose flour
¼ teaspoon salt
1 cup grated Cheddar cheese,
  loosely packed

½ cup shortening
¼ cup ice water
Filling for Apple Pie (page 166)

Sift flour and salt together, then work in the cheese thoroughly with a fork. Work in the shortening, then add the water, sprinkling it over the surface of the mixture. Stir lightly with a fork until pastry holds together. Divide pastry in half and line a 9-inch pie pan with one portion, saving the other for the top crust. Refrigerate both while you make the Apple Pie filling. Bake as directed for Apple Pie.

MARK TWAIN'S MUSH APPLE PIE

Pour cold Applesauce (page 141) into an unbaked 9-inch pastry shell (page 164), cover with thinly rolled pastry slashed in several places, seal edges securely, and crimp neatly. Bake in a preheated 450° oven for 20 minutes. Then reduce heat to 375° and bake 25 minutes or until crust is nicely browned. Serve warm with, if you wish, whipped or sweet cream.

COCONUT CUSTARD PIE

Pastry for a 1-crust pie (page 164)
Filling:
3 cups milk
1 cup sugar
4 tablespoons cornstarch
4 egg yolks
¼ cup butter
1½ cups grated coconut (fresh or canned)

1½ teaspoons vanilla
Meringue:
4 egg whites
½ teaspoon salt
¼ cup sugar
½ teaspoon vanilla
½ cup grated coconut (fresh or canned)

Line a 9-inch pie pan with pastry and bake in a preheated 450° oven 12 to 15 minutes. Pour coconut filling into chilled pastry shell. Cover with swirls of meringue and sprinkle ½ cup grated coconut on top. Bake in a preheated 425° oven for 5 to 6 minutes or until meringue is lightly browned.

To make the filling: Scald milk. Blend sugar and cornstarch together in the top of a double boiler. Pour in hot milk, a little at a time, and stir until smooth. Beat egg yolks in a bowl, then add the milk mixture, a little at a time. Pour back into top of double boiler and cook over boiling water, stirring constantly, until as thick as mayonnaise. Remove from heat and stir in butter, coconut, and vanilla. Cool.

To make meringue: Beat egg whites and salt together until they hold a soft shape. Beat in sugar, a little at a time, until meringue is smooth and stands in peaks. Stir in vanilla.

RHUBARB PIE

Setting forth her recipe for Rhubarb Pie in *The American Frugal Housewife,* Lydia Child cautioned: "These are dear pies, for they take an enormous quantity of sugar."

Pastry for a 2-crust pie (page 164)
3 cups sliced rhubarb
1½ cups sugar
2 tablespoons flour

¼ teaspoon salt
1 tablespoon lemon juice
2 egg yolks

Line a 9-inch pie pan with half the pastry. Save remaining pastry for top crust. Chill both while you prepare the filling. Cut rhubarb in slices about ½ inch thick and place in pie shell. Make a smooth paste of sugar, flour, salt, lemon juice, and slightly beaten egg yolks. Spoon on top of rhubarb and cover with top crust, slashed in several places. Bake in a preheated 400° oven for 20 minutes. Reduce heat to 350° and continue baking about 20 minutes or until pastry takes on a rich gold color. In some sections of the country rhubarb is known as pie plant.

PUMPKIN PIE

"Pumpkin pie," according to *The House Mother,* "if rightly made, is a thing of beauty and a joy—while it lasts....Pies that cut a little less firm than a pine board, and those that run round your plate are alike to be avoided. Two inches deep is better than the thin plasters one sometimes sees, that look for all the world like pumpkin flap-jacks. The expressive phrase, 'too thin', must have come from these lean parodies on pumpkin pie. With the pastry light, tender, and not too rich, and a generous filling of smooth spiced sweetness—a little 'trembly' as to consistency, and delicately brown on top—a perfect pumpkin pie, eaten before the life has gone out of it, is one of the real additions made by American cookery to the good things of the world. For the first pumpkin pie of the season, flanked by a liberal cut of creamy cheese, we prefer to sit down, as the French gourmand said about his turkey: 'with just two of us; myself and the turkey!'"

Pastry for a 1-crust pie (page 164)
2 cups cooked pumpkin (fresh, canned, or frozen)
⅔ cup brown sugar, firmly packed
2 teaspoons cinnamon
½ teaspoon ginger

½ teaspoon salt
¾ cup milk
2 eggs, well beaten
1 cup heavy cream
¼ cup brandy

Prepare pastry, line a 9-inch pie pan, and refrigerate while you make the filling. Combine pumpkin, sugar, spices, and salt in a mixing bowl. Then beat in milk, eggs, cream, and brandy with a rotary beater or an electric mixer. Pour into unbaked pastry shell and bake in a preheated 325° oven for 1 hour or until a knife inserted in center comes out dry. Cool. Serve plain, or with Cheddar cheese or whipped cream mixed with ginger (use 1 cup heavy cream and 2 tablespoons chopped crystallized ginger).

SUNNYSIDE MINCEMEAT PIE

This recipe is from the cookbook of Catherine Richardson, the daughter of Marion McLinden, who was in charge of the family kitchen at Sunnyside, Washington Irving's New York home.

2 pounds lean beef, ground
1 pound suet, ground
2 pounds sugar
5 pounds tart apples (pared, cored, and chopped)
2 pounds muscat raisins
1 pound currants
1 pound sultana raisins
½ pound citron, chopped

½ pound orange peel, chopped
1 tablespoon salt
1 teaspoon cinnamon
1 teaspoon allspice
1 teaspoon mace
1 quart boiled cider (about)
Brandy
Pastry for a 2-crust pie (page 164)

Mix beef, suet, sugar, fruit, salt, spices, and cider in a large kettle. Cover and simmer, stirring frequently, for 2 hours. Add cider if needed. Stir in brandy to taste. Pack into sterilized 1-quart jars, seal securely, store in a cool place, and allow to mellow at least 1 month before using. Makes 5 jars.

To make the pie: Line a 9-inch pie pan with pastry. Spoon in enough mincemeat to fill the pan and cover with remaining pastry, rolled thin. Seal securely and slash top in several places so steam can escape. Bake in a preheated 450° oven for 30 minutes. Serve warm.

SHOO-FLY PIE

There are many types of Pennsylvania Dutch Shoo-fly Pie. Those who dunk prefer a dry version like the recipe here. Others prefer what is called wet-bottom Shoo-fly. All varieties contain molasses, and the presence of molasses is responsible for one widely held theory about the way Shoo-fly Pie was named—that flies are partial to molasses and have to be chased away while the cook is making the pie.

Pastry for a 1-crust pie (page 164)
Crumb mixture:
1½ cups all-purpose flour
½ cup brown sugar, firmly packed
Pinch of salt
½ teaspoon cinnamon
Big pinch each ginger and nutmeg
¼ cup soft butter

Filling:
½ teaspoon baking soda
½ cup molasses
½ cup boiling water
⅔ of crumb mixture

Line an 8-inch pie pan with pastry. Refrigerate while you prepare the crumb mixture and filling. Combine flour with brown sugar, salt, and spices. Pinch in the butter until the mixture looks mealy. Set aside. Stir baking soda and molasses into boiling water. Add two-thirds of the crumb mixture and pour into the unbaked pie shell. Sprinkle top with remaining crumbs and bake in a preheated 375° oven for 30 to 40 minutes or until crust and crumbs are golden brown.

CHERRY PIE

Pastry for a 2-crust pie (page 164)
4 cups tart red cherries
2⅔ tablespoons quick-cooking tapioca
1¼ cups sugar

1 tablespoon lemon juice
¼ teaspoon almond extract
1½ tablespoons butter

Prepare pastry and line a 9-inch pie pan. Save remaining pastry for top and refrigerate both while you make the filling. Pit cherries and toss thoroughly with tapioca, sugar, lemon juice, and almond extract. Let stand about 10 minutes, then pour into unbaked pie shell, and dot with butter. Cover with top crust (or make a lattice top) and seal edges. Bake in a preheated 450° oven for 10 minutes. Reduce heat to 350° and continue baking 40 to 45 minutes.

To keepe Cherries yt [so that] you may have them for tarts at Christmas without Preserving: Take ye fayrest cherries you can get, fresh from ye trees, wth out bruising, wipe them one by one with a linnen cloth, yn [then] put ym [them] into a barrel of hay & lay them in ranks, first laying hay on the bottom, & then cherries & yn hay & yn cherries & then hay agayne, stop them close up yt noe ayre get to ym. then set them under a fether bead where one layeth continually for ye warmer they are kept ye better it is soe they be neere no fire. Thus doeing you may have cherries any time of ye yeare. You allsoe May keep Cherries or other fruits, in glasses close stopt from ayre.

—From Martha Washington's cookbook,
Collection of the Historical Society of Pennsylvania

VINEGAR PIE

Pastry for 1-crust pie (page 164)
¼ cup flour
½ teaspoon nutmeg
½ teaspoon cinnamon
½ teaspoon allspice
½ teaspoon cloves
Dash of salt
4 egg yolks

2 egg whites
1 cup sugar
1 cup commercial sour cream
3 tablespoons melted butter
3 tablespoons cider vinegar
1 cup coarsely chopped walnuts or pecans
1 cup raisins

Prepare pastry and line a 9-inch pie pan. Chill while you make the filling. Sift together flour, spices, and salt. Set aside. Beat egg yolks thoroughly. Wash and dry the beater, then beat the 2 whites until they stand in peaks. Gently fold sugar into egg whites and stir into yolks. Add flour mixture alternately with the sour cream. Combine butter, vinegar, nuts, and raisins and stir into the filling. Pour into pie shell and bake in a preheated 450° oven for 10 minutes. Reduce heat to 400° and bake 5 minutes. Then turn heat to 350°, and continue baking for about 15 minutes or until filling is set. Cool. May be served with whipped cream.

CHESS TARTS

Pastry for a 2-crust pie (page 164)
3 eggs
¾ cup sugar

Pinch of salt
2 tablespoons melted butter
Grated rind and juice of 1 lemon

Line 12 small fluted tart shells with pastry. Refrigerate while you make the filling. Beat the eggs vigorously, then add sugar and salt, beating until smooth. Stir in the butter, lemon rind, and juice. Spoon into chilled tart shells (fill them almost to the top of the pastry) and bake in a preheated 350° oven for 30 to 35 minutes or until tops are a pale gold color. Remove from oven and cool. The filling will sink slightly when tarts are completely cold.

BLACKBERRY PIE

Blackberries are cultivated in no other part of the world and, indeed, were not thought worth cultivating in this country until the 1830's. To the pioneers, blackberries were a nuisance, a weed spoken of in polite conversation only in terms of how it might best be removed. It crept hesitantly into the early cookbooks, frequently as a fruit for medicinal purposes ("Blackberry Syrup, for Cholera and Summer Complaint"). It was listed, however, as an alternate fruit to be used in some recipes, and gradually the weed became quite popular.

Pastry for a 2-crust pie (page 164)
4 cups fresh blackberries
3 tablespoons flour

1 cup sugar
1 tablespoon lemon juice
1 tablespoon butter

Line a 9-inch pie pan with half the pastry. Save remaining pastry for top crust. Chill both while preparing the blackberries. Combine berries, flour, sugar, and lemon juice. Spoon into pie shell and dot with butter. Cover with top crust slashed in several places. Bake in a preheated 450° oven for 15 minutes. Reduce heat to 350° and bake 35 to 40 minutes or until browned.

DEEP-DISH BLUEBERRY PIE

1 quart blueberries
1 cup sugar
3 tablespoons flour
1 tablespoon lemon juice

2 tablespoons butter
Pastry for a 1-crust pie (page 164) or
    Cream Biscuit dough (page 27)

In a deep pie dish, about 8 inches in diameter, toss berries with sugar and flour. Sprinkle with lemon juice and dot with butter. Cover with pastry or Cream Biscuit dough. Bake in a preheated 400° oven for 10 minutes, then reduce heat to 325°, and continue baking 15 to 20 minutes. Serve warm—either plain, with cream, or with vanilla ice cream.

SOUR CREAM RAISIN PIE

Pastry for a 1-crust pie (page 164)
2 eggs
¾ cup sugar
¼ teaspoon salt
1 teaspoon cinnamon

½ teaspoon nutmeg
¼ teaspoon cloves
1 cup commercial sour cream
1 cup seeded raisins

Prepare pastry and line an 8-inch pie pan. Refrigerate it while you make the filling. Beat eggs lightly, then stir in sugar, salt, cinnamon, nutmeg, and cloves. Stir in sour cream and raisins and pour into chilled pastry shell. Bake in a preheated 450° oven for 10 minutes, then reduce heat to 350°, and bake 30 minutes longer or until a knife inserted in center comes out dry. Serve warm.

CRANBERRY PIE

"I said my prayers and ate some cranberry tart for breakfast."
—From the diary of William Byrd, 1711

Pastry for a 2-crust pie (page 164)
3 cups fresh cranberries
1 cup raisins
2 tablespoons flour

1¼ cups sugar
½ cup water
1 teaspoon vanilla

Prepare pastry and line a 9-inch pie pan. Save remaining pastry for the top. Refrigerate both while you make the filling. Chop cranberries coarsely. Combine with raisins and all remaining ingredients. Place in chilled pie shell, cover with top crust (slashed in several places) and crimp edges together securely. Bake in a preheated 450° oven for 10 minutes. Then reduce oven temperature to 350° and continue baking a half hour longer. Cool before serving.

PECAN PIE

Pastry for a 1-crust pie (page 164)
3 eggs
¼ teaspoon salt
¾ cup sugar

½ cup melted butter
1 cup dark corn syrup
1½ cups pecan halves (about)

Prepare pastry, line a 9-inch pie pan, and bake in a preheated 450° oven for 5 minutes. Cool. Beat eggs and salt until very light and lemon colored. Beat in sugar a little at a time. With a wire whisk, fold in melted butter and syrup. Pour into partially baked shell and arrange pecan halves on top, broken side down. Bake for 10 minutes in a preheated 425° oven, reduce heat to 325°, and bake for 30 minutes. Serves 6 to 8. This pie can be baked in small fluted foil pans to make 8 to 10 individual pies. Reduce baking time slightly (bake until crust is golden).

SWEET POTATO PIE

Pastry for a 1-crust pie (page 164)
1¼ cups cooked, mashed sweet potatoes
½ cup brown sugar, firmly packed
½ teaspoon salt
¼ teaspoon cinnamon

2 eggs, well beaten
¾ cup milk
1 tablespoon melted butter
Pecan halves (optional)

Prepare pastry and line an 8-inch pie pan. Chill while you make the filling. Combine sweet potatoes, brown sugar, salt, and cinnamon in a bowl. Mix together eggs, milk, and butter and stir into sweet-potato mixture thoroughly. Pour into chilled pastry shell and arrange a circle of pecans around the edge. Bake in a preheated 400° oven for 45 minutes or until a knife comes out dry when inserted in the center.

CONCORD GRAPE TART

The grape has been the subject of more horticultural experiments than any other fruit in America: more than two thousand varieties had been introduced to America by the end of the nineteenth century. Possibly the most famous and most valuable of all varieties was the Concord grape, first planted in Concord, Massachusetts, by Ephraim W. Bull in 1849. In the century following its introduction, more Concord grapes were sold in the United States than all other species combined.

2 cups sifted all-purpose flour
½ teaspoon salt
¼ teaspoon baking powder
1 cup sugar
½ cup (1 stick) butter

4 cups Concord grapes
3 tablespoons flour
1 tablespoon lemon juice
2 egg yolks
1 cup commercial sour cream

Sift together flour, salt, baking powder, and *2 tablespoons of the sugar*. Pinch in butter with your finger tips until it appears mealy. Lift into an 8-inch square baking pan and press an even layer on bottom and about two-thirds of the way up the sides. Refrigerate until filling is prepared. Pinch off grape skins, separating pulp from skins. Cook pulp over a low heat for 7 minutes. Remove from heat and work thoroughly through a sieve (this is an easy way to remove the seeds). Combine pulp purée with grape skins, flour, remaining sugar, and lemon juice. Pour into prepared pastry and bake in a preheated 400° oven for 15 minutes. Mix egg yolks and sour cream together, then pour over the surface, and continue baking 25 to 30 minutes. Serve at room temperature. Serves 6.

CAKES

OLD-FASHIONED SEEDCAKE

2 cups sifted all-purpose flour
¼ teaspoon salt
¼ teaspoon nutmeg
1 cup (2 sticks) butter
1 cup sugar

2 teaspoons caraway seeds
6 eggs, separated
2 tablespoons brandy
Caraway comfits (sugared caraway seeds) or
    lump sugar, crushed

Sift together the flour, salt, and nutmeg. Set aside. Work butter until creamy, then gradually work in the sugar until mixture looks and feels fluffy. Stir in caraway seeds and beat in egg yolks, one at a time, beating hard after each addition. Add flour and brandy, alternately, and fold in the stiffly beaten egg whites, gently but thoroughly. Spoon batter into a greased and lightly floured 9-inch tube pan. Sprinkle caraway comfits or coarsely crushed lump sugar on top. Bake in a preheated 350° oven for 1 hour or until cake pulls away from sides of pan. Cool in pan about 10 minutes, then turn out onto cake rack, and cool completely. A day or two of mellowing, with the cake tightly wrapped, develops the delicious caraway flavor.

HONEY UPSIDE DOWN CAKE

Topping:
½ cup honey
¼ cup butter
4 to 5 cooking apples
Maraschino cherries
Cake batter:
1½ cups sifted all-purpose flour
1 teaspoon baking powder
¼ teaspoon baking soda
¼ teaspoon cinnamon

½ teaspoon nutmeg
Dash ginger
½ cup (1 stick) soft butter
¾ cup honey
1 egg
½ cup milk
Sauce:
½ cup honey
½ cup (1 stick) butter

To make the topping: Put honey and butter in a heavy 10-inch skillet (one that can go into the oven). Cook over a low heat until butter has melted. Core unpared apples and slice about ½ inch thick. Arrange enough of these slices in the honey mixture to fit comfortably. Simmer gently, turning once, until apples are partly cooked. Put a cherry in the center of each apple ring. Set aside for a moment.

To make the batter: Sift flour with baking powder, baking soda, cinnamon, nutmeg, and ginger. Set aside. Beat butter and honey together vigorously. Add the egg and beat thoroughly. Stir in flour mixture and milk alternately. Pour over apple rings and bake in a preheated 350° oven for 40 to 45 minutes or until a toothpick inserted in the center comes out dry. Turn upside down on a large platter and serve hot or cold with the sauce on the side.

To make the sauce: Combine honey with butter and heat until butter has melted. Do not boil.

KENTUCKY BOURBON CAKE

¾ pound (3 sticks) butter
2 cups white sugar
2¼ cups light brown sugar, firmly packed
6 eggs
5½ cups sifted all-purpose flour

¼ teaspoon salt
1 teaspoon mace
2 cups bourbon whiskey
3½ cups (1 pound) pecan meats

Cream butter until soft in your largest mixing bowl. Combine white and brown sugar thoroughly. Gradually work half the sugar mixture into butter, keeping it as smooth as possible. In a separate bowl beat eggs until light and fluffy. Then gradually beat in remaining sugar until you have a smooth, creamy mixture. Stir into butter mixture thoroughly. Sift flour, salt, and mace together. Add flour combination and whiskey to batter, alternating them and beginning and ending with flour. Break pecans into pieces and stir into batter. Pour into a well-greased 10-inch tube pan (batter should almost fill the pan) and bake in a preheated 300° oven for 1½ to 1¾ hours or until cake shrinks slightly from pan. Allow cake to cool in the pan about 15 minutes, then turn out onto cake rack, and cool completely. Bourbon Cake improves with age. It should be well-wrapped in foil and stored in the refrigerator. Do not freeze.

THE QUEEN OF ALL CAKES

This recipe is adapted from *Practical Housekeeping,* where it is called Ice-Cream Cake. The filling is made, the author explains, from thick sweet cream, beaten "until it looks like ice-cream." This elegant deception, the reader is instructed, "is the queen of all cakes."

½ cup sifted cake flour
¼ teaspoon salt
3 eggs, separated
1 teaspoon cider vinegar
½ cup sugar
¼ teaspoon almond extract

Filling:
1 can (3½ ounces) blanched almonds
¾ cup heavy cream
¼ cup sugar
½ teaspoon vanilla

Grease a jelly-roll pan, line with wax paper, and grease the wax paper. Sift flour and salt together and set aside. Beat egg yolks with an electric beater for 10 minutes. Wash the blades of the beater, then beat egg whites until frothy. Add vinegar and beat in the ½ cup sugar, a little at a time, until it becomes a satiny mixture that stands in peaks. Stir in almond extract, then fold into yolks gently. Sift flour over the surface and fold in until batter is well blended. Pour into pan and bake in a preheated 350° oven for 12 to 15 minutes or until cake begins to pull away from the sides of the pan. Do not overbake. Invert on a tea towel sprinkled lightly with confectioners' sugar and carefully pull off wax paper. Beginning with the broad side of the cake, roll it up. Keep towel around the cake as it cools, to hold the shape.

To make the filling: Chop almonds coarsely and toast in a 350° oven until golden. Beat cream until stiff, then stir in sugar, vanilla, and almonds. Unroll the cooled cake, spread the cream filling over the surface, and reroll. Chill before serving, then cut into slices.

VARIATION : To make an old-fashioned Jelly Roll, substitute jelly for cream filling.

GENERAL ROBERT E. LEE CAKE

This recipe is adapted from one used by Mrs. Robert E. Lee. The Lee Cake was especially popular in the nineteenth century, when a number of variations on the original recipe were published in cookbooks.

2 cups sifted all-purpose flour	2 cups sugar
½ teaspoon cream of tartar	Grated rind and juice of 1 lemon
1½ teaspoons baking powder	Dash of salt
8 eggs, separated	

To make the cake: Grease and flour four 9-inch cake pans. Sift together flour, cream of tartar, and baking powder four times. Beat egg yolks with a rotary or electric beater until very thick, light, and creamy. Add the sugar, a few tablespoons at a time, and continue beating until mixture is smooth and pale yellow. (This is a spongecake, essentially, so thorough beating is imperative.) Stir in lemon rind and lemon juice. Beat egg whites and salt until they stand in peaks. Fold into egg-yolk mixture alternately with the flour until well mixed. Spoon into cake pans and bake in a preheated 325° oven 20 to 25 minutes or until cake begins to pull away from sides of pans. Loosen edges with a knife and turn out on cake racks to cool while you prepare the filling and frosting.

Lemon Jelly Filling:	Grated rind of 2 lemons
6 egg yolks	Juice of 4 lemons
2 cups sugar	½ cup butter

To make the filling: Mix egg yolks with sugar, lemon rind, and lemon juice and cook over boiling water, stirring constantly, until sugar dissolves. Add butter and continue cooking, stirring constantly, for 20 minutes or until filling is smooth and very thick. Cool, then spread between layers of cooled cake.

Lemon-Orange Frosting:	2 tablespoons lemon juice
¼ cup butter	3 to 4 tablespoons orange juice
6 cups confectioners' sugar, sifted	Grated rind of 1 lemon
1 egg yolk	Grated rind of 2 oranges

To make the frosting: Beat or work butter until it has the appearance of thick cream, stir in confectioners' sugar, a little at a time, and continue working until mixture is very smooth. Beat in egg yolk and lemon juice. Stir in enough orange juice to make a spreadable frosting, then add grated lemon and orange rinds. Spread on sides and top of cake.

GLAZED COCONUT CAKE

1¾ cups sifted all-purpose flour	1 teaspoon almond extract
¼ teaspoon salt	
2½ teaspoons baking powder	*Glaze:*
½ cup (1 stick) butter	6 tablespoons melted butter
1 cup sugar	6 tablespoons brown sugar
2 eggs	3 tablespoons heavy cream
⅔ cup milk	½ cup grated or flaked coconut

Sift together flour, salt, and baking powder. Set aside. Cream butter until soft, add sugar, a little at a time, beating until smooth. Add eggs, one at a time, beating hard after each addition. Add milk and flour mixture, alternating them and beginning and ending with flour. Stir in almond extract and pour into an 8-inch square cake pan. Bake in a 350° oven for 45 minutes or until cake pulls away slightly from sides of pan. Turn out of pan and spread, while still warm, with glazed coconut.

To make the glaze: Mix together melted butter, brown sugar, heavy cream, and grated or flaked coconut. Spread on top of cake and place about 4 inches from broiling unit for several minutes or until nicely browned. Watch carefully because it takes only 3 to 4 minutes for the glaze to turn the right color.

HARTFORD ELECTION CAKE

A recipe for Election Cake—one of the first foods to be identified with American politics—was published as early as 1800 in Amelia Simmons' *American Cookery.* The cake was served at election time and, in the 1830's, this recipe became popularly known as Hartford Election Cake.

1 medium-sized potato
1 cup milk
1 teaspoon salt
1½ tablespoons sugar
2 tablespoons shortening

½ package active dry yeast or
   ½ cake compressed
1 egg, well beaten
3½ to 4 cups sifted all-purpose flour

Cook potato in boiling water until tender. Drain, peel, and work through a sieve or ricer, then set aside. Scald milk. Pour into a large bowl and stir in salt, sugar, shortening, and potato. When lukewarm, stir in yeast until dissolved. Add egg, then flour, a little at a time, to make a soft but still manageable dough. Turn out on a floured board and knead until smooth and elastic. Place in a greased bowl, brush with a little melted butter, cover with a tea towel, and put in a warm spot to rise. Let rise until a little more than double in size.

Ingredients for second step:
¾ cup (1½ sticks) softened butter
1 egg
1¼ cups light brown sugar, firmly packed
½ cup sherry
1 cup seedless raisins, chopped
1 cup sifted all-purpose flour

1 teaspoon ground cinnamon
¼ teaspoon ground cloves
¼ teaspoon ground allspice
¼ teaspoon ground mace
¼ teaspoon grated nutmeg
1 teaspoon salt
Milk Frosting (page 190)

When yeast dough has risen sufficiently, push down the dough with your fist and work in butter thoroughly. Then, using your hand as the mixer, stir in the egg, sugar, sherry, raisins (toss them, first, in 2 tablespoons of the flour), and remaining flour sifted with the spices and salt. Pour into a large greased Turk's-head or *gugelhupf* mold or a 10-inch tube pan, filling pan only two-thirds full. Cover with a tea towel and let rise about 1 to 1½ hours in a warm place. Bake in a preheated 325° oven for 50 to 60 minutes. Cool about 10 minutes, then turn out of the pan, and cool completely before frosting.

LINGONBERRY TORTE

4 squares (4 ounces) unsweetened chocolate
1 cup milk
1 cup flour
½ teaspoon salt
2½ teaspoons baking powder
4 eggs, plus 1 egg yolk

1½ cups sugar
2 teaspoons almond extract
Lingonberry jam (if unavailable, substitute
   currant, or whole cherry preserves)
Butter Cream Frosting,
   coffee variation (page 190)

Combine chocolate and milk in the top of a double boiler. Cook over hot water until chocolate melts. Stir frequently. Cool. Sift flour, salt, and baking powder together and set aside. Beat the eggs and additional egg yolk with a rotary or electric mixer until light and thick. Add sugar gradually and continue beating hard until mixture is very smooth (hard beating at this point is imperative). Stir in almond extract, then the chocolate-milk mixture. Sift flour mixture on top and fold in gently but thoroughly. Pour batter into 2 greased 9-inch cake pans and bake in a preheated 350° oven for 10 minutes. Reduce heat to 325° and continue baking 25 to 30 minutes longer or until a toothpick inserted in the center comes out dry. Cool several minutes, then invert on a cake rack to cool completely. Spread lingonberry jam between layers. Frost the top with Butter Cream Frosting, coffee variation.

MOTHER ANN'S BIRTHDAY CAKE

Ann Lee, founder of the Shakers, was born on February 29, 1736. To commemorate her birthday, each year on March 1 the Shakers held an afternoon meeting, followed by a supper at which this cake was served. The original recipe advises, "Cut a handful of peach twigs which are filled with sap at this season of the year. Clip the ends and bruise them and beat the cake batter with them. This will impart a delicate peach flavor to the cake."

3 cups sifted all-purpose flour
½ cup cornstarch
1 tablespoon baking powder
1 teaspoon salt
1 cup (2 sticks) butter
2 cups sugar

1 cup milk
2 teaspoons vanilla
12 egg whites
Peach jam
Butter Cream Frosting (page 190) or
   White Mountain Frosting (page 191)

Sift together flour, cornstarch, baking powder, and salt. Set aside. Cream butter until soft, then add sugar, a little at a time, and continue working until mixture is as smooth as possible. Add flour combination and milk alternately, beginning and ending with flour. Stir in vanilla, then fold in stiffly beaten egg whites very gently and thoroughly. Pour into 3 well-greased and lightly floured 9-inch cake pans. Bake in a preheated 350° oven for 25 to 30 minutes or until cake pulls away from sides of pan. Let stand several minutes before turning out onto cake racks. When cold, spread peach jam between layers and frost sides and top.

LEMON CHEESECAKE

2 tablespoons butter
¾ cup zwieback crumbs
¼ cup confectioners' sugar
4 eggs
1 cup granulated sugar
¼ cup all-purpose flour

¼ teaspoon salt
1 teaspoon grated lemon rind
3 tablespoons lemon juice
½ teaspoon vanilla
2 cups well-drained cottage cheese
1 cup heavy cream

Grease bottom and sides of an 8-inch spring-form pan with the butter. Blend zwieback crumbs and confectioners' sugar together, reserving 2 tablespoonfuls for the top of the cake. Sprinkle remaining crumb mixture on bottom and around sides of pan. Beat together eggs, granulated sugar, and flour thoroughly. Stir in salt, lemon rind, lemon juice, and vanilla. Mix in cottage cheese and heavy cream thoroughly. Pour into the crumb-lined pan, sprinkle with remaining crumb mixture, and bake in a preheated 325° oven for 1 hour. Cool in the pan, then chill. Makes 6 to 8 servings.

BURNT SUGAR CAKE

Caramel syrup:
½ cup sugar
½ cup boiling water
Batter:
2¼ cups sifted all-purpose flour
2½ teaspoons baking powder
Pinch salt
½ cup (1 stick) butter
1½ cups sugar
3 eggs, separated

4 tablespoons caramel syrup
1 cup milk
Frosting:
1½ cups sugar
4 tablespoons water
2 tablespoons caramel syrup
½ teaspoon cream of tartar
2 egg whites
½ teaspoon almond extract

To make caramel syrup: Pour sugar in a heavy skillet. Place over a moderate heat until sugar has melted and turned a rich caramel brown. Add boiling water (there will be a lot of sputtering, so stand back) and cook a minute or two longer until syrup is slightly thickened. Set aside and cool. This caramel syrup makes enough to use for both batter and frosting.

To make the batter: Sift together flour, baking powder, and salt. Set aside. Work butter until soft, then add ¾ *cup sugar*, a little at a time, and continue working the mixture until smooth. In a separate bowl, beat egg yolks thoroughly, then beat in remaining ¾ cup sugar until creamy. Stir yolk mixture into creamed butter along with the 4 tablespoons caramel syrup. Mix in flour combination, alternating with milk and beginning and ending with flour. Last of all, fold in egg whites beaten until they stand in peaks. Divide batter into 2 well-greased and floured 8-inch cake pans. Bake in a preheated 375° oven for 20 to 25 minutes or until cake shrinks from sides of pan. Remove from pans and cool on cake rack.

To make frosting: Put all ingredients, except almond extract, in the top of a double boiler and mix well. Place over rapidly boiling water and cook, beating constantly with a rotary or electric beater for *exactly* 7 minutes. Remove from heat, add almond extract, and beat until frosting is thick enough to spread. When cake is cold, spread frosting between layers, around sides, and over the top. Makes enough frosting to spread generously.

GINGERBREAD LOAF

John Adams once said—apparently in reference to the Molasses Act passed by the British Parliament in 1733—"Molasses was an essential ingredient in American independence." Molasses and ginger are inextricably linked with early American cooking; Amelia Simmons' *American Cookery* contained a recipe for molasses gingerbread.

2 cups sifted all-purpose flour	½ cup brown sugar, firmly packed
½ teaspoon salt	2 eggs, separated
1 teaspoon ground ginger	½ cup commercial sour cream
1 teaspoon baking soda	½ cup molasses
½ cup (1 stick) butter	

Sift together flour, salt, ginger, and baking soda. Set aside. Cream butter until soft. Add sugar, a little at a time, beating until smooth. Beat egg yolks vigorously and stir into butter-sugar mixture. Combine sour cream and molasses and add to the mixture, alternating with the flour combination. Finally, fold in stiffly beaten egg whites and pour into a greased loaf pan. Bake in a preheated 350° oven for 50 to 60 minutes or until a toothpick inserted in center comes out dry. Serve warm or cool, plain or with sweet butter, whipped cream, sweetened sour cream, or vanilla ice cream.

PRUNE CAKE

Plums were grown throughout America in colonial days, but the idea of raising them on a large scale for the purpose of making prunes came along late in the country's history. Pierre Pellier, a Frenchman, introduced Agen plums to California in 1856. Named for a district in France that is famous for its prunes, Agen plums are one of the oldest varieties under cultivation and excellent for prune making. The Santa Clara Valley, owing to Pellier's work, became a center for prunes in the late 1850's and has remained an important source.

⅔ cup prune pulp	½ cup shortening
1½ cups sifted all-purpose flour	1½ cups sugar
½ teaspoon cinnamon	2 eggs
½ teaspoon nutmeg	⅔ cup buttermilk
½ teaspoon allspice	⅓ cup chopped walnuts
¼ teaspoon salt	Sherry Frosting (page 190)
½ teaspoon baking soda	

Chop unsweetened cooked prunes, measure correct amount, and set aside. Sift together flour, all the spices, salt, and baking soda. Set this aside, too. Cream shortening until soft, then work in sugar, a little at a time, as thoroughly as possible. Add eggs and beat very hard, then stir in the prune pulp. Stir in flour combination and buttermilk, alternating them, and beginning and ending with flour. Last of all, stir in the nuts. Pour into a greased 10-inch tube pan and bake in a preheated 350° oven for 50 to 60 minutes or until cake pulls away from the sides of the pan. Cool about 10 minutes before turning out of pan. Cool completely before covering with Sherry Frosting.

MAPLE GINGERBREAD

2⅓ cups sifted all-purpose flour
1 teaspoon baking soda
1½ teaspoons powdered ginger
½ teaspoon salt
1 egg

1 cup maple syrup
1 cup sour cream
4 tablespoons melted butter
Maple Frosting (page 191)

Sift together flour, baking soda, ginger, and salt. Set aside. In a separate bowl beat egg vigorously, then stir in maple syrup, sour cream, and butter. Mix in the flour combination and pour into a greased and lightly floured 11 x 7 x 1½-inch baking pan. Bake in a 350° oven for 30 minutes or until cake pulls away from the sides of the pan. When cool, frost the top with Maple Frosting.

TWO-SPICE CAKE

1 cup butter
2¼ cups sugar
5 eggs
3 cups sifted all-purpose flour
1 tablespoon ground cloves

1 tablespoon cinnamon
Pinch of salt
1 cup buttermilk
1 teaspoon baking soda
Confectioners' sugar

Grease a 10-inch tube pan. Cream butter until soft and light, then gradually work in sugar until mixture is very light and fluffy. In a separate bowl beat eggs thoroughly and add to creamed mixture. Mix well. Sift flour with cloves, cinnamon, and salt. Beat about one-third of the flour combination into the batter, then stir in *half the buttermilk*. Add another third of the flour-spice combination and mix thoroughly. Stir baking soda into remaining half cup buttermilk and mix into batter along with the remaining flour. Pour into cake pan and bake in a preheated 350° oven 45 to 55 minutes or until cake tester comes out dry. Cool 10 minutes, then turn out on a cake rack, and cool completely. Sift confectioners' sugar over the top.

BISHOP'S BREAD

1¼ cups sifted all-purpose flour
1 teaspoon salt
1¼ cups (½ pound) mixed candied
   fruit, chopped
1¼ cups almonds or pecans, chopped

3 eggs
½ cup sugar
1 teaspoon vanilla
1 teaspoon orange extract

Sift flour and salt together and mix with candied fruit and nuts. Set aside. Beat eggs vigorously, then add sugar a little at a time, and continue beating hard until mixture is smooth and very thick. Stir in vanilla, orange extract, and flour combination. Pour into a greased and lightly floured loaf pan. Bake in a preheated 325° oven for 50 to 60 minutes or until toothpick inserted in center comes out dry. Remove from pan and cool on a cake rack. Cut in thin slices to serve. A cup (1 package) chocolate pieces may be added with the fruit and the nuts.

BOSTON CREAM PIE

Cake:
1½ cups sifted cake flour
2 teaspoons baking powder
¼ teaspoon salt
⅓ cup butter
1 teaspoon vanilla
¾ cup sugar
2 eggs
½ cup milk

Filling:
1 cup half-and-half (milk and cream)
¼ cup sugar
3 tablespoons flour
Dash of salt
1 egg, slightly beaten
½ teaspoon vanilla

To make the cake: Sift together flour, baking powder, and salt. Set aside. Work butter and vanilla together until creamy, then work in sugar, a little at a time, until smooth. Beat in eggs one at a time, beating hard after each addition. Stir in milk and flour combination alternately. Pour batter into 2 greased 8-inch round cake pans and bake in a preheated 375° oven for 25 minutes or until cake pulls away from sides of pan. Cool.

To make the filling: Scald half-and-half. Combine sugar, flour, and salt in a bowl and stir in the hot milk until smooth. Add to egg very slowly, beating constantly. Cook over boiling water, stirring constantly, until custard thickens. Remove from heat, stir in vanilla, and cool. When both cake and filling are cool, spoon filling between the layers and sprinkle top with confectioners' sugar, or frost with Chocolate Frosting (page 190).

VARIATION: To make Washington Pie, put raspberry jam or jelly between the layers in place of the custard, and shower the top with confectioners' sugar.

PLUMB CAKE

Four pounds flour, four pounds currants, four pounds butter, four pounds sugar, four pounds citrion, one half an ounce mace, one half pint brandy, forty eggs. Will make a devilish good wedding cake such as I had.
—Oliver Hazard Perry,
Collection of Newport Historical Society

SHAKER CIDER CAKE

3 cups sifted all-purpose flour
½ teaspoon baking soda
¼ teaspoon salt
½ teaspoon nutmeg

½ cup (1 stick) soft butter
1½ cups sugar
2 eggs, well beaten
½ cup cider

Sift together the flour, baking soda, salt, and nutmeg. Set aside. Work butter and sugar together as thoroughly as possible (mixture is never really smooth) and beat in the eggs. Stir in flour mixture and cider, alternating them and beginning and ending with flour. Spoon into a greased loaf pan and bake in a preheated 350° oven for about 1 hour or until toothpick inserted in the center comes out dry. Cool. To serve, cut in thin slices.

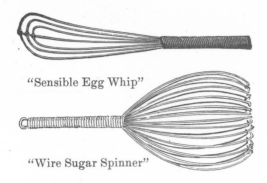

"Sensible Egg Whip"

"Wire Sugar Spinner"

LADY BALTIMORE CAKE

When Owen Wister chose Charleston for the setting of a novel, he made Mrs. Alicia Rhett Mayberry—one of the city's former belles—his central character. Mrs. Mayberry had created a cake called Lady Baltimore, which Wister duly described and made the title of his book, and, when *Lady Baltimore* was published in 1906, Mrs. Mayberry's cake became one of the most popular of American confections.

Cake batter:
2¾ cups sifted cake flour
4 teaspoons baking powder
¾ teaspoon salt
¾ cup butter
1½ cups sugar
4 egg whites
1 cup milk
1 teaspoon almond extract

Syrup:
1 cup sugar
½ cup water
½ teaspoon almond extract
Filling:
White Mountain Frosting (page 191)
2 cups pecans or walnuts, coarsely chopped
1 cup (6 or 8) figs, coarsely chopped
½ cup raisins
Brandy and sherry (optional)

To make the cake: Sift together flour, baking powder, and salt several times. Set aside. Cream butter until very soft, then work in *1 cup of the sugar,* a little at a time, until mixture is light and fluffy. Add flour and milk alternately, starting with *one-fourth of the flour.* Stir only until mixed, then stir in *one-third of the milk.* Follow this procedure, ending with flour. Beat egg whites until they stand in peaks, then beat in remaining sugar, a little at a time, making sure you incorporate all the sugar into the meringue. Fold meringue into batter, gently but thoroughly, until all white patches have disappeared. Mix in almond extract. Grease and coat with flour three 9-inch cake pans. Pour batter into pans, dividing it equally. Bake in a preheated 350° oven for 25 to 30 minutes or until cake pulls away from sides of pan or a toothpick inserted in center comes out dry. Cool for 5 minutes, then turn out on cake racks.

To make the syrup: While cake bakes, make a thick syrup with sugar and water. Bring slowly to a boil, then boil for 6 or 7 minutes. Flavor with almond extract. Spoon this syrup over the cake while it is still hot. Then cool the cake.

To make the filling: Prepare White Mountain Frosting and divide in half. Chop nuts, figs, and raisins (they may be soaked overnight in brandy or sherry) and add to half of the frosting.

To finish cake: Place bottom layer on a very large, flat cake plate, spread with half the nut-fruit filling, cover with second layer and the remainder of the filling. Place third layer on top. Frost sides and top with remainder of White Mountain Frosting.

ANGEL CAKE

Angel Cake was one of the favorite desserts of President Hayes's wife.

1 cup sifted cake flour	1 teaspoon cream of tartar
1½ cups egg whites (about 12)	1½ cups sugar
¼ teaspoon salt	1 teaspoon almond extract

After measuring flour, sift it three times and set aside. Put egg whites into your largest mixing bowl, add salt, and beat with a rotary or electric beater until foamy. Sprinkle cream of tartar over the eggs and continue beating until they stand in peaks. Sprinkle in the sugar, three or four tablespoons at a time, and fold it in gently but thoroughly. Use as few strokes as possible. When you add the last of the sugar, stir in the almond extract. Sift about ¼ *of the flour* over the entire surface of the batter and fold it in gently with a rubber spatula or with your hands. Continue sifting and folding until all flour is used. Do not overmix but make certain it is well mixed and all patches of flour have disappeared. Pour batter into an ungreased 10-inch tube pan and bake in a preheated 375° oven for 35 to 40 minutes or until cake springs back when pressed gently. To serve, tear apart with two forks. Do not cut with a knife.

TRADITIONAL POUNDCAKE

As cupcakes were named for having their ingredients measured by the cupful, so the ingredients of poundcake were first measured by the pound ("one pound sugar, one pound butter, one pound flour, one pound . . . eggs," as Amelia Simmons instructed). Poundcakes are of British origin, but they have enjoyed wide popularity in America.

3 cups sifted all-purpose flour	2 cups (4 sticks) butter
¼ teaspoon salt	2 cups sugar
1 teaspoon baking powder	9 eggs, separated
1 teaspoon mace	2 tablespoons cognac

Grease a 10-inch tube pan and coat lightly with flour. Sift together flour, salt, baking powder, and mace. Set aside. Cream butter until soft, then work in sugar a little at a time, and continue creaming until mixture is smooth. Beat egg yolks thoroughly and stir into creamed mixture. Add flour combination a little at a time, stirring until batter is free of lumps. Beat egg whites until they stand in peaks and fold into the batter along with the cognac. Mix only until all white patches have disappeared, working with a light hand. Pour into cake pan and bake in a preheated 350° oven for 35 minutes. Reduce oven heat to 325° and continue baking 25 minutes or until cake tester comes out dry. Let stand at least 10 minutes before turning out on a cake rack.

VARIATION I: You can substitute ½ teaspoon each of almond extract, lemon extract, and rose water, eliminating both the mace and cognac. Add the flavorings to butter when you cream it. The English often top poundcake with Almond Paste (page 191) and Milk Frosting (page 190). Cool the cake thoroughly before frosting.

VARIATION II: To make Lemon Poundcake, add grated rind of 2 lemons when you combine egg yolks and creamed mixture. Then add 6 tablespoons lemon juice, alternating with flour and beginning and ending with the flour. No other flavorings are necessary.

COCONUT POUNDCAKE

3 cups sifted all-purpose flour
¼ teaspoon salt
2 teaspoons baking powder
1 cup softened butter
1 pound (3½ cups) confectioners' sugar

1 teaspoon vanilla
4 eggs, well beaten
½ cup milk
1 can (4 ounces) grated coconut
Grated rind of 1 lemon

Sift together flour, salt, and baking powder. Set aside. Work butter until creamy, then add confectioners' sugar, a little at a time, beating until smooth. Beat in vanilla and the well-beaten eggs. Mix in flour combination and milk, alternating them and beginning and ending with flour. Finally, stir in coconut and lemon rind. Pour into a buttered and lightly floured 10-inch tube pan. Bake in a preheated 350° oven for 35 minutes. Reduce oven heat to 325° and continue baking 35 minutes longer or until cake pulls away from the sides of the pan. Cool about 10 minutes, then remove from pan, and cool completely on a cake rack. Serve cake without frosting, cut in very thin slices. This cake keeps well wrapped in foil.

CANDY CAKE

½ cup (1 stick) butter
½ cup sugar
3 eggs, well beaten
½ cup molasses
1½ teaspoons vanilla

1½ cups all-purpose flour
Pinch salt
1 cup (4-ounce can) black walnuts
Confectioners' sugar

Work butter until soft, then gradually work in the sugar until mixture is well blended. Beat in eggs, molasses, and vanilla. Mix in flour thoroughly. Add pinch of salt, then the nuts. Pour into a greased 11¼ x 7½ x 1½-inch baking pan and bake in a preheated 350° oven for 30 minutes or until a toothpick comes out dry. Sprinkle with confectioners' sugar and cut into thin fingers when cold.

HICKORY NUT CAKE

2 cups all-purpose flour
1 teaspoon baking soda
1 teaspoon cinnamon
1 teaspoon nutmeg
½ cup (one stick) butter
1 cup sugar

3 eggs, separated
1 teaspoon lemon juice
1 cup seedless raisins
2 cups coarsely chopped hickory nuts
3 tablespoons bourbon whiskey
½ teaspoon salt

Sift together flour, baking soda, cinnamon, and nutmeg and set aside. Cream butter until soft, then cream in sugar, a little at a time, until mixture is smooth. Beat egg yolks hard and add to mixture, then add lemon juice. Mix raisins and nuts with flour combination and add to batter alternating with the whiskey. Beat egg whites and salt together until they stand in peaks, then fold into batter gently but thoroughly. Pour into 2 well-greased loaf pans and bake in a preheated 250° oven for 2 to 2½ hours or until cake pulls away from the sides of pan.

MARTHA WASHINGTON'S GREAT CAKE

"Take 40 eggs & divide the whites from the youlks," reads the original recipe, now in the archives at Mount Vernon, "& beat them to a froth." Beating the whites of forty eggs to a froth with a little bundle of twigs would give any modern cook pause. This adaptation calls only for the ingredients available to Mrs. Washington, including "frensh" brandy. The cake was served at Mount Vernon on Christmas, Twelfth Night, and other "Great Days."

1 pound golden raisins
1 box (11 ounces) currants
1 cup (8 ounces) candied orange peel
¾ cup (6 ounces) candied lemon peel
1 cup (8 ounces) citron
⅓ cup (3 ounces) candied angelica
⅓ cup (3 ounces) candied red cherries
⅓ cup (3 ounces) candied green cherries
½ cup brandy

4½ cups sifted all-purpose flour
1 teaspoon mace
½ teaspoon nutmeg
1 pound (4 sticks) softened butter
2 cups sugar
10 eggs, separated
2 teaspoons fresh lemon juice
⅓ cup sherry

Pick over raisins and currants and soak them in water overnight. Chop orange and lemon peel quite fine; do the same with the citron, angelica, and both kinds of cherries. Pour brandy over fruit, cover, and allow to stand overnight. The following day, sift together flour, mace, and nutmeg. Set aside. Work butter until creamy, then add *1 cup sugar*, a little at a time, beating until smooth. Beat egg yolks until thick and light, then beat in remaining cup of sugar, a little at a time, and the lemon juice. Combine with butter-sugar mixture. Add flour and sherry alternately. Stir in all the fruit and, last of all, fold in stiffly beaten egg whites. Pour the batter into a well-greased and floured 10-inch tube pan, a 10-inch Turk's-head mold, or 2 large loaf pans. Place pan of hot water in the bottom of a preheated 350° oven. Place cake pans in oven and bake 20 minutes. Reduce heat to 325° and continue baking 1 hour and 40 minutes for large cake; 40 minutes for loaf cakes. Cakes are done when a toothpick, inserted at the center, comes out dry. Turn out on rack to cool, then wrap in cheesecloth soaked in sherry (or brandy), and store in an airtight crock or tin for a month or more. If, during this mellowing period, the cheesecloth dries out, soak it again with the same spirits and rewrap the cake. Recipe makes about 11 pounds of Great Cake.

STACK CAKE

This recipe is identified with the Smoky Mountain region, where the principal sweetening ingredient in use was—and still is—molasses. This cake resembles gingerbread, with applesauce between the layers.

4 cups sifted all-purpose flour
1 teaspoon salt
2 teaspoons baking powder
½ teaspoon baking soda
¾ cup shortening
1 cup sugar

1 cup molasses
3 eggs
1 cup milk
Applesauce (page 141)
    or canned applesauce
Confectioners' sugar

Sift together flour, salt, baking powder, and baking soda. Set aside. Work shortening until soft. Add sugar a little at a time while creaming the mixture. Mix in molasses thoroughly, then beat in the eggs, one at a time. Stir in flour combination and milk alternately. Spoon a thin layer of batter, about ⅓ inch, in greased 9-inch cake pans. Bake in a preheated 350° oven for 15 to 20 minutes or until cake pulls away from sides of pan. There will be six or seven thin layers of cake. When all layers are baked and cooled, stack with a generous amount of lightly spiced applesauce between each layer. Sprinkle confectioners' sugar on top.

BLACK FRUITCAKE

This recipe is of English origin and is known variously as Dark Fruitcake, English Fruitcake, Black Fruitcake, and Merry Christmas Cake.

¼ pound candied citron	¼ pound shelled walnuts or pecans
⅛ pound candied lemon peel	2 cups sifted all-purpose flour
⅛ pound candied orange peel	½ teaspoon mace
½ pound candied cherries	½ teaspoon cinnamon
1 pound candied pineapple	½ teaspoon baking soda
1 pound golden raisins	½ cup (1 stick) butter
½ pound seeded raisins	1 cup sugar
¼ pound currants	1 cup brown sugar, firmly packed
½ cup dark rum, cognac, sherry, or Madeira	5 eggs
	1 tablespoon milk
¼ pound blanched shelled almonds	1 teaspoon almond extract

The fruits and nuts should be prepared a day ahead as follows: sliver the citron, lemon, and orange peel into very thin strips; cut the cherries in half and the pineapple in thin wedges. Set aside. Pick over the raisins and currants to eliminate stray stems or seeds, add rum, cognac, sherry, or Madeira, and soak overnight. Chop the almonds and the walnuts or pecans coarsely. Set them aside, too. The following day, prepare the pan. Grease a 10-inch tube pan, four 1-pound coffee cans, or 2 bread pans, measuring 9 x 5 x 3 inches. Line with brown paper.

To make the cake: Mix ½ *cup of the sifted flour* with all the fruits and nuts in a large bowl. Sift remaining flour with spices and baking soda. Cream butter until soft, then work in granulated sugar and brown sugar, a little at a time, until mixture is smooth. Stir in the eggs, milk, almond extract, and, finally, the flour mixture. Mix thoroughly. Pour over the fruit and nuts and work together, with your hands, until batter is very well mixed. Lift the batter into the pan or pans and press it down firmly to make a compact cake when cooked. Bake in a preheated 275° oven. A tube pan that uses all the batter will take 3¼ hours; the bread pans, which will each hold half the batter, 2¼ hours; the coffee cans, which each hold one-fourth of the batter, 2 hours. Remove cakes from oven, let stand half an hour, then turn out onto cake racks. Peel off the brown paper very carefully. The four small, round cakes make attractive Christmas presents.

To age fruitcakes: Allow at least four weeks. Wrap each cake in several layers of cheesecloth well soaked in rum, cognac, sherry, or Madeira. Place in an airtight container, such as a large crock or kettle, and cover tightly. If cheesecloth dries out, moisten it with a little of the wine or spirits. Do not overdo it. The cakes should be firm, not soft, at the end of the aging period. This will make them easy to slice in neat, compact slices. If you wish to frost fruitcakes after they have been properly aged, cover the top first with Almond Paste (page 191), then with Milk Frosting (page 190). To decorate, make a garland of candied cherries, slivered angelica, and blanched whole almonds around the edge of the cake.

MARBLE CAKE

Get out all ingredients for both cakes, measure them accurately, and grease and flour a 10-inch tube pan. Set the oven at 350°, and follow the directions below.

To make white cake:
2½ cups sifted cake flour
2 teaspoons baking powder
¼ teaspoon salt
½ cup (1 stick) softened butter
1 teaspoon vanilla
1 cup sugar
½ cup milk
4 egg whites
To make dark cake:
2 cups sifted cake flour

1 teaspoon baking soda
¼ teaspoon salt
1 teaspoon cinnamon
1 teaspoon cloves
½ teaspoon nutmeg
½ cup shortening
1 cup brown sugar, firmly packed
4 egg yolks, beaten
½ cup molasses
1 cup buttermilk
Chocolate Frosting (page 190)

First make the white cake: Sift flour, baking powder, and salt together. Work butter until creamy, stir in vanilla, then gradually beat in the sugar. Beat until mixture is as smooth as possible. Stir in milk and flour mixture alternately. Last of all, fold in stiffly beaten egg whites, gently but completely. Set batter aside.

To make the dark cake: Sift flour, baking soda, salt, cinnamon, cloves, and nutmeg together. Set aside. Work shortening until soft. Gradually work in the brown sugar. When mixture is as smooth as possible, beat in egg yolks and molasses. Then stir in buttermilk and flour mixture alternately.

To fill the pan: Put a heaping tablespoon of white batter next to same amount of dark batter all around the bottom of the pan. Make a second layer with white batter on top of dark batter. Follow this pattern until all batter is used. Work quickly. Bake in a preheated 350° oven for 60 to 65 minutes or until cake tester comes out dry when inserted into center of cake. Cool completely before covering sides and top with Chocolate Frosting.

BROWNSTONE-FRONT CAKE

2 cups sifted all-purpose flour
1 teaspoon baking soda
Dash salt
1 cup boiling water
2 squares (2 ounces) unsweetened
   chocolate

½ cup (1 stick) butter
1¾ cups brown sugar, firmly packed
2 eggs
½ cup commercial sour cream
1 teaspoon vanilla
Chocolate Frosting (page 190)

Sift together flour, baking soda, and salt. Set aside. Pour boiling water over chocolate and let stand until cool. Cream butter until soft, then work in brown sugar, a little at a time, until smooth. Beat eggs vigorously and stir into sugar combination. Add flour mixture and sour cream alternately, beginning and ending with flour. Finally, stir in the chocolate-water mixture and vanilla. Pour batter into a greased 9 x 5 x 3-inch loaf pan and bake in a 325° oven 50 to 60 minutes or until cake begins to shrink away from sides of pan. Cool for a few minutes, then turn out on a cake rack. When completely cooled, frost with Chocolate Frosting.

APPLESAUCE CAKE

1½ cups sifted all-purpose flour
1 teaspoon baking soda
Pinch of salt
1 teaspoon cinnamon
1 teaspoon cloves
½ cup shortening

¾ cup brown sugar, firmly packed
1 egg
1 cup applesauce
1 cup nuts, chopped
1 cup raisins
½ cup pitted dates, chopped

Sift together flour, baking soda, salt, cinnamon, and cloves. Set aside. Work shortening until soft, then stir in sugar, a little at a time, working the mixture until smooth. Beat in the egg vigorously. Alternately stir in flour mixture and applesauce. Then add nuts, raisins, and dates. Pour batter into a greased loaf pan and bake in a preheated 350° oven for 50 to 60 minutes or until cake pulls away from sides of pan. Cool several minutes before turning out onto a cake rack.

CINNAMON CUPCAKES

1½ cups sifted all-purpose flour
2 teaspoons baking powder
Pinch of salt
1 tablespoon cinnamon
½ cup (1 stick) butter

1 cup sugar
2 eggs
½ cup milk
Whipped Cream Frosting,
    cinnamon variation (page 191)

Sift together flour, baking powder, salt, and cinnamon. Set aside. Work butter until soft, then gradually work in sugar as thoroughly as possible. Beat in eggs, one at a time, beating hard after each addition. Stir in the flour combination and milk alternately. Spoon into greased muffin pans and bake in a preheated 350° oven for 25 minutes or until a toothpick inserted in center comes out dry. Frost with Whipped Cream Frosting, cinnamon variation. Makes 18.

NAPLES BISCUITS

This recipe for Naples Biscuits, or Ladyfingers, is adapted from Mary Randolph's *Virginia Housewife.*

3 eggs, separated
⅓ cup confectioners' sugar
⅓ cup flour

Pinch salt
½ teaspoon vanilla

Beat egg yolks long and hard, preferably with an electric mixer. Wash blades of mixer, dry thoroughly, then beat egg whites until they hold a soft shape. Add sugar, a little at a time, and continue beating until mixture stands in peaks. Fold into yolks gently, then sift flour and salt over the top and fold in, then add the vanilla. Shape into thin fingers with a spoon or decorating tube on a cooky sheet lined with brown paper. Bake in a preheated 350° oven for 10 to 12 minutes. Cool on a cake rack and sprinkle with a little confectioners' sugar. Makes 16 to 18.

CHOCOLATE FROSTING

2 squares unsweetened chocolate
2 tablespoons softened butter
½ teaspoon vanilla
Pinch of salt

1 cup confectioners' sugar
1 egg
¼ cup milk

Melt chocolate over hot, not boiling, water. Combine butter, vanilla, and salt in a bowl. Stir in confectioners' sugar, a little at a time, until smooth, then beat in egg, milk, and the melted chocolate. Beat hard until creamy and stiff enough to spread.

BUTTER CREAM FROSTING

½ cup softened butter
1½ cups confectioners' sugar

2 tablespoons milk
½ teaspoon vanilla

Combine all ingredients and beat with an electric beater at high speed until smooth and thick. If the frosting is too thin, add additional confectioners' sugar.

VARIATION I: To make Coffee Butter Cream Frosting, substitute 1 teaspoon instant coffee for vanilla.

VARIATION II: To make Chocolate Butter Cream Frosting, melt ½ cup semi-sweet chocolate pieces over hot, not boiling, water. Beat frosting, then stir in melted chocolate.

SHERRY FROSTING

Combine ⅓ cup softened butter, 1 egg white, 1 tablespoon sherry, and 2 cups confectioners' sugar in a bowl. Beat with a rotary or electric beater until frosting is smooth and of a spreading consistency, then stir in 1 tablespoon orange rind grated fine.

MILK FROSTING

Combine 1½ cups sugar, ½ cup milk, and 1 teaspoon butter in a saucepan. Cook, stirring constantly, until mixture begins to boil. Then boil, without stirring, until a few drops tested in cold water form a soft ball. Remove from heat, stir in ½ teaspoon vanilla, and beat until frosting is of a spreading consistency. Spread over top of cake, letting it dribble down the sides. If frosting becomes too stiff to spread, melt in top of double boiler over boiling water, then beat again.

WHIPPED CREAM FROSTING

Combine 1 cup heavy cream with ¼ cup sugar. Chill in refrigerator at least two hours, then beat with a rotary or electric beater until stiff. Flavor with vanilla, almond extract, orange extract, etc.

VARIATION I: To make Cocoa Whipped Cream Frosting, substitute ¼ cup brown sugar, firmly packed, for the sugar and add ¼ cup cocoa.

VARIATION II: To make Cinnamon Whipped Cream Frosting, add ½ teaspoon cinnamon.

MAPLE FROSTING

2 cups confectioners' sugar
Pinch of salt
1 tablespoon softened butter

3 tablespoons maple syrup
1 tablespoon heavy cream

Combine all ingredients. Beat until mixture is smooth and of a spreading consistency.

WHITE MOUNTAIN FROSTING

3 cups sugar
1 cup water
¼ teaspoon cream of tartar

3 egg whites
Dash of salt
Flavoring (vanilla, orange extract, etc.)

Cook together sugar, water, and cream of tartar until candy thermometer reaches 238° or until syrup spins a long thread when dripped from a spoon. Pour a thin, slow stream of the syrup into stiffly beaten egg whites, beating constantly until frosting stands in peaks. Stir in salt and flavoring to taste.

ALMOND PASTE

1 pound blanched almonds
1 pound confectioners' sugar, sifted
3 egg whites

1 teaspoon almond extract or
2 teaspoons rose water

Work almonds through a food grinder or blend in an electric blender. Thoroughly mix in confectioners' sugar. Beat egg whites slightly, then stir into the almond mixture. Add almond extract or rose water, using your hands to blend the heavy mixture.

COOKIES

NEW YEAR'S COOKIES

Christmas and New Year's have always called for special recipes, and the Dutch New Year's *koekjes*, traditionally baked in molds that produced the design of an eagle or the name of a famous person like Washington, were once among the most ornate. In 1808, Washington Irving's *Salmagundi: Or, The Whim-Whams and Opinions of Launce-lot Langstaff, Esq., and Others* claimed: "These notable cakes, hight [called] new-year-cookies . . . originally were impressed on one side with the burly countenance of the illustrious Rip [Van Winkle]."

3 cups sifted all-purpose flour	2 eggs
1 tablespoon baking powder	1 cup sugar
½ teaspoon salt	1 cup heavy cream
1 teaspoon nutmeg	1½ tablespoons caraway seeds

Sift together flour, baking powder, salt, and nutmeg. Set aside. Beat eggs until very light, beat in sugar, a little at a time, and then the cream. Stir in flour combination and caraway seeds. Refrigerate for several hours until dough is firm enough to handle. Roll about ¼ inch thick on a lightly floured board and cut with a small cooky cutter. Sprinkle tops with sugar and bake on greased cooky sheets in a preheated 350° oven for about 10 minutes. Makes about 8 dozen.

APEES

These cookies, especially popular at Christmastide in Pennsylvania, were probably named for Ann Page, a famous nineteenth-century Philadelphia cook. In his *Annals of Philadelphia*, published in 1830, J. F. Watson wrote: "Philadelphia has long enjoyed the reputation of a peculiar cake called the apee . . . Ann Page, still alive . . . first made them, many years ago, under the common name of cakes. . . . On her cakes she impressed the letters A. P., the letters of her name."

1 cup (2 sticks) butter	2⅓ cups sifted all-purpose flour
1 teaspoon vanilla	¼ teaspoon cream of tartar (scant)
1⅓ cups sugar	¼ teaspoon salt
2 eggs	⅔ cup commercial sour cream

Work butter and vanilla until soft, then work in sugar a little at a time, and continue mixing until very smooth. Add eggs, one at a time, beating hard after each addition. Sift together flour, cream of tartar, and salt. Stir into mixture, alternating with sour cream. Drop by teaspoonfuls onto a greased cooky sheet and bake in a preheated 375° oven for 10 minutes. Cookies should be very pale. Makes about 6 dozen.

CINNAMON STARS

1 pound unblanched almonds
5 egg whites
Dash of salt

2 cups sifted confectioners' sugar
2 teaspoons cinnamon
1 teaspoon grated lemon rind

Work almonds through a nut grinder or blend in an electric blender. Set aside. Beat egg whites and salt until they hold a shape. Beat in confectioners' sugar, a little at a time, and continue beating until the mixture stands in peaks. Stir in the cinnamon and grated lemon rind. Transfer about one third of the mixture to another bowl to use later as a glaze. Fold ground almonds into remaining mixture and blend thoroughly. Pat half the mixture at a time on a board or pastry cloth lightly sprinkled with additional confectioners' sugar. Pat about 1/3 inch thick, dusting the palm of your hand frequently with confectioners' sugar if mixture seems sticky. Cut with a small star or round cutter and place on a greased cooky sheet. Brush tops with reserved egg-white mixture and bake in a preheated 300° oven for 20 minutes or until edges begin to firm (the color remains the same). Makes about 5 dozen.

SAND TARTS

2 cups sifted all-purpose flour
1/2 teaspoon salt
1 teaspoon baking powder
1/2 cup (1 stick) butter
1/2 teaspoon vanilla

1 cup sugar
1 egg
1 egg yolk
1 teaspoon cinnamon
3 tablespoons sugar

Sift together flour, salt, and baking powder. Cream butter and vanilla until soft, then add the sugar a little at a time. Work the mixture until light and fluffy. Add unbeaten egg and extra egg yolk, beating well. Mix in the flour mixture and beat hard. Chill dough in refrigerator for several hours or, preferably, overnight. Divide the dough into portions and roll one portion at a time on a sugar-sprinkled board until paper thin. If possible, use a pastry cloth and a rolling pin in a knitted sleeve. If dough becomes too soft to handle easily, return to refrigerator and chill. Cut with cooky cutters, place on an ungreased cooky sheet, and brush tops with a little milk. Mix the sugar and the cinnamon together and sprinkle on each cooky. Bake in a preheated 350° oven for 8 to 10 minutes or until edges of cookies turn a delicate brown. Makes about 3 dozen.

ANISE CAKES

1/2 cup (1 stick) butter
1 1/2 cups sugar
3 eggs

1 teaspoon aniseed
3 cups sifted all-purpose flour
1/2 cup blanched almonds

Cream butter until soft, then gradually add sugar, and continue working until well blended. Add eggs, one at a time, beating hard after each addition. Stir in aniseed and flour. Drop batter from a teaspoon onto greased cooky sheet and place an almond on top. Bake in a preheated 350° oven for 10 to 12 minutes or until bottoms of cookies turn a golden brown. The tops should be pale. The cakes improve in flavor if allowed to ripen in an airtight container for several days before serving. Makes 3 to 4 dozen.

THE BUTTER DROP

The Butter Drop, forerunner of the Toll House Cooky, appears in a great number of old cookbooks, beginning with *American Cookery* by Amelia Simmons.

1 cup plus 2 tablespoons sifted
  all-purpose flour
½ teaspoon salt
½ teaspoon baking soda
½ cup (1 stick) butter

6 tablespoons brown sugar
6 tablespoons granulated sugar
1 egg
½ teaspoon vanilla

Sift together flour, salt, and baking soda and set aside. Work butter until soft, then add both kinds of sugar, a little at a time, beating until creamy. Beat in egg and vanilla vigorously. Then stir in flour combination. Drop batter from a teaspoon onto a greased cooky sheet, allowing plenty of room for expansion. Bake in a preheated 375° oven for 8 to 10 minutes. Makes about 48.

To make Toll House Cookies: Stir in 1 cup chocolate pieces and ½ cup coarsely chopped nuts before you spoon batter onto the baking sheet.

CREOLE KISSES

3 egg whites
2 cups confectioners' sugar

1 teaspoon vanilla
½ cup chopped pecans

Beat egg whites with a rotary or electric beater until they stand in peaks. Beat in the sugar and vanilla a little at a time. Stir in pecans. Cover a cooky sheet with brown wrapping paper. Drop the Kisses from a teaspoon onto the ungreased paper and bake in a preheated 350° oven for 15 to 20 minutes. Makes about 45.

SNICKERDOODLES

New England cooks had a penchant for giving odd names to their dishes—apparently for no other reason than the fun of saying them. Snickerdoodles come from a tradition of this sort that includes Graham Jakes, Jolly Boys, Brambles, Tangle Breeches, and Kinkawoodles.

3¼ cups sifted all-purpose flour
½ teaspoon salt
1 teaspoon baking soda
1 teaspoon cinnamon
1 cup (2 sticks) butter

1½ cups sugar
3 eggs, well beaten
1 cup hickory nuts or walnuts, coarsely chopped
½ cup currants
½ cup raisins, chopped

Sift together flour, salt, baking soda, and cinnamon. Set aside. Work butter until creamy, then add sugar, a little at a time, beating until smooth. Beat in eggs thoroughly. Stir in flour combination, nuts, currants, and raisins. Drop from a teaspoon onto a greased cooky sheet about 1 inch apart, and bake in a preheated 350° oven for 12 to 14 minutes. Cookies keep well in an airtight container. Makes about 10 dozen.

EDENTON TEA PARTY CAKES

On October 25, 1774, fifty-one ladies of Edenton, North Carolina, met at the behest of one Penelope Barker, in the home of Elizabeth King, to express their indignation over the British tax on tea. They resolved at this tea party (with tea made from dried raspberry leaves): "We the Ladys of Edenton do hereby solemnly engage not to conform to the pernicious practice of drinking tea." At this gathering cookies, made according to this recipe of Penelope Barker's, were served.

3½ cups sifted all-purpose flour
1 teaspoon baking soda
½ teaspoon salt
¾ cup butter

1 teaspoon vanilla
2 cups brown sugar, firmly packed
3 eggs

Sift together flour, baking soda, and salt. Set aside. Work butter and vanilla until soft, then add the sugar, a little at a time, while continuing to cream the mixture. Beat in eggs, one at a time, and stir in flour combination thoroughly. Divide dough in half, wrap each half in wax paper, and chill for several hours or until firm enough to handle easily. Roll out one portion at a time as thin as possible on a lightly floured board and cut with a cooky cutter. Place several inches apart on a greased cooky sheet and bake in a preheated 400° oven for 7 to 9 minutes. Makes 6 dozen cookies when a 2½-inch cooky cutter is used.

BENNE CAKES

Benne (sesame) seeds, brought to the South by African slaves, were thought to bring good luck. The seeds were planted as a border around cotton fields and were used in desserts, candies, and cookies.

Dough:
3 cups sifted all-purpose flour
2 teaspoons baking powder
½ teaspoon salt
½ teaspoon nutmeg
¾ cup butter
½ cup sugar

Grated rind of 1 orange
1 egg
½ cup milk
Glaze:
2 tablespoons butter
¾ cup honey
3 tablespoons benne (sesame) seeds

Sift together flour, baking powder, salt, and nutmeg. Cream the butter until soft, then work in sugar, a little at a time, until light and fluffy. Finally, stir in orange rind. Beat egg and milk together slightly. Mix into sugar-butter combination alternately with the flour mixture. Dust your hands with a little flour, pinch off pieces of the dough, and roll into small balls the size of a walnut. Bake on ungreased cooky sheets in a preheated 350° oven for 10 minutes or until lightly browned. Cool on a rack. Makes about 5 dozen.

To make the glaze: Cook butter, honey, and benne seeds until a few drops tested in cold water separate into threads that are hard but not brittle (290° on a candy thermometer). Cool until foam settles. Dip the top of each cooky in the glaze. Work quickly. If the glaze hardens, reheat over hot water. Stir the glaze occasionally to keep seeds from floating on top. These cookies are best when fresh.

MUSTER DAY GINGERBREAD

Muster Day, or Training Day, Gingerbread is named for a New England tradition. Before the Civil War, the first Tuesday of every June was set aside as Training Day for all men from ages eighteen to forty-five. This military training began at nine o'clock in the morning, and the men were usually accompanied by wives, children, cousins, aunts, uncles, sisters, grandfathers, and friends. It became, of course, an occasion for festivity, and this Gingerbread was one of the indispensable ingredients of the day.

⅔ cup brown sugar, firmly packed
⅔ cup molasses
1 teaspoon ginger
1 teaspoon cinnamon
½ teaspoon cloves

¾ tablespoon baking soda
⅔ cup butter
1 egg
5 cups all-purpose flour

Heat brown sugar, molasses, ginger, cinnamon, and cloves to the boiling point. Remove from heat, add baking soda, and pour over butter in a mixing bowl. Stir until butter has melted, then stir in the egg and flour thoroughly. Knead for a few minutes, then gather dough into a ball. Refrigerate dough until firm enough to roll easily, then roll on a lightly floured board, and cut with fancy cooky cutters. Place on greased cooky sheet and bake in a preheated 325° oven for 8 to 10 minutes.

CASHEW SHORTBREAD

2 cups sifted cake flour
½ teaspoon baking powder
1 cup (2 sticks) butter

½ cup confectioners' sugar
1 cup salted cashews, chopped

Sift flour and baking powder together and set aside. Cream butter until soft, then work in sugar with your hands until smooth. Stir in flour and, last of all, the cashews. Chill in refrigerator for at least 1 hour. Divide dough in half and roll one portion at a time about ⅓ inch thick on a lightly floured board. Refrigerate other half until needed. Work fast. Cut into 1½-inch squares and place on an ungreased cooky sheet. Bake in a preheated 375° oven for 15 minutes. Makes about 4 dozen.

COCONUT JUMBLES

⅔ cup butter
1 cup sugar
1 egg, well beaten

1 cup flour
1 can (4-ounce size) grated coconut

Cream butter, then work in sugar, a little at a time, and continue working until well blended. Stir in egg thoroughly. Mix in flour and coconut with your hands. The batter will be very stiff. Drop from a teaspoon onto a greased cooky sheet, allowing plenty of room for expansion. Bake in a preheated 425° oven for 10 to 12 minutes. Makes about 40.

GINGERSNAPS

These Gingersnaps, Miss Harland instructed in Common Sense in the Household, *"will keep for weeks, if locked up."*

¾ cup butter
¾ cup shortening
2¾ cups sugar
2 eggs
½ cup molasses

4 cups sifted all-purpose flour
2 teaspoons baking soda
2 teaspoons cinnamon
2 teaspoons cloves
2 teaspoons ginger

Cream the butter and shortening until soft and light, then add *2 cups of the sugar,* a little at a time, and continue creaming until mixture is very fluffy. Beat in the eggs and molasses thoroughly. Sift together all the dry ingredients and mix, little by little, with the creamed batter, beating hard. The batter will be quite soft. Roll pieces of the dough into balls about 1 inch in diameter, then roll each ball in the remaining sugar. Place on greased baking sheet about 3 inches apart to allow for spreading and bake in a preheated 375° oven for 12 to 15 minutes. After you take Gingersnaps from the oven, let them stand a minute before cooling on a wire rack. Makes about 100. Do not make these in hot, humid weather because they will remain soft.

MORAVIAN CHRISTMAS COOKIES

½ cup brown sugar, firmly packed
¾ teaspoon baking soda
½ teaspoon salt
¾ teaspoon ginger
¾ teaspoon cloves
¼ teaspoon nutmeg

¾ teaspoon cinnamon
¼ teaspoon allspice
1 cup molasses
½ cup shortening
4 cups sifted all-purpose flour

Sift together the brown sugar, baking soda, salt, and all the spices. Heat molasses just to the boiling point but *do not boil.* Stir in the shortening until absolutely smooth. Cool slightly, then beat in the sugar-spice mixture. Now knead in the flour with your hands until dough holds together. Shape into a big ball and chill in the refrigerator until firm. This dough will keep for weeks so you can bake as many cookies as you want at a time. Break off pieces of the dough and roll paper-thin on a lightly floured board. Cut into circles, place on a greased cooky sheet, and bake 6 to 8 minutes in a preheated 375° oven. Makes about 10 dozen.

BROWNIES

2 squares (2 ounces) unsweetened chocolate
½ cup butter
1 cup sugar
2 eggs, well beaten

1 teaspoon vanilla
½ cup sifted all-purpose flour
Pinch of salt
½ cup chopped walnuts

Melt chocolate over hot water. Work butter until soft, then gradually beat in sugar. When mixture is as smooth as possible, beat in eggs and vanilla. Stir in flour, salt, melted chocolate, and chopped nuts. Pour into a greased 8-inch square cake pan and bake in a preheated 350° oven for 25 to 30 minutes (brownies should remain soft). Cut in squares.

CANDY

PECAN NOUGAT

1½ cups coarsely chopped pecans
2 cups sugar

2 tablespoons fresh lemon juice

Spread pecans over a shallow baking pan and toast in a 350° oven about 10 to 15 minutes. Combine sugar and lemon juice in a heavy skillet. Cook over a low heat, stirring constantly with a wooden spoon, until melted sugar has a deep golden color. Stir in pecans and pour into a large, oiled pan or on a marble slab. Work fast, spreading the nougat with an oiled spatula as thin as possible. Cool until solid, then break into pieces.

HONEY POPCORN BALLS

3 quarts popcorn, popped
1 cup honey

1 cup sugar
Pinch of salt

Pop the corn and measure correct amount into a large bowl. Cook honey, sugar, and salt in a saucepan over medium heat until syrup reaches 245° on candy thermometer or until a few drops tested in cold water form a firm ball which does not flatten when removed from the water. Pour over popcorn in a very thin, steady stream. (Fork the syrup through the popcorn thoroughly while you pour.) When mixture is cool enough to handle, butter your hands and shape it into balls, pressing it together firmly. Makes about 2 dozen.

DOTTY DIMPLE'S VINEGAR CANDY

Rebecca Sophia Clarke (Sophie May) of Norridgewock, Maine, wrote more than forty books for children, including the six-volume series, published from 1867 to 1869, called the *Dotty Dimple Stories*. Miss Clarke's books were distinguished by their lack of plot, overweening presence of moralizing, cute naughtiness, and baby talk. They were distinguished, too, by talk of this candy, which became as popular with children as did the books and was, unlike the stories, enduringly cherished by children.

Combine 3 cups sugar with 1½ cups vinegar and cook over a low heat, stirring constantly, until sugar is dissolved. Continue cooking until syrup reaches the soft-crack stage (270° to 290° or until a few drops tested in cold water separate into threads which are hard but not brittle). Pour onto a large buttered platter and let cool until candy can be handled comfortably. Butter your hands and pull the taffy until it is white and almost firm. Stretch into a rope about 1 inch in diameter and snip off pieces with scissors.

VASSAR FUDGE

Fudge was popular in the late nineteenth century in women's colleges. Sometimes cooked over the gaslight which hung from the center of the ceiling, it was used as the excuse for parties after "lights-out." These fudge recipes were given by Maria Parloa in a booklet distributed by Walter Baker & Co. in 1905.

2 cups sugar
2 squares (2 ounces) unsweetened chocolate

1 cup light cream
1 tablespoon butter

Combine sugar, coarsely chopped chocolate, and cream. Cook over a moderate heat, stirring only until sugar and chocolate have melted. Continue cooking until mixture reaches 238° or until a few drops tested in cold water form a soft ball. Remove from heat, add butter, and cool slightly. Beat until fudge begins to harden, then transfer to a buttered platter. Cut into squares before the fudge is absolutely firm. Makes a little more than 1 pound.

VARIATION: To make Wellesley Fudge, add ½ pound of marshmallows when the candy is removed from the heat.

SMITH COLLEGE FUDGE

1 cup granulated sugar
1 cup brown sugar, firmly packed
¼ cup molasses
½ cup light cream

2 squares (2 ounces) unsweetened chocolate
¼ cup butter
1½ teaspoons vanilla

Combine the 2 sugars, molasses, cream, and coarsely chopped chocolate in a saucepan. Cook over a moderate heat, stirring until sugar and chocolate have melted. Continue cooking, without stirring, until mixture reaches 238° or until a few drops tested in cold water form a soft ball. Remove from heat, stir in butter and vanilla, cool slightly, then beat until fudge begins to harden. Pour onto a buttered platter and cut into squares before the fudge is completely hard. Makes about 1¼ pounds.

SECRETS

Take glazed paper of different colours, and cut into squares of equal size, fringing two sides of each. Have ready, burnt almonds, chocolate nuts, and bonbons or sugar-plums of various sorts; and put one in each paper with a folded slip containing two lines of verse; or what will be much more amusing, a conundrum with the answer. Twist the coloured paper so as entirely to conceal their contents, leaving the fringe at each end.

—Eliza Leslie, *Directions for Cookery*, 1837

PEANUT BRITTLE

2 cups sugar
1 cup light corn syrup
½ cup water
2 cups peanuts

1 tablespoon butter
1 teaspoon vanilla
2 teaspoons baking soda

Combine sugar, syrup, and water in a heavy skillet. Cook over a low heat until mixture reaches 230° or until it spins a thread about 2 inches long when dropped from a spoon. Stir in peanuts and continue cooking to 300° or until a few drops tested in cold water separate into threads which are hard and brittle. Remove from heat and stir in remaining ingredients. Pour onto a greased platter, spreading as thin as possible. When cold, break into pieces.

PRALINES

Pralines were named for the French diplomat César du Plessis-Praslin, later Duc de Choiseul. It is said that Praslin's butler advised him that almonds coated with sugar would not cause indigestion. In Louisiana, the Creoles adapted Pralines, substituting native pecans for almonds and brown sugar for white.

3 cups light brown sugar, firmly packed
¼ cup water

1 tablespoon butter
1 cup pecan meats

Combine sugar, water, and butter in a saucepan. Cook over a low heat until candy thermometer indicates 238° or until a little syrup dropped into cold water forms a soft ball which flattens when taken out of the water. Add pecans and stir until mixture adheres to the nuts. Remove from heat and continue stirring until candy is thick and opaque. Drop from a tablespoon onto wax paper, making small patties. Makes about 2 dozen.

CREAM PRALINES

1½ cups sugar
⅓ cup light molasses
1 cup light cream

1 tablespoon butter
Dash of nutmeg
1½ cups pecan meats, coarsely chopped

Combine sugar, molasses, cream, butter, and nutmeg in a large saucepan. Bring to a boil and cook over medium heat, stirring occasionally, until mixture reaches 240° on candy thermometer or until a little syrup dropped in cold water forms a firm ball. This takes from 35 to 40 minutes. Remove from heat and let stand 3 minutes, then add the nuts, and drop from a teaspoon onto wax paper or foil. Makes about 2½ dozen.

SALT WATER TAFFY

This famous candy is sold all along the Boardwalk at Atlantic City and, it is claimed, is made with sea water.

1 cup sugar
1 tablespoon cornstarch
⅔ cup white corn syrup
1 tablespoon butter
½ cup water

¼ teaspoon salt
Food coloring
Flavoring extracts (vanilla, almond, orange, peppermint, etc.)

Mix sugar and cornstarch in a saucepan. Stir in corn syrup, butter, water, and salt. Cook over a moderate heat until mixture reaches 254° or until a few drops tested in cold water form a ball which holds its shape. Remove from heat, add a few drops of food coloring and flavoring extract, and pour onto a buttered platter. Cool until it can be handled comfortably. Butter your hands and pull the taffy until it is light in color and firm enough to hold a shape. Stretch into a roll about 1 inch in diameter and snip off bits with kitchen shears. Wrap each piece in wax paper.

Taffy pull

SUGARED NUTS

Measure out 2 cups of nut meats (walnuts, black walnuts, hickory nuts, pecans, etc.), place in a saucepan, and warm the nut meats slightly. Combine 1 cup sugar with ½ cup water and cook, stirring constantly, until sugar is dissolved. Continue cooking until syrup reaches 238° or until a little syrup, dropped into cold water, forms a soft ball which flattens when taken out of the water. Remove from heat and pour very slowly over the warm nuts, shaking the nuts back and forth vigorously. The intended result is a relatively even coating of sugar over all the nuts.

COBBLERS

In *The Bon-Vivant's Companion*, Jerry Thomas wrote, "Like the julep, this delicious potation is an American invention, although it is now a favorite in all warm climates. The 'cobbler' does not require much skill in compounding, but to make it acceptable to the eye, as well as to the palate, it is necessary to display some taste in ornamenting the glass after the beverage is made."

Fill a tall glass with shaved ice, add 2 jiggers (3 ounces) spirits (whiskey, applejack, brandy, or rum) or wine (sherry, Rhine wine, Bordeaux, or sauterne) and 1 teaspoon sugar dissolved in a little water. Stir well. Add 2 or 3 orange slices and serve with a straw.

VARIATION I: To make Cobblers with champagne, fill four tall glasses ⅓ full with shaved ice, then add 1 teaspoon sugar dissolved in a little water. Fill glasses with champagne and decorate each glass with a piece of orange or lemon peel.

TODDIES AND SLINGS

Toddies and Slings are essentially the same. The word "toddy" is derived from *tari*, a Hindu word, and means fresh or fermented sap from various species of palm trees. When "toddy" was adopted by traders, it became a specific potion made by man rather than by nature. "Sling"—originally English slang for any drink or draught—also came to mean a particular drink. During the summer, according to John Bernard's *Life in the Old Dominion*, a southern gentleman would "rise about nine, when he exerted himself to walk as far as his stables to look at the stud he kept for the races; at ten he breakfasted on coffee, eggs, and hoe-cake, concluding it with the commencement of his diurnal potations—a stiff glass of mint sling. . . . He then sought the coolest room and stretched himself on a pallet in his shirt and trousers. . . . Between twelve and one his throat would require another emulsion, and he would sip half a pint of some mystery termed bumbo, apple toddy, or pumpkin flip." The Mint Sling and Apple Toddy Bernard speaks of are variations on the more traditional Slings and Toddies given here.

To make a hot Whiskey Toddy: Dissolve 1 lump of sugar in a glass half full of boiling water. Add 1 jigger of whiskey and a small twist of lemon peel. Sprinkle with nutmeg.

VARIATION I: To make a Whaler's Toddy, dissolve 1 teaspoon sugar in a small mug half full of boiling water. Add ½ slice lemon, 3 whole cloves, 1 small piece of cinnamon, and ¼ cup rum. Stir with a spoon, then sprinkle with grated nutmeg.

VARIATION II: To make a Kentucky Toddy, dissolve 1 lump of sugar in a little water, then combine with 1 jigger bourbon and a twist of lemon peel. Add an ice cube and stir well.

MINT JULEP

Although versions of the Julep (called *julab* in Arabic and *gulab* in Persian) can be traced back as far as 1400 A.D., the drink is now identified with the southern United States. "I must...descant a little upon the mint-julep," Captain Frederick Marryat wrote in his diary while traveling through the South in 1838, "as it is, with the thermometer at 100°, one of the most delightful and insinuating potations that ever was invented, and may be drunk with equal satisfaction when the thermometer is as low as 70°."

The Julep has been made with rum, brandy, bourbon, and other potent liquors. It is generally agreed, however, that the classic Julep is the one made with bourbon, which has been popularized in Kentucky. There are two principal unresolvable arguments about the Mint Julep: whether the mint in a Julep should be crushed or not, and whether or not a Julep drinker should use a straw or bury his nose in the mint. Such arguments notwithstanding, Julep drinkers do agree, as Charles Dickens noted during his travels through the American South in 1842, "that...the mounds of ices, and the bowls of mint-julep and sherry cobbler they make in these latitudes, are refreshments never to be thought of afterwards, in summer, by those who would preserve contented minds."

To make a Kentucky Mint Julep: Chill silver mugs or goblets or heavy cut-crystal tumblers on ice in the refrigerator for as long as possible. Dissolve sugar (allow 1 lump per mug) in a little water. Fill each mug with finely crushed ice, add enough bourbon to cover the ice, and stir until the outside of the mug is heavily frosted. Then stir in the sugar syrup to taste. Tuck 5 or 6 sprigs of fresh mint into the ice so that they protrude above the rim.

VARIATION I: To make a Georgia Mint Julep, substitute equal amounts of cognac and peach brandy for the bourbon.

VARIATION II: To make a Louisiana Mint Julep, substitute rum for bourbon.

VARIATION III: To make a Major Bailey, muddle 1 teaspoon confectioners' sugar, 4 dashes fresh lime juice, and 6 mint leaves in a tall goblet. Fill with shaved ice, then add 1 jigger of gin. Stir until outside of glass is frosted.

CLARET CUP

3 tablespoons sugar
Grated rind of 1 lemon
3 slices of lemon
1 tablespoon Angostura bitters
1 strip cucumber peel

½ jigger each of brandy, maraschino, and white curacao
1 quart soda water, chilled
2 bottles red wine, chilled
Mint leaves

Combine all ingredients *except soda, wine, and mint,* cover, and let stand for about one hour. When ready to serve, place a block of ice in a chilled punch bowl. Strain punch into bowl, add wine, and garnish with mint leaves.

COCKTAILS

There are a number of theories concerning the origin of the word "cocktail" and, although none is completely reliable, one story from New Orleans seems quite plausible. Monsieur A. A. Peychaud arrived in New Orleans in 1793, opened an apothecary shop, and dispensed—according to a secret family formula—a tonic he called "bitters." Occasionally, for customers suffering severely from a malady, Peychaud would serve a mixture of cognac and bitters, presented to customers in an eggcup, or *coquetier*, as it was called in French. It is said that Americans—who soon insisted on having bitters with other combinations of liquors—slurred *coquetier* into "cocktail." Among the earliest references to such a mixed drink is one in a periodical called *The Balance*, dated May 13, 1806, describing the cocktail as "a stimulating liquor composed of spirits of any kind, sugar, water, and bitters. It is vulgarly called *bitter sling*, and is supposed to be an excellent electioneering potion."

Virtuoso at the bar

THE MARTINI, 1862

Jerry Thomas, author of *The Bon-Vivant's Companion*, claims to have originated the Martini while tending bar at San Francisco's Occidental Hotel between 1860 and 1862. Thomas called it the Martinez, and later chroniclers have said it was named for a chilly traveler on his way to Martinez, California.

1 dash of bitters	1 wineglass of vermouth
2 dashes of maraschino	2 small lumps of ice
1 jigger of gin	

Shake thoroughly and strain into a large cocktail glass. Put ¼ slice lemon in the glass and serve. To make the cocktail very sweet, add 2 dashes syrup.

OLD-FASHIONED WHISKEY COCKTAIL

The Old-Fashioned Whiskey Cocktail is said to have been invented by the bartender at the Pendennis Club in Louisville, Kentucky.

Mix together ¼ lump of sugar and 2 teaspoons water. Add a dash of Angostura bitters, 1 jigger whiskey, and 1 piece lemon peel. Add ice and stir.

NEW ORLEANS SAZERAC

"The planter 'takes a drink' a dozen times in the forenoon," Nathaniel Parker Willis wrote from New Orleans in 1852, "but he does not *drink* it. He seldom calls for it when alone. It is with him a matter of etiquette. Wherever he meets friend or acquaintance, there is a drinking saloon near by—and he would feel as much at a loss to exchange the compliments of the day, without stepping in to do it over a glass, as to bow to a lady without his hat, or manage an interview without mention of health or weather." It seems likely that the planter in New Orleans most often exchanged the compliments of the day over Sazerac, which originated in the Vieux Carré and was one of the most famous New Orleans drinks.

Muddle 1 lump sugar with 1 teaspoon water, a dash each of Angostura and orange bitters, 3 dashes of absinthe or Pernod. Then add 1 jigger bourbon, 1 ice cube, and a twist of lemon peel. Stir, then strain into an old-fashioned glass and serve.

RAMOS GIN FIZZ

Henry C. Ramos arrived in New Orleans in 1888 and purchased the Imperial Cabinet saloon, where this famous drink was served. The drink requires such a great deal of shaking—at least five minutes—that one of the distinctive features of Ramos' establishment was its corps of young boys who did nothing but stand behind the bar to attend to shaking Gin Fizzes. During the Mardi Gras of 1915, the corps reached the prodigious size of thirty-five lads.

1 tablespoon confectioners' sugar
3 to 4 drops orange-flower water
Juice of ½ lime
Juice of ½ lemon
1 jigger dry gin

1 egg white
1 jigger rich milk or cream
1 squirt Seltzer water
2 drops vanilla (optional)

Put all the ingredients, in the order given, in a cocktail shaker. Fill with crushed ice (the ice should not be too fine since lumps are needed to whip the egg white and cream to a froth). Shake long and steadily until mixture thickens. Strain into a tall, thin highball glass.

FLIP

Flips were originally hot drinks concocted in the winter and were warmed by thrusting an iron flip dog or loggerhead into the mug, which produced a pleasant sizzle and a burnt taste. Gradually they became cold drinks, and the flip dogs that hung by the fireplace were of no use except for poking large logs. A Yard of Flannel is a hot Flip which, when properly made, looks fleecy. In the eighteenth century, Myles Arnold reported the drink to be a favorite with the riders on the Boston Post route: "and indeed, 'tis said they sometimes wrap themselves warmly with it."

To make a Yard of Flannel: Heat 1 quart ale in a saucepan. Beat 4 eggs with 4 tablespoons sugar and 1 teaspoon grated nutmeg or ginger, then add ½ cup dark rum. Pour into a pitcher. When ale is almost boiling, pour it into another pitcher. To combine the two mixtures, pour hot ale, a little at a time, into egg mixture, stirring briskly to prevent curdling. Then pour the contents of the two pitchers back and forth until the mixture is as smooth as cream.

To make a cold Flip: dissolve 1 teaspoon confectioners' sugar in a little water in a cocktail shaker. Add 1 jigger spirits or 2 jiggers wine, 1 egg, and 2 or 3 lumps of ice. Shake thoroughly and serve with a little grated nutmeg on top.

SHRUBS AND BOUNCES

Shrubs and Bounces belong to the same family—both are made with a fruit base and brandy or rum—and they are part of the heritage of colonial America. There seems to be little rationale for their names (although "shrub" may derive from the Arabic *shurb,* meaning drink), but, then, there is little rationale for many old colonial drinks, like the Mam, Meridian, the Bogus, Bombo, Rombo, Rumbullion, and Rattle-Skull, the Tiffs and Toddies, Sampsons and Stone Fences, and Whistle Belly Vengeance. The Indians had a rum drink called Coow-woow, which some said was their customary war whoop. The recipes here are eminently palatable, in contradistinction to many of the quaint-sounding old potions.

To make Lime Rum Shrub: Dissolve 1½ cups sugar in 2½ cups water, then combine with 1 quart dark rum and 1 cup fresh lime juice. Mix well, bottle, and let stand in a cool place at least 7 days before using.

To make Orange Brandy Shrub: Dissolve 2 cups sugar in 2½ quarts fresh orange juice. Add 1 quart brandy. Mix well, bottle, and let stand in a cool place at least 7 days before using.

To make Cherry Bounce: Mash 5 pints cherries and crack the stones. Pour 1 quart dark rum over them and let the mixture stand at least 7 days. Strain through several layers of cheesecloth, then sweeten to taste with brown sugar. Mix well, bottle, and let stand at least another week before using.

To serve a Shrub or a Bounce, pour into a highball glass filled with shaved ice or ice cubes.

STONE FENCE

In 1809, Washington Irving, in his *History of New York...by Diedrich Knickerbocker,* told how the Dutch "lay claim to be the first inventors of the recondite beverages, *cock-tail, stone-fence,* and *sherry-cobbler."* The first Stone Fence appears to have been made with sweet cider and applejack; it was later made with sweet cider and bourbon.

Pour ¼ cup bourbon into a highball glass, add 2 or 3 ice cubes, and fill the glass with sweet cider.

BENJAMIN FRANKLIN'S ORANGE SHRUB

To a Gallon of Rum two Quarts of Orange Juice and two pound of Sugar—dissolve the Sugar in the Juice before you mix it with the Rum —put all together in a Cask & shake it well—let it stand 3- or 4-Weeks & it will be very fine & fit for Bottling—when you have Bottled off the fine pass the thick thro' a Philtring paper put into a Funnell—that not a drop may be lost. To obtain the flavour of the Orange Peel paire a few Oranges & put it in Rum for twelve hours—& put that Rum into the Cask with the other—For Punch thought better without the Peel.
— From the Franklin Papers,
American Philosophical Society

SANGAREE

The essential characteristic of Sangaree (from the French *sang,* meaning "blood") is its deep red color, derived from red wine. In colonial days, this mild drink was valued as a bracer.

To make Peach Sangaree: Combine ½ cup sliced peaches, 2 tablespoons lemon juice, pinch of salt, 3 tablespoons sugar, pinch of cinnamon, 1 whole allspice, and ½ cup red Bordeaux wine. Mix well and chill for one hour. Strain into a tall glass and fill with sparkling water.

To make Strawberry Sangaree: Combine ½ cup crushed strawberries, 2 tablespoons sugar, 1 teaspoon lemon juice, and ½ cup red Bordeaux wine. Mix well and chill for one hour. Strain into a tall glass and fill with sparkling water.

To make Pineapple Sangaree: Combine ½ cup diced pineapple, 2 tablespoons sugar, 1 whole allspice, 1 tablespoon orange juice, 1 teaspoon lemon juice, and ½ cup red Bordeaux wine. Mix well and chill one hour. Strain into a tall glass and fill with sparkling water.

To make Orange Sangaree: Combine ¼ cup orange juice, 2 tablespoons lemon juice, 2 tablespoons sugar, 1 clove, 2 whole allspice, and ½ cup red Bordeaux wine. Mix well and chill for one hour. Strain into a tall glass and fill with sparkling water.

HAYMAKER'S SWITCHEL

In the haying season farmers used to take their "nooning" (midday dinner) with them, which included a jug of Switchel to wash the meal down. Although a Switchel was usually straight, farmers have been known to spike it with hard cider, or even brandy, which Down Easters used to say got the hay in the barn in half the time.

To make Haymaker's Switchel: Combine 1 cup brown sugar, ½ teaspoon ginger, ½ cup molasses, ¾ cup vinegar, and 2 quarts of water. Mix together, add ice, and chill.

MAY WINE BOWL

2 quarts white wine, well chilled
3 sprays fresh (1 ounce dried) woodruff

½ cup fine granulated sugar
1 cup small strawberries

Sprinkle sugar over woodruff and let stand in a tightly covered glass jar for several hours. Add *2 cups of the wine* to the woodruff, cover again, and let stand overnight. Place a large lump of ice in a punch bowl. Add woodruff and the wine in which it soaked. Pour the remaining cold wine over the ice and stir. Garnish with strawberries. Fills 20 punch cups.

There's a little place just out of town,
Where, if you go to lunch,
They'll make you forget your mother-in-law
With a drink called Fish-House Punch.
— From *The Cook*, 1885

FISH HOUSE PUNCH

This punch is the specialty of Philadelphia's famed fishing and social club, the State in Schuylkill, which was founded in 1732, during the reign of George II, by a group of amateur anglers and cooks. When William Black visited Philadelphia in 1744, he reported in his journal that he and his company were welcomed at Gray's Ferry with a bowl of punch large enough to have "swimm'd half a dozen young geese."

¾ to 1 pound sugar
1 quart lemon juice (scant)
2 quarts Jamaica rum

1 quart cognac
½ cup peach brandy

Dissolve the sugar in the smallest possible amount of cold water, then stir in the strained lemon juice. Pour this mixture over a large solid lump of ice, then add the rum, cognac, and peach brandy, in that order. Allow the mixture to mellow for several hours, giving it an occasional stir.

ROMAN PUNCH

It was customary, in the nineteenth century, to serve an ice or sherbet mixed with liquor just after the roast. At some of the formal banquets given by President Grant as many as thirty courses were served, and such middle-course fortification was no doubt necessary. This Roman Punch was the favorite "cup" of the period. During the administration of President Hayes, his wife forbade any liquor to be served at dinners at the White House. As long as Mrs. Hayes was hostess, there were no wineglasses, no fragrance of bourbon, no champagne coolers in evidence at state dinners. Mrs. Hayes's singlehanded temperance movement was not generally appreciated; Secretary of State Evarts stated he would not permit the diplomatic corps to have their annual dinner at the White House if there was to be no wine. At a dinner party given by the Hayeses some of the company eventually noticed that platters of oranges were being consumed with dispatch. They would then try an orange and discover it contained what they thought was Roman Punch. But President Hayes wrote in his diary: "The joke of the Roman punch oranges was not on us but on the drinking people. My orders were to flavor them strongly with the same flavor that is found in Jamaica rum. This took! There was not a drop of spirits in them!"

To make Roman Punch: Mix quickly 1 quart lemon sherbet with 1 cup Jamaica rum. Spoon into chilled punch glasses or scooped-out oranges and serve at once.

An orange filled
with Roman Punch

PLANTER'S PUNCH

Dissolve 1 tablespoon sugar in the juice of 1 lime. Add 2 jiggers (½ cup) rum and cracked ice. Shake well. Strain into a tall glass half filled with finely cracked ice and decorate with a maraschino cherry, a sliver of fresh pineapple, and half a slice of orange.

PINK LEMONADE

3 lemons
¾ cup sugar
12 to 14 ice cubes

3 cups cold water
½ bottle maraschino cherries and juice

Scrub lemons, trim off ends, and cut into very thin slices, discarding seeds. Place slices in a bowl, add sugar, and press hard with the back of a wooden spoon until all sugar is dissolved. Add ice cubes, water, and cherry juice. Strain into glasses and garnish with whole maraschino cherries. Makes 6 to 8 servings.

OLD-FASHIONED EGGNOG

Eggnog is descended from the English sack posset, a hot drink made with ale or with dry Spanish wine called sack. Like posset, Eggnog was originally made with ale ("nog" is an English word for a strong ale), but—as it was adopted by Americans—it came to be made with more typical American liquors, like rum, bourbon, and even cider. The earliest American cookbooks relegated Eggnogs to a section of recipes for the sick and the weak. An Eggnog-type milk punch given in *American Practical Cookery Book* was accompanied by the note: "This must be used only with advice."

12 eggs, separated
1 cup sugar
1 quart milk
2 cups bourbon

1 cup Jamaica rum
1 quart heavy cream, whipped
Nutmeg

Beat egg yolks slightly, add sugar, a little at a time, and continue beating until smooth. Pour in milk, bourbon, and Jamaica rum. Beat egg whites until they stand in peaks. Fold egg whites and whipped cream into yolk mixture, gently but thoroughly. Serve cold with freshly grated nutmeg on top. Serves 25 to 30.

BALTIMORE EGGNOG

The Bon-Vivant's Companion, from which this was adapted, notes: "Egg Nog made in this manner is digestible, and will not cause headache. It makes an excellent drink for debilitated persons, and a nourishing diet for consumptives."

16 eggs, separated
¾ cup sugar
⅔ of a whole nutmeg, freshly grated

1 cup brandy or rum
1 cup Madeira
3 quarts half-and-half (milk and cream)

Beat egg yolks until very thick and creamy, then thoroughly beat in the sugar, a little at a time. Beat in the nutmeg, then mix in the brandy or rum and Madeira. Beat egg whites until they stand in peaks, then fold into the yolk mixture. Stir in the half-and-half. Serve in a chilled punch bowl. Serves 20 to 30.

KENTUCKY EGGNOG

24 egg yolks
1½ cups sugar
1½ cups Jamaica rum

2 bottles (fifths) bourbon
1 quart heavy cream, whipped
1 quart vanilla ice cream

Beat egg yolks until light, then beat in sugar, and continue beating steadily for 20 minutes. Stir in the rum and allow the mixture to stand at least 1 hour or until rum has "cooked" the eggs. Then add bourbon. Just before serving, stir in the whipped cream and ice cream. Pour into a well-chilled punch bowl. Serves 30 to 35.

SYLLABUS

Syllabub is closely related to Eggnog. The name is derived from wine that came from Sillery in the Champagne region of France, and from "bub," an Elizabethan slang word for bubbling drink. Although Eggnog called for strong liquors, Syllabub has always been made with wine—some men eschewed this weak potation, considering it a lady's drink. Traditionally a Christmas drink, Syllabub was often made "under the cow"—as shown in a recipe from Richard Brigg's *New Art of Cookery*, published in Philadelphia in 1792, which instructed that a bowl filled with wine be placed under a cow, and the cow milked "till [the Syllabub] has a fine froth at the top."

2 cups white wine	3 cups milk
5 tablespoons grated lemon rind	2 cups light cream
⅓ cup lemon juice	4 egg whites
1½ cups sugar	Nutmeg

Combine wine, lemon rind, and juice. Stir in *1 cup of the sugar* and let stand until sugar dissolves. Combine milk and cream, add wine mixture, and beat with rotary beater until frothy. Beat egg whites until stiff, add remaining ½ cup sugar, a little at a time, beating constantly until whites stand in peaks. Pour wine mixture into punch bowl, top with puffs of egg white, and sprinkle whites with nutmeg. Traditionally served with New Year's Cookies (page 192). Syllabub is so mild, children are allowed to share it. Makes 16 punch cups.

Barroom brawl

CAFÉ BRÛLOT

Brûlot, literally translated, means burnt brandy. In Louisiana, and particularly in New Orleans, *Café Brûlot* was frequently served with the room in darkness, as, according to Lafcadio Hearn, "The crowning of a grand dinner . . . the *pièce de résistance*, the greatest *pousse-café* of all."

Brew three large cups of strong, drip coffee and keep it very hot. Heat, by rinsing in boiling water, a *brûlot* bowl, earthenware bowl, or chafing dish, and a silver ladle. Place 2 very thin strips of lemon rind and the same amount of orange rind in the bowl. Add 4 whole allspice, 2 whole cloves, 1 small stick of cinnamon, 8 small lumps of sugar, and 1½ cups of brandy. Ladle out several lumps of sugar and a little of the brandy. Ignite this ladleful and, when blazing well, slide contents back into the bowl. Keep ladling mixture in and out of bowl while brandy flames. Add the hot coffee, a little at a time, and continue to ladle the mixture until the flame dies. Serve at once in demitasse cups.

HOT BUTTERED RUM

Nicholas Cresswell wrote in his journal in 1777 that the people of New England "import large quantities of Molasses from the West Indies, which they distill and sell to Africa and the other Colonies, which goes by the name of Yankee Rum or Stink-e-buss." Rum had become an important part of the American economy by the early seventeenth century, and the passage of the Molasses Act by the British Parliament in 1733 had done much to lay the foundation for revolution.

Once independence was won, rum found its way into domestic politics. It was used by politicians to influence voters, a practice once dubbed by Theodorick Bland, Jr., as "swilling the planters with bumbo." The honored tradition of feasting voters on food and drink originated quite early in the history of America. When George Washington ran for the legislature in 1758—though a Virginia statute expressly forbade the treating of voters and declared all elections obtained in this manner illegal—Washington's agent supplied the voters of Frederick County, Virginia, with 160 gallons of rum, beer, wine, and cider, or about a quart and a half per voter. The list included 28 gallons of rum, and 50 gallons of rum punch. After the election, Washington wrote his agent, "My only fear is that you spent with too sparing a hand."

Warm a heavy tumbler. Combine 1 teaspoon confectioners' sugar, ¼ cup boiling water, ¼ cup dark rum, and 1 tablespoon butter in the tumbler, fill with boiling water, and stir until well mixed. Serve immediately with freshly grated nutmeg on top.

TOM AND JERRY

The Tom and Jerry has been such a popular American drink that many a bartender, up to the present century, laid claim to inventing or naming it. Pierce Egan, the great dean of British boxing, wrote a book in 1821 called *Life in London, or the days and Nights of Jerry Hawthorne and his Elegant Friend Corinthian Tom,* from which some authorities insist the Tom and Jerry received its name. Egan, it is said, popularized the drink to such an extent that taprooms became known as Tom and Jerries.

It is often alleged in America that the originator of the drink was Professor Jerry Thomas, author of *The Bon-Vivant's Companion* (from which this recipe is taken) and bartender for a time at San Francisco's El Dorado bar. As is so often the case in saloon discussions, solid historical documentation has become somewhat befogged. What can be said with certainty is that the Professor at the El Dorado did popularize the drink in America.

Use 1 egg for each drink. Separate the eggs and beat the whites until frothy. Then beat in 1 heaping teaspoon sugar for each egg white and continue beating until whites stand in peaks. Beat egg yolks separately until thick and lemon-colored. Mix the two together with a pinch of baking soda. Place 2 tablespoons of the egg mixture in each mug. Add ½ jigger brandy and ½ jigger rum, then fill to the top with hot milk, cream, or boiling water. Give it a stir, then grate a little nutmeg on top.

BLUE BLAZER

However dubious the claim that Professor Jerry Thomas invented the Tom and Jerry, it is certain that he was responsible for the Blue Blazer. While keeping bar at San Francisco's El Dorado, the Professor was confronted by a miner who was burdened down with a brace of pistols, several months' worth of gold dust, and a rambunctious thirst. When the miner demanded a drink that would compensate for his many months away from civilization, Thomas asked him to come back in an hour. The Professor then called upon all his experience and inventiveness and, when the miner returned, took down from behind the bar two silver mugs that had been put on a special rack only for show. At this signal all the El Dorado patrons gathered around the bar. Thomas put whisky and boiling water into one of the mugs, set a match to it, and tossed the flaming mixture back and forth between the two mugs, quashing the blue flame after about ten seconds. It is reported that the miner missed three days of civilization after quaffing the Blue Blazer. In *The Bon-Vivant's Companion,* the Professor cautions, "The novice in mixing this beverage should be careful not to scald himself. To become proficient in throwing the liquid from one mug to the other, it will be necessary to practise for some time with cold water."

Put 1 wineglass Scotch whisky and 1 wineglass boiling water in a mug. Ignite the liquid and, while it is blazing, pour ingredients 4 or 5 times from one mug to the other. Properly done, this will have the appearance of a continuous stream of liquid fire. Sweeten with 1 teaspoon pulverized white sugar. Serve in a small bar tumbler with a piece of lemon peel.

Mixing a Blue Blazer

THE COCKTAIL PARTY

The cocktail party, with its rounds of drinks and trays of hors d'oeuvres, did not come into vogue until the twentieth century. Previously, guests were invited for dinner rather than just for drinks. Appetizers and canapés were rarely served, except, perhaps, for a half-dozen oysters before the soup. The dishes listed below (with the pages of the recipe section on which they may be found), are especially adaptable for serving at cocktail parties or as appetizers before dinner.

MENUS

NEW YEAR'S DAY COLLATION

Baked Ham*   *Boned Turkey*   *Daube Glacé**   *Oyster Pan Roast**

Squab in Compote*   *Lobster Salad*   *Chicken Salad**

Watercress or Bread-and-Butter Sandwiches   *Cream Biscuits**

Finger Rolls   *Molded Jellies*

Blancmange*   *Small Cakes*   *New Year's Cookies**

Marzipan in Shapes of Fruits, Vegetables, and Flowers   *Fruits*   *Ices*

Eggnog*   *Champagne*   *Coffee*   *Chocolate*   *Tea*

The custom of paying New Year's calls originated in New York, where the Dutch held open house on New Year's Day and served cherry bounce, *olykoeks* steeped in rum, cookies, and honey cakes. From New York the custom spread throughout the country. On the first New Year's after his inauguration, George Washington opened his house to the public, and he continued to receive visitors on New Year's Day throughout the seven years he lived in Philadelphia. On January 1, 1791, a senator from Pennsylvania noted in his diary: "Made the President the compliments of the season; had a hearty shake of the hand. I was asked to partake of the punch and cakes, but declined. I sat down and we had some chat. But the diplomatic gentry and foreigners coming in, I embraced the first vacancy to make my bow and wish him a good morning."

Eventually, it became *de rigueur* for those who intended to receive company to list in newspapers the hours they would be "at home." It was a disastrous practice: parties of young men took to dashing from house to house for a glass of punch, dropping in at as many of the homes listed in the papers as they could. Strangers wandered in off the streets, newspapers under their arms, for a free drink and a bit of a meal.

The custom of having an open house on the first day of the year survived the assaults of the newspaper readers. The traditional cookies and cakes continued to be served, along with hot toddies, punches, eggnogs, tea, coffee, and chocolate. But public announcements of at-home hours were dropped at the end of the nineteenth century, and houses were open only to invited friends.

A TALBOT COUNTY HUNT BREAKFAST

Bourbon and Branch

Scrambled Eggs in Cream   *Country Sausage with Fried Apple Rings**

Creamed Sweetbreads and Oysters*   *Capitolade of Chicken**   *Kidney Stew**

Bacon and Fried Tomato Slices*   *Waffles**   *Hominy Pudding**

Broiled Salt Roe Herring*   *Baked Country Ham**

Spoon Bread*   *Beaten Biscuits**   *Buttermilk Biscuits**

Jellies   *Apple Butter**   *Honey*   *Damson Plum Preserves*

Coffee

Chesapeake bounty

Chesapeake Bay, in Maryland, is one of the most richly endowed areas in the eastern United States. The landed gentry who settled there (in manorial holdings with names like Betty's Love, Lloyd's Landing, Wye House, Fairview, Haphazard, Mary's Delight, Crooked Intention, and Troth's Fortune) dressed their tables with the bay's oysters, fish, and shellfish and with game, fish, and waterfowl from the surrounding tidal rivers and marshes.

Hunt breakfasts were held each spring and fall in Maryland. In the fall, hunters went out for duck and wild goose before sunup and returned to one of the manor houses for breakfast. Preceded by ample quantities of bourbon and other drinks, breakfast was usually served at midday. This menu is typical of breakfasts served in Talbot County, located across the bay from Annapolis.

LA CUISINE CRÉOLE

MALCOLM F. J. BURNS

At the French market

In the New Orleans *Item* for July 8, 1880, Lafcadio Hearn lamented, "We fear that the good old Creole lore is rapidly disappearing. . . . Many of these secrets are kept with something of religious awe. Neither love nor money nor menaces could extort them from the owners. If childless, it is more than likely the secret will die with their owners; if they have children, these generally inherit the mystical power, but hardly ever do they seem in this generation to obtain the success of their fathers and mothers. We have often suggested that all the extant knowledge in regard to Creole cookery and herb medicine, so far as it is possible to obtain it, should be collected and published." Fortunately, in 1885 Hearn listened to his own wisdom and published the first basic book of Creole cookery. At about that same time Charles Gayarré had written in *Harper's* "Good heavens! with what supreme, indescribable contempt would Aunt Henriette or Uncle Frontin have looked down upon the best French *cordon bleu* that had presumed to teach her or him! Sufficient to say that Marc Antony, if he had known a creole cook of the old *régime*, would have given him two or three of his best Asiatic provinces as a reward for feasting Cleopatra." It was in those Saturnian days that meals like the three shown here were common in New Orleans. They include a substantial dinner, an elaborate feast for New Year's Day, and a simple treat of sweet cakes and coffee.

218

CREOLE FAMILY DINNER

Shrimp with Creole Sauce Remoulade*

Mushroom Bisque

Veal Grillades*

Hominy Pudding*   *Artichokes with Lemon Butter**   *Glazed Baby Carrots**

Salad   *Cheese*

Coconut Custard Pie*   *Demitasse*

LOUISIANA NEW YEAR'S DAY DINNER

Oysters Rockefeller*

Celery   *Radishes*   *Olives*   *Salted Almonds*

Consommé Julienne

Stuffed Baked Fillets Creole*

Roast Stuffed Turkey*   *Cranberry Sauce**   *Green Peas*

Yams with Apples*   *Mashed Potatoes*   *Cauliflower with Brown Butter Sauce*

Daube Glacé*   *Sauce Piquante**

Green Pepper and Tomato Salad with French Dressing*

Toasted Crackers and Cheese

Vanilla Ice Cream* with Bananas Flambé*   *Assorted Small Cakes*

Café Brûlot*

COFFEE IN THE VIEUX CARRÉ

Calas*

A Nun's Sigh*   *Crullers*

Café au Lait

Turtle Soup

Ham Mousse*   *Salmon*

Fillet of Beef or Baby Turkey Bordelaise or Crown Roast of Lamb*

Sweetbreads Toulouse

Pâté en Bellevue*   *Asparagus with Hollandaise Sauce**

Sorbet*

Russian Salad*   *Camembert Cheese with Crackers*

Nesselrode Pudding*   *Demitasse*

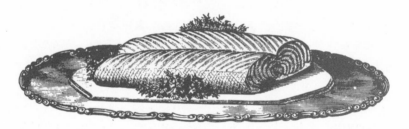

Poached salmon

In the days of Ward McAllister, the self-appointed Boswell of New York's Four Hundred, society was composed of men notable more for their wealth than for their discrimination. Many of McAllister's dicta, therefore, seem to preserve social graces in a setting of disingenuousness ("The highest cultivation in social manners enables a person to conceal from the world his real feelings") and to render truisms as clichés ("A dinner wholly made up of young people is generally stupid. You require the experienced woman of the world, who has at her fingers' ends the history of past, present, and future").

When the chronicler of the Four Hundred presented this menu for a successful dinner party in his *Society As I Have Found It,* he advised, "Success in entertaining is accomplished by magnetism and tact. It is the ladder to social success. If successfully done, it naturally creates jealousy." But, McAllister added, "In planning a dinner the question is not to whom you owe dinners, but who is most desirable. The success of the dinner depends as much upon the company as the cook. Discordant elements—people invited alphabetically, or to pay off debts—are fatal.... So much for your guests."

220

LINCOLN'S INAUGURAL LUNCHEON

Mock Turtle Soup

Corned Beef and Cabbage*   *Parsley Potatoes*

Blackberry Pie*   *Coffee*

Abraham Lincoln was partial to corn bread, honey, and a good cup of coffee. Aside from these preferences the President seems to have evinced little interest in cuisine—and often to have forgotten altogether about eating. One morning, while the artist Francis B. Carpenter was at the White House painting *The First Reading of the Emancipation Proclamation,* Lincoln heard the clock strike noon and interrupted Carpenter's work with, "I believe, by the by, that I have not yet had my breakfast, —this business has been so absorbing that it has crowded everything else out of my mind."

The conduct of the Civil War preoccupied Lincoln, of course, but his tastes predated his White House years. Leonard Swett, a lawyer who worked with Lincoln in the eighth judicial circuit in Illinois, once said, "I never, in the ten years of circuit life I knew him, heard him complain of a hard bed or a bad meal of victuals." Lincoln's last law partner, William H. Herndon, said more pointedly that Lincoln "filled up and that is all." Noah Brooks, one of Lincoln's friends from Illinois, recalled having been invited to breakfast one morning by Lincoln and noting that "the President would appear to forget that food and drink were needful for his existence, unless he were persistently followed up by some of the servants." Brooks remarked to Lincoln that he was surprised to see that the President preferred milk to coffee for breakfast. Lincoln replied, "eyeing his glass of milk with surprise, as if he had not before noticed what he was drinking, 'Well, I do prefer coffee in the morning, but they don't seem to have sent me in any.'"

Surprisingly enough, Lincoln showed enough interest in his food to plan the above menu. The luncheon was served at Willard's Hotel in Washington at midday on March 4, 1861, immediately following the inaugural ceremonies at the Capitol. After lunch, the Lincoln family went from the hotel directly to the Executive Mansion.

A SOUTHWESTERN DINNER

*Meatball Soup**

*Baked Avocado Stuffed with Crab Meat**

*Refried Beans**   *Summer Squash, Mexican Style**

Chicken Tamales   *Stuffed Beets**

*Pineapple-Yam Turnovers**   *Coffee*

The states bordering on Mexico—Texas, New Mexico, Arizona, and California—share a cuisine that is generally called Spanish. In fact, the cuisine is basically that of the American Indians who lived in the Southwest, flavored by additions from the Mexican Indians and from the Spanish conquistadors. The mixing process began in 1519, when the Aztec emperor Montezuma II offered the Spaniards some tomatoes and chilies. The New World was also able to provide the cuisine with three indigenous foods known as the American agricultural triad: corn, beans, and squash. The Spanish contributed their culinary mastery of onions and garlic. In addition to these ingredients, the food of the Southwest makes conspicuous use of seasonings like basil, thyme, rosemary, and oregano.

Two obligatory items in any southwestern dinner are chili peppers and frijoles. Frijoles may refer to a number of different beans, although pinto, or painted, beans are favored. They are served for dinner and for supper and are eaten—warmed-over, or refried—for breakfast (giving rise to the saying, *"Frijoles—frijolitos y frijoles refritos,"* or "Beans—more beans, and warmed-over beans"). Chili peppers provide most of the necessary heat in the cuisine.

Tamales, too, are essential ingredients (and are now commercially packaged). It is said that tamales saved Hernando Cortes and his men from starvation in Mexico. When the Aztecs realized that the Spanish soldiers were not (as had been thought because of their "pure" white skin) high priests from Quetzalcoatl, the god of plenty, they stopped giving the invaders food. Cortes, however, had won the love of a woman named Malinche and told her he would have to leave if his men could not obtain food. Malinche told Cortes to storm the gates of the city on a certain evening. He did, and Malinche led a group of friends who bombarded the Spaniards with tamales.

222

DINING AT SHAKERTOWN

Shakers at dinner

Shaker Flank Steak*   **Cold Tongue**

Shaker Spinach with Rosemary*   **Fried Tomato Slices***

Shaker Potato Salad*   **Corn Pudding***

Shaker Daily Loaf*   **Blueberry Muffins***   **Graham Gems***   **Buttermilk Biscuits***

Rose Haw Preserves   **Pickles**   **Strawberry Jam**   **Tomato Preserves***

Grape Conserve*   **Pear Marmalade***   **Honey**   **Carrot Pickles***

Mother Ann's Birthday Cake*   **Shaker Cider Cake***

Milk   **Tea**   **Coffee**

The Shaker settlement at Pleasant Hill, in Kentucky's bluegrass country, was organized in 1806. Almost from its beginning, the settlement attracted visitors from neighboring Danville and Harrodsburg. Young couples drove to Pleasant Hill in surreys and carryalls to share (for a modest price) in lavish meals. One Shaker sister wrote in 1866, "As to our fare in general, we have the cream of the earth; plenty of flour, meal, milk and butter . . . strawberries, asparagus, lettuce, radishes, peas, preserves, honey, molasses . . . buttered waffles, fritters, doughnuts, baked dumplings, peach pies, apple pies." The list of comestibles continued to prodigious lengths. Two of the most distinctive parts of Shaker menus were the breads and preserves. In an era when bleaching flour was common practice, the Shakers spoke against killing the "live germ of the wheat." (In an 1871 edition of the Shaker *Manifesto,* an article by Henry Ward Beecher charged that "what had been the staff of life for countless ages had become a weak crutch.") Shaker tables always had an abundance of freshly baked breads and muffins, and jams and jellies.

Engraving of Monticello

"Never before," it was said of Thomas Jefferson's eight years in the White House, "had such dinners been given in the President's house, nor such a variety of the finest and most costly wines. In his entertainments republican simplicity was united with epicurean delicacy; while the absence of splendor, ornament and profusion was more than compensated by the neatness, order and elegant simplicity that pervaded the whole establishment."

Jefferson's superb dinners were occasionally equaled by some of his successors in the White House, but they were rarely excelled. All three of the menus given here use foods that were available at Monticello during April, a bountiful month for crops on the plantation. A maigre, or fast day menu, is included (at bottom), since the custom of Friday and Lenten abstinence from meat was well rooted in Virginia and since Jefferson, a deist, had continued his connection with the Anglican church.

224

Deviled Crab*

Consommé Julienne

Roast Saddle of Lamb* with Brown Gravy   Conserve of Whole Currants

Pilau with Pignon Nuts*

Green Peas with Mint*

Salad of Mixed Garden Stuff* with Monticello Dressing*

Beaten Biscuits* with Assorted Cheese

Crème Brûlée*   Coffee   Fruit   Nuts

Deviled Eggs with Anchovies*

Celery   Radishes   Olives   Small Green Onions

Sorrel Soup*

Standing Ribs of Beef* au Jus   Horse-radish Sauce*

Spinach Timbales*   Scalloped Tomatoes*

Small Roast Potatoes or Macaroni and Cheese Pudding*

Salad

Pots de Crème*   Macaroons   Meringues

Fruit   Coffee   Nuts

Oysters on the Half Shell

Mock Turtle Soup

Baked Shad with Roe Soufflé*

Fresh Asparagus with Virginia Boiled Dressing*   Scalloped Potatoes*

Blancmange* with Brandied Apricots*   Small Cakes

Coffee   Fruit   Nuts

A PENNSYLVANIA DUTCH DINNER

Corn Chowder*

Chicken Potpie*   *Red Cabbage**   *Scalloped Potatoes**

<u>*Seven Sweets:*</u>   <u>*Seven Sours:*</u>

Sweet Pickled Peaches*   *Red-Beet Eggs**

Apple Butter*   *Pickled Jerusalem Artichokes**

Quince Honey   *Pickled Yellow Beans*

Ginger Pears*   *Cantaloupe Pickle**

Grape Conserve*   *Piccalilli*

Rhubarb Jam   *Corn Relish**

Tomato Preserves*   *Carrot Pickles**

Homemade Bread

Shoo-fly Pie*   *Applesauce Cake**

Coffee

William Penn, in a pamphlet in 1681, commended the "province of Pennsilvania" with great restraint: "I shall say little in its praise.... This shall satisfie me, that by the Blessing of God, and the honesty and industry of Man, it may be a good and fruitful Land." In 1686, James Harrison, a Quaker minister, was less reserved in his praise of the new land: "The Peach-Trees are much broken down with the weight of Fruit this Year...Rasberries, Goosberries, Currans, Quinces, Roses, Walnuts and Figs grow well.... Our Barn, Porch and Shed, are full of Corn this year." Dr. Nicholas More wrote in 1686, "We have had admirable English Pease this Summer; every one here is now persuaded of the fertility of the ground, and goodness of the climate, here being nothing wanting, with industry, that grows in England . . . and we have this common advantage above England, that all things grow better, and with less labour." It was in this exceptionally fertile country that the Pennsylvania Dutch nurtured a cuisine that has always reflected the generosity of the land on which they live.

Hermann, Missouri, was founded in 1837 by the German Settlement Society of Philadelphia. The purpose of the settlers was to establish a German community in which the language and customs of Germany might be preserved. The site chosen on the banks of the Missouri River was reminiscent of the Rhine Valley; the land was suitable for vineyards, and Hermann became, for a time, the second largest wine-producing center in America. One of the limestone cellars of Hermann's wine company contained the "twelve apostles," casks of 1,500- to 3,000-gallon capacity, carved with likenesses of the apostles.

Winegrowers customarily celebrated in late spring (when the major work in the vineyards had been completed) or in the fall (when the summer sun had done its work and the grapes had been harvested). The May festival became traditional in Hermann after 1844, when the settlers produced their first wine, and the wine drinking was accompanied by dancing, singing, pageants, band concerts, and feasts. Below is a *Maifest* menu, followed by a picnic for the children.

May Wine Bowl*

Chicken Fricassee*   *Dumplings**   *Green Peas*   *Fried Mushrooms**

German Rye Bread   *Cheese*   *Coleslaw**   *Pickles*

Lemon Cheesecake*   *Coffee*   *Sour Cream Raisin Pie**

Spring picnic

Pink Lemonade*   *Cream Potato Salad**   *Buns with Knackwurst*

Slices of Brick Ice Cream with Sand Tarts* and Cinnamon Stars*

Soft-Shelled Crabs* on Toast   *Chicken Croquettes* with Green Peas*

Lamb Cutlets with Tartare Sauce*   *Aspic of Beef Tongue*

Woodcock and Snipe on Toast   *Salad with Mayonnaise*

Strawberries with Cream   *Orange Baskets Garnished with Strawberries*

Charlotte Russe*   *Nesselrode Pudding**   *Blancmange**

Ice Cream* Garnished with Preserved Fruits   *Water Ices*

Wedding Cake   *Small Fancy Cakes*

Roman Punch*   *Chocolate*   *Coffee*

A wedding cake

The marriage of Nellie Grant, President Ulysses Grant's only daughter, took place at eleven o'clock on the morning of May 21, 1874. It was the first wedding to be held in the White House in thirty years, since President Tyler married Julia Gardiner. Nellie married a young Englishman, Algernon Sartoris (to whom, at first, her father objected), in an elaborate ceremony in the East Room of the White House. The bride wore a white satin dress, with a white veil and a wreath of white flowers, green leaves, and orange blossoms. The wedding breakfast was served in the state dining room.

Although the press was not admitted, a reporter from the New York *Herald* managed to be present, and it is from his account of the breakfast that the menu is taken. "It is said," the journalist recounted, "by those who have long been frequenters of the White House, nothing to equal it was ever before witnessed."

A SYLVAN REPAST

Cream of Celery Soup (Colored Green)

Grilled Trout*

Mushrooms in Cream* on Toast

Roast Rack of Venison*   Plum Sauce*

Saratoga Chips*   Green Peas served in Patty Shells

Salpicon of Fruits*

Quail* in Nests of Puréed Chestnuts*

*English Walnuts and Celery Mixed with Green Mayonnaise
in Cups of Molded Tomato Jelly*

*Small Balls of Cream Cheese, Colored Green to Imitate Birds' Eggs,
in Nests of Shredded Lettuce*

Pistachio Ice Cream Molded in a Ring, Center Filled with Whipped Cream

White Cakes with Green Icing   Fruits   Coffee

"Of late it has been the fashion to have one prevailing color," Mary Ronald wrote in her *Century Cook Book*, published in 1895. She referred not simply to table decorations, but to the food itself. It was possible, in the 1890's, to find directions for serving a dinner composed almost entirely of foods of a single color. Miss Ronald said, "In many cases this is very suitable as well as complimentary to the guests entertained. For instance, a white dinner to a bride, pink to young people, red to a Harvard company, or yellow to those with Princeton affiliations." Miss Ronald's Sylvan Repast, or "Al Fresco" dinner, an evocation of a woodland scene, was her green dinner. "Of all colors," she said, "green is the easiest to carry out, and perhaps the most pleasing...." The ceiling was decorated to resemble a blue sky dotted with little white clouds. Palms, bay trees, and rubber plants were set about the dining room, and the center of the large round table was filled with ferns, primroses, and moss. Light was provided by green candles covered with green shades. The menu is composed largely of "products of the forest," Miss Ronald said. "The aspect of this dinner was really sylvan."

Turtle Soup

*Broiled Salmon Steaks or New England Poached Salmon with Egg Sauce**

Green Peas   Small Boiled New Potatoes in Jackets

Indian Pudding or Apple Pandowdy**

Coffee   Tea

When John Adams signed the Declaration of Independence, he wrote to his wife, Abigail, that the day of the signing "will be the most memorable epocha in the history of America. I am apt to believe that it will be celebrated by succeeding generations as the great anniversary Festival. It ought to be commemorated, as the day of deliverance by solemn acts of devotion to God Almighty. It ought to be solemnized with pomp and parade, with shows, games, sports, guns, bells, bonfires and illuminations from one end of this continent to the other, from this time forward, forevermore."

Though the Adamses celebrated the Fourth of July each year with enthusiasm, their tastes at the dinner table reflected New England thrift and simplicity. They reflected, too, Mrs. Adams' concern with practical matters. On June 23, 1797, she wrote from Philadelphia to her sister, "To day will be the 5th great dinner I have had, about 36 Gentlemen to day, as many more next week, and I shall have got through the whole of Congress, with their apendages. Then comes the 4 July which is a still more tedious day, as we must have then not only all Congress, but all the Gentlemen of the city, the Govenour and officers and companies, all of whom the late President used to treat with cake, punch and wine. What the House would not hold used to be placed at long tables in the yard. As we are here we cannot avoid the trouble or the expence...."

The Adamses' neighbors in Massachusetts had no such problems on the Fourth of July; they just served the traditional New England dinner of salmon with egg sauce, along with the first new potatoes and early peas. The salmon along the eastern seaboard began to run in late June and were readily available for Independence Day.

The Waldorf-Astoria, 1899

Cape Cod Oysters

Chicken Gumbo Filé*

Celery   Assorted Nuts

Fillet of Flounder, American Style*

Roast Wild Duck*   *Currant Sauce**

Wild Rice Sauté   Alligator Pear Salad

Pumpkin Pie* with American Cheese   Coffee

Oscar Tschirky, the maître d'hôtel of the Waldorf-Astoria, was known simply as Oscar—in much the same way (and with similar deference) as one of his contemporaries was referred to as Victoria. Oscar shared his throne with other social arbiters such as Ward McAllister, but in the Palm Garden of the Waldorf-Astoria the greatest measure of recognition a socialite could receive was to have Oscar personally suggest the wines and food for dinner.

Oscar differed from royalty in that he recognized the *nouveaux riches* as equals of the established American "aristocracy." George Boldt, the manager of the Waldorf, would have preferred to cater only to the Four Hundred. But Oscar realized that such people, regardless of their wealth, could not support a large modern hotel, and that such exclusivism was, in any event, obsolescent. Early in this century, Oscar reached beyond the boundaries of the Palm Garden to publish his own cookbook, which became a best seller. Later, he was asked to outline what he considered a dinner typical of American tastes and traditions; his answer was the above menu.

"The Bibulous Loafer," 1882

The Reverend Thomas Dixon, Jr., in an article in *Leslie's Illustrated* of March 3, 1892, declaimed, "All signs seem to point now to the temporary triumph of the saloon over the forces of Christian civilization in America." Speaking of the Hotel Vendôme bar in New York, Reverend Dixon said, "At the extreme end of the room, and separated from the bar by twenty or thirty feet, stands the free-lunch counter, built of African marble and Mexican onyx! It is loaded with the most tempting food cooked by master hands."

The free lunch was an innovation from the West in the early nineteenth century. Throughout the century, as the institution of the free lunch spread across the country, a man could walk into almost any saloon in America and for the price of a drink (or two) help himself to the inexhaustible supplies of the free-lunch counter. The institution reached its zenith between 1890 and 1910, and it was, in those favored years, a boon to the bachelor, the young college student, and the junior clerk, who could dine sumptuously, within their modest means, in the congenial atmosphere of the saloon. This menu (published by The Book Club of California) is taken from San Francisco's Palace of Art, whose proprietor, Ernest Haquette, maintained a lunch counter esteemed as especially generous. The more typical free-lunch counter contained an assortment of salty edibles intended to stimulate thirst. Haquette's spread, although it must have provoked thirst, had some culinary pretensions, too. The Palace of Art was decorated with tasteful oil paintings (its nudes inviting, but modest), a collection of European glass, and ladies. The fact that Haquette admitted ladies to his saloon may account for the special lavishness of his lunch spread.

Yet other free-lunch counters, though they may appear frugal compared with that of the Palace of Art, were no mean affairs of cheese and crackers. In 1896, the New York *Daily Tribune* revealed, "Millions of money are annually expended in this seeming gratuity, and over fifty thousand regulars depend upon what they can gather from our counters for their daily subsistence." Even some of the least distinguished saloons in New York laid out as much as ten thousand dollars per year for their lunches. In 1907, the New York *Herald* reported, in an article giving advice on how a man might live in New York without any money at all: "The man who would live on nothing a year could actually become something of a connoisseur. He could study the cooking of the various chefs and learn where to find the best chicken or salad or roast, fish or oysters, and by carefully selecting his courses he could make an excellent dinner within a radius of a few blocks. . . . he would enjoy the cooking of the best chefs in America."

Radishes   *Crab Salad*   *Celery*

Clam Juice

Pig's Head   *Bolinas Bay Clams*   *Headcheese*

Homemade Sausage, Country Style*   *Beef à la Chili Colorado*

Chili con Carne*   *Honolulu Beans*

Chicken Croquettes*   *Veal Croquettes**   *Terrapin Stew*

Fried Clams   *Sardines*   *Baked Ham**

Saratoga Chips*   *Corned Beef*

Tongue in Spicy Aspic*   *Beef Stew**   *Boston Baked Beans**

Frizzled Beef*   *Smoked Salmon*

Cheese   *Crackers*

Cracked Crab   *Holland Herring*

Almonds   *Popcorn*   *Apples*

A NANTASKET BEACH CLAMBAKE

New England Clam Chowder* or Codfish Chowder*

Baked Clams with Melted Butter Dressing

Baked Blue Fish   Baked Cod*   Fried Perch

Nantasket Chips   Boiled Potatoes   Sweet Potatoes

Clam Fritters*   Corn on the Cob*   Cucumber Salad*

Brown and White Bread

Watermelon   Pie   Tea   Coffee

One of the chief contributions the Indians made to the cuisine of New England was the clambake. Later, New England clambakes, like Kentucky burgoos, were put on to attract voters to election rallies, and became the excuse for innumerable social outings. In the latter half of the nineteenth century, upper Narragansett Bay in Rhode Island was crowded with clambake resorts like Rocky Point and Crescent Park. Bakes were served every day, and fleets of steamboats operating out of Providence and the neighboring area ran excursions to these clambake sites along the shore.

A fire was (and still is—the system used by the Indians on the shores of Rhode Island has not been improved upon) built on a foundation of large stones. When the stones were white-hot, the fire was swept away, and a layer of rockweed was placed on the stones. Clams were placed on the rockweed, then another layer of weed, a layer of potatoes and corn (covered by a layer of husks), then fish enveloped in cloth or paper bags. (The ingredients in a clambake varied somewhat; although not shown on this menu, sausages, lobsters, and even chickens were often added to a bake.) The bake was then blanketed with a wet canvas, which was covered with rockweed and held down at the edges with stones to keep in the steam. The canvas was kept moist throughout the cooking. It took about an hour to heat the stones, and forty-five minutes for the heat from the stones to cook the bake.

The menu here, dating from the late nineteenth century, is taken from the Arlington Hotel at Nantasket Beach, Massachusetts, which advertised this full dinner for fifty cents with "Clams Baked on Heated Rocks . . . No steam pipes are used."

Littleneck Clams

Grilled Trout*   *Cucumbers, Sautéed**

Omelette* with Mushrooms in Cream*   *Grilled Plover*

Filet Mignon*   *Potatoes*   *Asparagus with Hollandaise Sauce**

Tomato and Lettuce Salad

Ice Cream*   *Strawberries*   *Cakes*   *Coffee*

"Waiter!"

The opening sentence of Dr. Oliver Wendell Holmes's *The Autocrat of the Breakfast-Table* is characteristic of the book and of the man who spoke with the gentle art—now considered lost—of the conversationalist: "I was just going to say, when I was interrupted..."

Dr. Holmes was often interrupted, but it was never a permanent condition. He was considered the poet laureate of both the breakfast and the dinner tables. Holmes was a member of the Saturday Club, founded in Boston in 1855. The club was devoted to the discussion of literature and to monthly banquets which the members unabashedly gave in honor of one another. Holmes's fellow members included Henry Wadsworth Longfellow, Ralph Waldo Emerson, Nathaniel Hawthorne, James Russell Lowell, Louis Agassiz, Richard Henry Dana, Jr., Francis Parkman, John Greenleaf Whittier, William Dean Howells, Henry Adams, and Henry James.

The menu presented here is from a breakfast given in honor of Holmes in 1879.

In the early days of American politics, candidates for office resorted to an eminently successful device to get out the voters: they supplied the electorate with food and drink.

Electioneering—beginning even before 1758, when George Washington served voters rum, punch, beer, wine, cider, and cakes—was always carried on in the midst of great outdoor feasts. Election cannon would roar, banners would fly, and a band would blare an inspiring march as speakers mounted the platform to speak—interrupted only by a midday repast—until well into the evening. In 1840, the rallies reached their zenith in the "Log Cabin and Hard Cider" campaign of William Henry Harrison. At Albany, the Whigs raised a log cabin and feasted on corn bread, cheese, and hard cider. At Columbus, Ohio, there was ginger cake, hoecake, and bacon with the cider. At Wheeling, West Virginia, Harrisonites entertained 30,000 at a rally with 360 hams, 26 sheep, 20 calves, 1,500 pounds of beef, 8,000 pounds of bread, over 1,000 pounds of cheese, and 4,500 pies.

George P. Prentice, an editor of a New England magazine who went south to write a biography of Henry Clay, described what he saw of southern politics: "I have just witnessed that strange thing, a Kentucky election. . . . Whiskey and apple toddy flowed in the cities and villages like the Euphrates through ancient Babylon. . . . drunkenness stalked triumphant. . . . Runners, each with a whiskey bottle poking its long, jolly neck from his pocket, were employed in bribing voters, and each party kept half-a-dozen bullies . . . to flog every poor fellow that should attempt to vote illegally; a half-hundredweight of mortar would scarce fill up the chinks in the skulls that were broken."

Year after year Kentucky voters ran the risk of having their skulls broken in order to share in some food and drink and hear an orator. The entry for July 24, 1844, in the diary of Henry Baxter speaks of a Democratic rally in Walnut Lick, Kentucky, which was attended by about two thousand people: "Mr. O'Hara an old Irish lawyer of Owen Co. Ky. followed, and from him we had the whole history of Whiggery and Democracy, from the very beginning of our government until the present time...We then adjourned to dinner which is the first of the kind I ever was at. Here were five or six ditches dug two and a half feet deep, and about as wide, in which had been built fires, which when burned down to the coals, they had put over their quarters of veal and mutton upon spits of wood....Further on was a table about two hundred feet long...strewed from end to end with...meat."

Baxter was, of course, describing a barbecue (from the Spanish *barbacoa,* meaning a "frame"). The Mexican Indians had used frames of green wood to dry and smoke fish, and the Spaniards adapted the method to roast the meat of large animals. Colonists as far north as Pennsylvania used barbecue frames to cook fish, pigs, and sheep, but in Texas, the main feature was always beef, in great quantities. (Westerners distinguish between real barbecues and the lamb barbecues of the sheepherders by calling the latter Basque barbecues, since so many of the sheep farmers were of Basque ancestry.)

A menu adapted from a standard Texas barbecue appears below. With it is a menu built around burgoo, one of the most popular dishes at rallies in Kentucky in the latter half of the nineteenth century.

*Barbecued Spareribs**

*Four-Bean Salad**   *Buttermilk Biscuits**

*Individual Pecan Pies**   *Coffee*

"Hard Cider Triumphant"

*Mint Juleps**

*Burgoo**

*Corn Sticks**   *Coleslaw**

Apple Pie or Deep-Dish Blueberry Pie**

Hickory Nut Cake or Kentucky Bourbon Cake**

Coffee

Oysters on the Half Shell

Celery   *Radishes*   *Olives*

Consommé

Roast Turkey* with Chestnut Stuffing*   *Giblet Gravy**

Roast Suckling Pig*   *Cranberry Sauce**   *Spiced Crab Apples**

Spinach   *Mashed Potatoes*   *Onions in Cream**   *Brussels Sprouts*

Salad

Mincemeat Pie*   *Pumpkin Pie**   *Vanilla Ice Cream**

Nuts   *Fruits*   *Chocolate Dragées*   *Coffee*

Along with the turkey and other traditional dishes, the Thanksgiving table at Sagamore Hill always featured suckling pig, a favorite food of Roosevelt and his eldest daughter, "Princess Alice." Except for such special occasions, however, the meals at the Roosevelt home were not elaborate. They featured the harvest of the family gardens, orchards, and bayshore; fresh milk, cream, and butter from the dairy herd; and home-baked breads to be eaten with preserves, jams, and jellies. "At Sagamore Hill," Roosevelt once said, "we love a great many things—birds and trees and books, and all things beautiful, and horses and rifles and children and hard work and the joy of life."

Roosevelt dined simply—often content with no more than bread and milk—but he consumed his edibles in great quantities. O. K. Davis recalled, "I have seen him eat a whole chicken and drink four large glasses [of milk] at one meal, and chicken and milk were by no means the only things served." Lloyd Griscom remembered Roosevelt as "stoking up prodigiously, as though he were a machine." And Theodore Roosevelt, Jr., said that his father's coffee cup "was more in the nature of a bathtub." Roosevelt was as fond of sweets (his Thanksgiving dinner is topped here with chocolate candies) as he was of a whole chicken, or half a suckling pig; Richard Henry Dana III once noticed that Roosevelt put as many as seven lumps of sugar in his coffee, "and I bethought me of the humming bird which lives on sweets, and is one of the most strenuously active of vertebrates."

Adolphus François Gerard, who was born in Alençon, France, about 1844, spent some time in a French seminary, dissipated a small fortune enjoying the pleasures of Paris, and became a journalist in London and New York. Then, cavalierly, Gerard joined the United States Army and was assigned to a post in Cheyenne, Wyoming. He deserted—and became Louis Dupuy, one of the most famous chefs of the West in the nineteenth century. Dupuy was the proprietor of the Hotel de Paris in Georgetown, Colorado (the second largest city in the state at that time, owing to the silver-mining boom). The rich and renowned from all over the world traveled out of their way to delight in the cuisine at the Hotel de Paris. The dinner below was served in March, 1879; the nine men who had journeyed to Georgetown solely for the purpose of dining at Dupuy's hotel were Jay Gould (who later said it was the best meal he had ever had) and his son George, General Grenville M. Dodge, Sidney Dillon, Russell Sage, Captain G. H. Baker, Oliver Ames, W. A. H. Loveland, and E. K. Berthoud. Together, the nine men represented over two hundred million dollars.

Galantine of pheasants

Oysters on the Half Shell

Soup

Ptarmigan or Pheasant in Casserole*   **Venison Cutlet**   **Sauce Piquante***

Sweetbreads Eugénie*

Vegetables   **Apple Fritters***   **Salad**

French Bread

Peach Charlotte* with Brandy Sauce*   **Petits Fours**   **Coffee**

Thanksgiving dinner

Haunch of Venison*   *Roast Chine of Pork**

Roast Turkey*   *Pigeon Pasties*   *Roast Goose**

Onions in Cream*   *Cauliflower*   *Squash*

Potatoes   *Raw Celery*

Mincemeat Pie*   *Pumpkin Pie**   *Apple Pie**

Indian Pudding*   *Plum Pudding**

Cider

This menu for a New England Thanksgiving dinner is taken from a letter written in 1779 by Juliana Smith to her "Dear Cousin Betsey." As Thanksgiving Day approached, Grandmother Smith (the great-granddaughter of the Reverend Richard Mather of Dorchester, Massachusetts), "who is sometimes a little desponding of Spirit as you well know, did her best to persuade us that it would be better to make it a Day of Fasting & Prayer in view of the *Wickedness of our Friends & the Vileness of our Enemies,* I am sure you can hear Grandmother say that and see her shake her cap border. . . . But my dear Father brought her to a more proper frame of Mind, so that by the time the Day came she was ready to enjoy it almost as well as Grandmother Worthington did, & she, you will remember, always sees the bright side."

240

While it would be difficult to set forth a single "traditional" Thanksgiving menu, the preparations related by Juliana Smith that went into this dinner were certainly typical of early New England Thanksgivings. "This year it was Uncle Simeon's turn to have the dinner at his house, but of course we all helped them as they help us when it is our turn, & there is always enough for us all to do. All the baking of pies & cakes was done at our house & we had the big oven heated & filled twice each day for three days before it was all done. & *everything was* GOOD, though we did have to do without some things that ought to be used. Neither Love nor (paper) Money could buy Raisins, but our good red cherries dried without the pits, did almost as well & happily Uncle Simeon still had some spices in store. The tables were set in the Dining Hall and even that big room had no space to spare when we were all seated." Apparently roast beef was part of the traditional menu for this family, but "of course we could have no Roast Beef. None of us have tasted Beef this three years back as it all must go to the Army, & too little they get, poor fellows. But, Nayquittymaw's Hunters were able to get us a fine red Deer, so that we had a good haunch of Venisson on each Table." There was an abundance of vegetables on the table, including "one which I do not believe you have yet seen. Uncle Simeon had imported the Seede from England just before the War began & only this Year was there enough for Table use. It is called Sellery & you eat it without cooking." Cider was served instead of wine, with the explanation that Uncle Simeon was saving his cask "for the sick." Juliana added that "The Pumpkin Pies, Apple Tarts & big Indian Puddings lacked for nothing save *Appetite* by the time we had got round to them."

Counting the Reverend Mr. Smith, his wife, two grandmothers, and the six Livingstons from next door, there were forty people at the dinner. "Uncle Simeon was in his best mood, and you know how good that is! He kept both Tables in a roar of laughter with his droll stories of the days when he was studying medicine in Edinborough, & afterwards he & Father & Uncle Paul joined in singing Hymns & Ballads. You know how fine their voices go together. Then we all sang a Hymn & afterwards my dear Father led us in prayer, remembering all Absent Friends . . . We did not rise from the Table until it was quite dark, & then when the dishes had been cleared away we all got round the fire as close as we could, & cracked nuts, & sang songs & told stories. At least some told & others listened. *You know nobody* can exceed the two Grandmothers at telling tales of all the things they have seen themselves, & repeating those of the early years in New England . . ."

A BISHOP HILL SMÖRGÅSBORD

Marinated Salmon   Sardines   Pickled or Smoked Herring

Herring Salad   Pickled Oysters   Crayfish   Shrimp Mayonnaise

Lutfisk   Dill and Mustard Sauce*   Stuffed Celery   Cream Potato Salad*

Aspics Molded and Decorated with Vegetables, Meats, Fish, and Fruits

Smoked or Pickled Tongue   Baked Ham*   Swedish Beans*

Liverwurst Sausages   Swedish Meatballs*   Pickled Pig's Feet

Spiced Crab Apples*   Pâté* and Cheese Balls   Chicken Liver Balls

Janson's Temptation*   Stuffed Cabbage*   Pickled Beets

Swedish Rye Bread*   Crisp Rye Bread   Saffron Bread*

Sharp Wisconsin Cheese   Caraway Seed Cheese   Edam Cheese

Swedish Christmas Cookies   Lingonberry Torte*   Swedish Mints

Coffee   Chocolate

Bishop Hill was founded in the 1840's in Illinois by the prophet Eric Janson and his followers. The prophet had been a purist in Sweden, burning books and calling for a return to the more austere early days of the Church; finally, King Oscar I was moved to contribute to a fund to help the Jansonists leave Sweden for America.

Janson's asceticism, and the rigors of pioneer life, showed in the early cuisine of Bishop Hill, and much of the austerity has persisted. However, as the Jansonists became more settled, the early strictures were softened.

Though Bishop Hill *smörgåsbords* remained coffee-drinking affairs, with none of the *aquavit* and beer and ale found in other Swedish communities in America, the feast gradually came to reflect the riches of the Illinois farm land rather than the privations extolled by the prophet. The menu given here, then, is typical of Swedish *smörgåsbords* throughout the country.

Traditionally, a *smörgåsbord* (meaning "bread and butter table") was only a preliminary to a full meal. Eventually, however, the informal preliminary grew into a buffet meal to be served on holidays.

MORAVIAN LOVE FEAST

Love feast in a Moravian Church

Love Feast Buns   *Christmas Cookies*   *Sugar Cake*

Coffee with Milk

Moravian settlers in Pennsylvania and North Carolina brought with them their old custom of the love feast, a tradition that originated in the agapae, feasts held by early Christians in commemoration of the Last Supper. The custom does not replace holy communion, nor is it considered of equal importance. It is intended merely to rekindle a spirit of love and unity and to remove—at least for a time—all social distinctions. To the accompaniment of singing by the choir, the sweet love feast buns are served from baskets, and a substantial cup of coffee (usually made by brewing the coffee with the sugar and milk) is passed to each participant.

In old Salem, North Carolina, love feasts were celebrated at least five times a year: at New Year's, during Lent, at Christmas, and on August 13 and November 13 (two special Moravian feast days). In 1783, when the community celebrated the Fourth of July for the first time, the observance included a love feast.

In Moravian households, a type of love feast was often held as a quiet celebration of a birthday or as a thank offering to those who had befriended a family in distress or in bereavement. Rather than offering only coffee and the buns, as in the church version, these love feasts included Moravian sugar cake, cheese and biscuits, cookies, and coffee or tea; cider was served when in season.

Commemorative medal

An Onion Soup Call'd the King's Soup*

Oysters on the Half Shell   *Broiled Salt Roe Herring**   *Boiled Rockfish*

Roast Beef* and Yorkshire Pudding*   *Mutton Chops*

Roast Suckling Pig*   *Roast Turkey* with Chestnut Stuffing**

Round of Cold Boiled Beef with Horse-radish Sauce*   *Cold Baked Virginia Ham*

Lima Beans   *Baked Acorn Squash**   *Baked Celery with Slivered Almonds**

Hominy Pudding*   *Candied Sweet Potatoes**

Cantaloupe Pickle*   *Spiced Peaches in Brandy**   *Spiced Cranberries*

Mincemeat Pie*   *Apple Pie**   *Cherry Pie**   *Chess Tarts**

Blancmange*   *Plums in Wine Jelly**   *Snowballs**   *Indian Pudding**

Great Cake*   *Ice Cream**   *Plum Pudding**

Fruits   Nuts   Raisins

Port   Madeira

Christmas was an especially meaningful holiday at Mount Vernon. George and Martha Washington were married on Twelfth Night in 1759, and throughout their lives they tried to spend the Christmas holiday season together. Even during the Revolution, Martha Washington traveled the winter roads with a military escort to join the General in his winter quarters.

Dinner at Mount Vernon was customarily served at three o'clock in the afternoon—an hour about which the General was altogether precise. He was likely to tell late guests, "Gentlemen... I have a cook who never asks whether the company has come, but whether the hour has come." (Martha was equally punctual. In 1790, she concluded an evening party promptly at nine o'clock by rising and announcing to her company, "The General always retires at nine, and I usually precede him.")

In the prevailing fashion, dinner was served in three courses and on two tablecloths. One cloth was removed between each course, and the fruit, nuts, and wines were served on the bare table. In the center of the table was an elegant epergne, and handsome platters containing meats and fish were placed symmetrically about the table—with a suitable assortment of vegetables and "corner dishes" of sauces, relishes, and preserves located at other appropriate spots.

Dinners were customarily concluded with toasts around the table. In 1789 William Maclay, a senator from Pennsylvania, was guest at a dinner party with the President and Mrs. Washington, Vice-President and Mrs. Adams, and several others. At the end of the meal, Maclay reported, "the President, filling a glass of wine with great formality drank to the health of every individual name by name round the table. Everybody imitated him, charged glasses, and such a buzz of 'health, sir,' and 'health, madam,' and 'thank you, sir' and 'thank you, madam,' never had I heard before. Indeed, I had liked to have been thrown out in the hurry; but I got a little wine in my glass, and passed the ceremony. The ladies sat a good while, and the bottle passed about; but there was a dead silence almost. Mrs. Washington at last withdrew with the ladies."

The Christmas menu opposite is a composite of meals served at Mount Vernon, made up of dishes that were available there in winter. Visitors to Mount Vernon were given to incomplete accounts, like that of Amariah Frost, who dined with the Washingtons in 1797 and reported, "The dinner was very good, a small roasted pigg, boiled leg of lamb, roasted Fowles, beef, peas, lettice, cucumbers, artichokes, etc. puddings, tarts, etc. etc." In compiling this menu the etceteras have been replaced by recourse to various guests' reports, garden books, farm records, and invoices of goods ordered from merchants.

INDEX

C

N

O